Varieties of Protestantism

Varieties of
Protestantism

John B. Cobb, Jr.

THE WESTMINSTER PRESS

Philadelphia

PRINTED IN THE UNITED STATES OF AMERICA

TO JEAN

Contents

Preface

THIS BOOK is the product of one Protestant's effort to understand himself in terms of his religious heritage. It is offered to the reader, Protestant or not, with the hope that it may help him also to gain a deeper appreciation of what remains, despite all competitors, the greatest spiritual dynamic in America.

On the one hand, I long ago became convinced that many of our denominational divisions are, from the religious point of view, accidental and irrelevant. On the other hand, I have been equally convinced that, partly related and partly unrelated to our institutional loyalties, there is a very real diversity at a deep level of spiritual orientation and commitment — a diversity that cannot be brushed aside in the interest of apparent unity. I felt increasingly driven to classify these basic orientations and to try to feel my way into each so that I might understand, and to some degree be grasped by, its spiritual appeal.

I realize keenly that in every chapter there are failures of discernment and distortions of meaning for which the limitations of my knowledge, and still more of my spiritual experience and imagination, are responsible. I hope, nevertheless, that each chapter may introduce the reader sympathetically and appreciatively into a world of thought and feeling that he may pursue at leisure by reading, by imagination, by worship, and in personal contacts.

I am indebted to many books and many individuals for such

insights as I have attained. Two persons I must single out above all to whom I would express my heartfelt thanks. Prof. William Beardslee of Emory University read drafts of all these chapters and with his wonted generosity and deep sensitivity made many wise suggestions that have affected the final form of the book. If still more of his thought had been incorporated, the resulting book would have been further improved. Mr. Andrew L. Floyd read the manuscript painstakingly and perceptively both in its earlier and in its penultimate forms and made incalculable contributions to its form and to its content.

Among others who gave helpful counsel with regard to one or another of the following chapters are Prof. T. J. J. Altizer of Emory University, Prof. Hugh Caldwell of the University of the South, Pres. E. C. Colwell of the Southern California School of Theology, Prof. Harold Oliver of Southeastern Baptist Theological Seminary, Prof. Martin Schmidt of San Francisco Theological Seminary, and Prof. Claude Thompson of Candler School of Theology. All these men have helped to protect me from what would otherwise have been embarrassing blunders, but for those which remain I alone am responsible.

A succession of patient and competent typists worked on drafts of the manuscript, and to all of them I am grateful. In this connection I wish to make special mention of Mrs. John M. Atthowe, Jr., who took a helpful interest in the manuscript altogether beyond the call of duty.

My debt to my wife is quite beyond acknowledgment. I would, however, make special mention of her patient labor on the Index and in reading proof in the late evening hours after strenuous days of care for a household including four active and demanding boys.

Much of the material under the heading of "Popular and Postscientific Protestantism" was published in an article in *Religion in Life,* under the title "Protestant Theology and Church Life," in the Winter issue, 1955–1956.

J. B. C., JR.

CHAPTER I

Introduction

IN THE PAST few decades American Protestants have become painfully aware that their fragmentation places them at a serious disadvantage in their relations with other religious bodies, especially the Roman Catholics. Protestant denominations are often treated as a unit by secular and political agencies, but they have difficulty even in understanding one another. They encounter baffling problems when they seek to achieve a common witness of spiritual and theological depth. Yet the concern to make a common witness has found expression in councils of churches, participation in the ecumenical movement, and in mergers of denominations. A large literature has been produced, and a spirit of good will among denominations prevails. Nevertheless, there still exists widespread confusion as to the positive significance of Protestantism, and considerable misunderstanding among Protestant groups. It is hoped this book may contribute something toward the overcoming of this confusion and misunderstanding.

The positive significance of Protestantism cannot consist in its opposition to Roman Catholicism or its relationship to capitalism or democracy. Protestantism is essentially a religious movement grounded in affirmations rather then negations. Its true interpretation, therefore, must be in religious terms.

When one undertakes to present the religious affirmations

of Protestantism, he is immediately confronted by a dilemma. On the one hand, he may select one tradition within Protestantism as normative and treat all other forms as partial or confused expressions of the true Protestant spirit. On the other hand, he may acknowledge the multiplicity of his subject and abandon the quest for any inner unity.

The first alternative has been followed by a number of recent introductions to Protestantism directed to the general public. The problem in this approach is to determine which tradition in Protestantism is truly normative. The contrasting presentations of two widely used primers illustrate this problem. Clarence Seidenspinner in *A Protestant Primer* presents the Protestant spirit in terms of individualistic freedom. In his view, Luther's distinctive contribution was his assertion of the authority of the informed conscience against all external authority. From this point of view recent liberalism is the full and consistent expression of the spirit only partially developed in the Reformation period. On the other hand, James H. Nichols in *Primer for Protestants* presents such Reformation emphases as the unconditional primacy of God's act and justification by faith alone as normative for Protestantism. In this account modern individualism appears as a temporary and one-sided expression of the true Protestant spirit.

The historical record, as such, cannot determine whether modern individualism is a one-sided expression of the Protestant spirit or its full and consistent fruition. Such a judgment is necessarily dependent upon the commitments of the author. If the essence of Protestantism is the right of each individual to act freely in religious matters as his private judgment directs, as Seidenspinner affirms, the Reformers can be credited with but a tenuous hold upon Protestant truth. If, on the other hand, as Nichols prefers to think, the heart of Protestant faith is obedience to God's will objectively revealed in his Word, much of modern Protestantism is scarcely as "Protestant" as is Roman Catholicism.

It would seem, therefore, that the advantages of simplifying the variety of forms of Protestantism for popular presentation are counterbalanced by the danger that many Protestants will not be able to recognize the portrait that is drawn of them. Simplification may be justifiable if we are committed in advance to the superior truth of one Protestant tradition and desire to recall to its fold our erring brethren, but if our purpose is to understand Protestantism in its actual variety of expression, we cannot make the assumption that any one tradition is normative.

A number of recent writers, recognizing the difficulties involved in presenting Protestantism as a unity, have followed the second alternative. Their works range from encyclopedic listings of all organized religious bodies and their most obvious distinctive features to more detailed studies of the dominant characteristics of the major families of denominations. All these books serve important functions, but their chosen approaches to Protestantism have inherent limitations.

Most of the authors who describe Protestantism in its diversity approach it through its institutional expressions. This approach results in emphasis on the organization and official teaching of the Protestant bodies. These are important matters, but they cannot comprise the whole of the living significance of Protestantism, nor even its deepest reality. Such studies display Protestant denominations as objects for inspection, but they cannot lay bare the heart of the faithful member. They rarely lead the reader to a personal understanding of the appeal of a given tradition for its adherents or of the inner relationship between thought, worship, and life which constitutes the heart of religion.

The understanding that can be gained from the study of Protestant institutions is limited, not only because it focuses on organization and official pronouncements rather than personal religion, but also because in the contemporary scene denominational lines are not always useful guides to the spiritual life of individual members. Within such large denominations as the Methodist, Baptist, Presbyterian, or Episcopalian one finds a wide range of religious understanding. Spiritual unity may often be found as much across denominational lines as within them. Furthermore, some important contemporary emphases, such as those on the social gospel and on the quest for abundant life, are not formally organized, though they constitute the real religion of tens of thousands of earnest Protestants.

What is still needed is an approach to Protestantism that recognizes its diversity but that does not identify its diversity with organized groups. This book is written to meet this need. It seeks to differentiate Protestant traditions in terms of their inner meaning to believers or, in other words, in terms of their distinctively religious character. It also recognizes that there are profound divergences in thought and spirit resulting from different responses to the problems with which advancing knowledge has confronted Protestants. These divergences cut across traditional lines and are treated separately from them.

This approach need not ignore or minimize the importance of institutional embodiments. Many institutions arose out of distinctive personal apprehensions of spiritual reality, gave expression thereto, and have done much to perpetuate special types of religious life. Hence, many denominational lines do provide useful clues to fundamental spiritual principles, and many varieties of the religious spirit are distinctively related to particular denominations. But by starting the investigation from the side of personal religion rather than formal organizations the limitations of the institutional approach can be overcome.

Commitment to the study of Protestantism in its variety postpones, but does not prejudge, the question as to unity. We should not speak of Protestantism as a unity until we have dealt honestly with its multiplicity, accepting each expression on its own terms. If unity is to be affirmed at all, it must be discovered and not imposed.

In advance of such discovery we cannot assume that any significant positive unity exists. Perhaps there is no single religious principle that characterizes all branches of Protestantism in any way that clearly distinguishes it from Roman Catholicism on the one hand or secularism on the other. Indeed, it seems quite possible that the quest for any common denominator that is at the same time distinctive is doomed to failure.

Nevertheless, another kind of unity may be found. Perhaps what is really vital to each form of Protestantism is compatible with what is really vital to all the others. Perhaps the apparent contradictions among them are not ultimate, but arise understandably, although not inevitably, from the special concern of each to protect distinctive principles that are intrinsically capable of harmonious relations. Perhaps, then, such a study of Protestantism may give some clues for the formulation of a truly ecumenical theology which can protect what is dear to all without sacrifice of its own integrity.

We should not assume that the spiritual perspectives in terms of which we classify Protestantism are unique to it. Indeed, we may safely suppose that at the deepest level there is extensive overlapping between the forms of Protestantism and those of Eastern Orthodoxy and Roman Catholicism. If this overlapping should prove even greater than anticipated, if, that is, this book should lead to the recognition that the resemblances of the spiritual principles of Protestants and other Christians are greater than generally supposed, we may indeed rejoice. Nevertheless, this book is written with non-Roman Catholic Christians of Western Europe and America chiefly in mind.

The major initial problem in carrying out this project was the formulation of a classification of the forms of Protestantism. This problem is rendered acute by the extreme multiplicity of forms that Protestantism actually exemplifies. Rarely can one find two Protestants who do not differ in some of their religious views. Hence, very few readers are expected to find

their personal attitudes identical with those represented as
characterizing any one of the nine types of Protestantism.
However, this does not mean that the selection of these patterns is arbitrary.

Most Protestants, at least in America, are vague and confused about their religious convictions. They are products of a
variety of religious influences which have molded their attitudes in more or less inconsistent ways. On the other hand,
a few Protestants have achieved a clear understanding of the
alternative religious patterns that they are offered and strive
for a personal synthesis among them. In neither of these
groups can one find individuals who clearly embody any one
typical pattern.

However, both groups are affected by such patterns. The
forces that mold, somewhat inconsistently, the attitudes of the
majority may be analyzed into a number of self-consistent
patterns of thought and life. Likewise, the careful synthesis
of the thoughtful leader may be analyzed into the simpler and
often clearer patterns that have been the subjects of synthesis.
The patterns that have, in chance interaction, molded the
half-unconscious attitudes of the ordinary Protestant and the
patterns that provide the starting point for thoughtful synthesis are essentially the same. They are patterns dictated by
the inner logic of fundamental convictions and emphases that
provide the alternative living centers for Protestant spirituality.
In some cases, these patterns have received classic expression
in major thinkers of the past and have been self-consciously
maintained by major denominations. In other cases, the patterns have appeared more as deep-lying tendencies of thought,
pervasively influential but rarely achieving full articulation in
organized groups or even in individuals.

A "methodological note" is appended to this introduction
to explain to the critical reader the principles of classification
employed in this book. Here it is sufficient to state quite simply the structure adopted as it may be seen at a glance in the
table of contents.

Protestantism is divided into four major forms which are treated in Chapter II through V. The first three are further divided into two types each, and the fourth into three. The first section in each chapter consists in a statement of the role of that form of Protestantism in the modern world, the unity of the types grouped together, and the basic sources of their differences. This is followed by sections devoted to the specific types of Protestantism in which the central principles of each are presented and the ways in which other doctrines and attitudes fall into place are indicated.

The goal in Chapters II through V is to display each of the nine types of Protestantism in terms of its inner meaning to its adherents. Therefore, each position is presented appreciatively, uncritically, from the point of view of the assumption of its truth. This kind of presentation not only should make the appeal of each type objectively evident, but also should help the reader to experience the approach subjectively. Only as one personally experiences the attractiveness of each position can one know that he has at least partially understood its meaning for believers.

This manner of presentation necessarily leaves the impression that the author accepts as true all details of whichever position he is presenting. Complete agreement with all the positions presented is obviously impossible. The reader is asked, in reading these chapters, to seek the meaning of each type of Protestantism and not the author's private views.

In Chapter VI the subject is the response of Protestantism to the rise of science and "the scandal of eschatology." These topics are intrinsically more impersonal and intellectual. Hence, they are treated in a more detached and critical spirit. Still, the author's personal views are not important.

In the final chapter, the meaning for Protestants of the diversity of Protestantism is discussed. At issue especially is the direction in which unity may be sought. Here the author's own views are presented in the hope that the reader of the preceding chapters may come to share his basic attitudes.

METHODOLOGICAL NOTE

The classification employed has been adopted in the conviction that there is a close relationship between systematic alternative possibilities for spiritual life and those historically exemplified and currently effective. This means that as one seeks to distinguish the basic possible ways in which, given the common Christian history, Protestants might understand themselves religiously, one at the same time discovers corresponding historical divisions within Protestantism.

The common Christian heritage of all Protestants includes as central the understanding of Christianity as the means or way of salvation. Within this common understanding, lines of division may be drawn in a number of ways. The way chosen here is to begin with the concept of salvation. Salvation can be understood essentially in terms of the life now lived on the planet earth or in terms of a life that begins after physical death. The this-worldly view need not reject the idea that life continues beyond the grave, and the otherworldly view need not deny that eternal life begins before death. But the difference remains and deeply affects the total outlook of the Christian.

This division within Protestantism is employed in this book to distinguish what is treated in Chapter V as liberalism from what is treated in Chapters II through IV. The more extensive treatment of otherworldly Protestantism is justified by its much greater historical importance.

Given the understanding of Christianity as having to do with man's attainment of eternal life, the deepest division seems to be between those who focus attention upon the salvation proffered by God and those who focus attention upon how man must respond in order that he may benefit from God's offer. The former group asks, " How does God save me? " The latter group asks, " What must *I* do to be saved? " The former concentrates attention upon the objective work of God, rejoicing in what he has already done. The latter concentrates upon the subjective response of the self, questioning whether it has been adequate for the personal appropriation of God's gift.

The emphasis upon the subjective, personal acceptance of the saving work of God by each one separately produces the " individualistic Protestantism " treated in Chapter IV, whereas the alternative preoccupation with what is done for us by God provides the context for the forms of Protestantism discussed in Chapters II and III. This more " objectivistic " Protestantism can be further distinguished according to how the effective work of God is understood.

One understanding of God's saving work is its identification with the Word once spoken in Jesus' life, death, and resurrection as recorded in Scripture. The other alternative is to see God's working in the Christian church called into being through Christ but continuing to mediate truth and grace throughout the ages. Chapter II treats of those types of Protestantism which proclaim the final decisiveness of the Word once spoken, whereas Chapter III deals with those who are chiefly concerned with the church as the mediator of redemptive power.

This fourfold classification of forms of Protestantism is then subdivided into nine types. Each of these types can be identified systematically as an alternative interpretation within one of the four forms now distinguished. Each may also be seen as embodied at least partially in some Protestant institutions or important historical movements. The actual presentation in each case is guided, in the first place, by concern for the inner consistency of the development of a particular principle, but, in the second place, also by concern to throw light upon historical movements that have embodied to varying degrees one or another of the systematic positions. Concern for adequacy of historical expression plays its largest role in Chapter II. Elsewhere, concern for the systematic positions will be seen to predominate.

However, the dual concern need not create grave difficulties.

There is an inner logic in the religious life that tends to cause the most earnest individuals to work out the consistent implications of their special emphasis and concern. Often, at least, important movements or institutions originate from the work of such relatively consistent leaders. Followers in later generations, seeking to recapture the distinctiveness of their faith, move toward the same kind of consistent pattern. Therefore, despite the fact that most religious men are not primarily interested in systematic consistency, there is a kind of consistency that is effective in their life and thought whether or not it is ever immaculately embodied. The nine types of Christian self-understanding articulated in this book are intended to express the major alternative forms of religiously consistent Protestantism that have in the past been available for faith.

Chapter II, which is distinguished by its focus on the Word, is further divided according as the Word is identified chiefly with the work of Christ or chiefly with the Scriptural record. Clearly it is in the churches of the Reformation that the authority of the Word is most vigorously proclaimed, and the alternative interpretations of the Word correspond roughly to the distinctive emphases of Luther and Calvin.

Chapter III, which deals with " churchly Protestantism," is distinguished into two types, according to the kinds of concern for the church that are possible. The church may be understood primarily as a place of public worship through participation in which the believer finds eternal life; or the church may appear as an authoritative institution capable of giving guidance and direction in all the problems of life and thought. These systematic distinctions have profoundly affected historical movements, but they have not received decisive institutional expression. In this book they are referred to somewhat artificially as " liturgical " and " authoritarian " Protestantism.

Chapter IV, which treats of " individualistic Protestantism," is subdivided according to the understanding of the criteria of salvation by which the individual judges his condition. The individualist may answer the question as to what one must do to be saved either by demanding belief and obedience as acts of will or by requiring an actual change of heart that transcends all acts of will. Usually some combination of these provides the actual answer, but relative emphases vary greatly. In general, the Baptists have tended to stress belief and obedience, whereas Wesleyans have stressed the inward experience and change of heart as the work of the Holy Spirit. " Biblicism " and " experientialism " are the terms chosen to identify these positions.

Chapter V, entitled "Liberal Protestantism" and distinguished by its understanding of salvation as transforming the conditions of life in the here and now, might have been subdivided much further. Actually, many persons have reinterpreted each of the other traditions with decreasing emphasis on the belief that individual life continues beyond the grave. Thus there is a liberal Lutheranism, a liberal Calvinism, a liberal liturgicalism, and so forth. Yet most of the liberal forms of these great traditions have yet to achieve any stable or consistent expression except in the minds of a few leading thinkers. These forms may, therefore, point the way for the future, but they are not yet effective types of Protestantism. Hence, the systematic subdivision of liberalism is worked out on lines that point to its more developed and popular expressions.

The salvation in this world which is sought may be either individual or social. According to the choice at this point, the social gospel may be distinguished from other forms of liberalism. Those persons who seek salvation on an individual basis may be distinguished further according to whether they understand salvation as personal union with God or as abundant life, healthful, happy, and constructive, at the ordinary temporal level. The former is called " mystical Protestantism," the latter, " the quest for abundant life."

Again it must be stressed that the method employed cannot lead to the presentation of positions that individual Protestants will recognize as identically their own. Almost all of us find ourselves drawn in varying degrees to several types. Yet it should assist self-understanding and basic religious decision to see separately the fully developed implications of the alternative emphases that appeal to us.

Furthermore, the typology of Protestantism developed in this book is not a classification of contemporary Protestant theologians. Some of them, it is true, accept as their responsibility the recovery and clarification of their heritage. This typology has relevance for their work, and in some instances their books are listed in the "Selected Readings." For the most part, however, the greater names in Protestant theology stand beyond their own traditions. The traditions from which they come, Calvinist in the case of Karl Barth, Lutheran in the case of Paul Tillich, still color their thought; but these men must be understood in their own terms.

In the same way, many creative thinkers in the liberal traditions stand far beyond the kinds of popular orientations characterized in the chapter on "Liberal Protestantism." For example, a great deal of fruitful work is now in progress among psychologically trained theologians and theologically trained psychologists that is yearly pressing back the frontiers of knowledge about man and his "quest for abundant life." The kind of Protestantism described below under this heading, however characteristic of a widespread popular movement, would satisfy few of the intellectual leaders. In this case, an introduction to the thought of these leaders is provided by a few of the volumes listed in the "Selected Readings."

Thus, emphatically, this book is *not* an account of the major alternatives in contemporary creative religious thought. It is intended to provide light upon the traditions out of which this pioneering work develops and to pose afresh some of the problems with which it must wrestle. But my major concern remains that of illuminating the differences and agreements that divide and unite Protestants, and of encouraging the continued growth of mutual understanding and respect.

No footnotes have been used. The primary purpose of documentation is to justify statements made in the text by reference to their authoritative source. In a work undertaking to describe the historical or contemporary convictions of an empirically distinguishable group, such documentation would be indicated. In the present work, however, which treats of "motifs" or "ideal types," statements are not justified in this way. For example, to claim warrant for a statement in the section on experientialism because it accurately describes Wesley's position would imply that Wesley's thought as such was normative for this movement. This would be quite false since, although Wesley did give classical expression to this position, much that Wesley taught on baptismal regeneration, for example, is in severe tension with the experientialist orientation. Consequently, it has seemed more honest and more useful to replace footnotes with bibliographies.

The bibliographies relevant to the topics discussed would include virtually the entire corpus of works written by Protestants or about Protestantism. From this vast library a very few books have been chosen for inclusion in " Selected Readings " which will be found at the end of each chapter. These lists include both primary works that give clear expression to major aspects of each tradition and secondary works selected for their profundity, simplicity, and accessibility. In many cases books equally suitable by all these criteria are arbitrarily omitted since all cannot be included. Many of the books listed contain extensive bibliographies which will enable the serious student to pursue his research indefinitely. Any book specifically mentioned in a chapter is listed in " Selected Readings," as are those books whose influence on the statement of the positions is most apparent to the author.

Only one more-extended bibliography is included. It is at the back of the book and is a list of general works on Protestantism, which, while not exhaustive, does include most of the books dealing with Protestantism as a whole or treating of the multiplicity of divisions within it that have been published in English since 1940. Special listings of books treating of the American scene are included. However, general philosophical, phenomenological, and sociological studies of religion are omitted, even though some do include treatments of Protestantism.

CHAPTER II

Reformation Protestantism

IN ITS BROADEST SENSE Protestantism refers to all Christian movements, other than the Roman Catholic Church, that share the heritage of Western Christianity. It is with this meaning that the term is generally used throughout this book. But in a much more definite sense Protestantism is that movement which stems from the Reformation, and especially from the work of Luther and Calvin. Despite all the changes that time has wrought, there is still present in the Presbyterian, the Reformed, and the Lutheran Churches a special quality of life and spirit that reflects the power of those towering personalities of the sixteenth century.

In much of the eighteenth and nineteenth centuries many of the most distinctive elements of Reformation faith seemed foreign to the spirit of the day. Yet that faith continued vital in the lives of countless thousands. In the reaction against the earlier optimism that has swept Western Europe since the end of the First World War, many of the characteristic emphases of the Reformation have enjoyed a vigorous revival. This has occurred especially in those churches which have never lost sight of their Reformation heritage; but so dynamic has been the theological movement that they have produced that thoughtful Christians in other traditions as well have been gripped by the Reformation way of understanding the faith. Not only have many Presbyterians and Congregationalists ceased to apologize for their Calvinist heritage or compromise it with the more individualistic spirit dominant in recent times, but also many Anglicans, Baptists, and Methodists have felt the sting of their sharp criticism, have reappraised their own traditions in terms of a deeper appreciation of the Reformation, and have incorporated into their own lives something of the distinctive spirit of the Reformation.

A reader of the vast literature of the Reformation may be impressed primarily either by the unity of the spirit it reflects or by its diversity. When viewed either against the common background of the sixteenth century or in contrast with eighteenth- and nineteenth-century patterns of thought, it is the unity that is paramount.

Both Lutheranism and Calvinism center about a relationship to God in Christ that is personal and immediate. No human intermediary, no institution, no tradition, can stand between a man and his Lord. In the supernatural sphere as well, no principality or power can separate us from him, and no saint, not even Mary herself, can help us to bring before him our needs and desires.

There is something stark and fearful about this relationship. The God into whose presence we come without aid and without recourse is not only the God of merciful love we see in Jesus. He is also the God of power, of judgment, of wrath. He is a God revealed, but he is also unfathomable mystery.

The immediacy of our relationship with God gives us freedom in our relationship with nature and our fellow man. Before God we acknowledge no spiritual superior. We recognize no ultimate dependence upon signs or symbols, or upon the natural world in which we live. The world is ours to use freely for our own good.

But the immediacy of our relationship to God also destroys every vestige of our complacency and self-confidence. The mediators that the Roman Catholic Church had provided for the pious had afforded them a sense of security before God.

It seemed that there were those who understood human frailty
and could interpret it before God while still interposing their
own virtue against his wrath. The shock of confrontation with
God had been eased by the gradual stages through which it
was to be attained. Means were provided appropriate to the
stage of development in which each found himself. There
were ways to compensate for one's sins and ways to obtain the
grace that was needed before confronting God. Above all,
the church itself offered shelter and comfort.

At one stroke all this was wiped away. The human soul stood
naked before God, and in its nakedness it saw itself in the
totality of its rebellion against God. It saw its very virtue as
pretense and this pretense as the worst of sins. It saw its wisdom as ignorance and its refusal to acknowledge ignorance as
contempt of God. It saw its self-respect as self-deceit and its
inability to abandon this deceit as a sign of its total depravity.

We find that the difference between ourselves and God is
not one of degree. Hence our alienation cannot be overcome
by stages of progress. There is not *more* in God of what *we*
call " goodness," " power," " love," or " justice " in human relationships. God is something wholly different from all these. He
is goodness, but his absolute goodness is not comparable to
human goodness. He is power, but his omnipotence is not related to what we call " power." He is love, but his love is of a
kind that does not exist in us. He is justice, but no man can
understand his judgments. The gulf between God and man is
total, so there can be no mediation. No means can be provided
by which we can attain fellowship with God. Only God can
initiate such a relationship, and for him to do so would be an
act of unimaginable grace.

But just this act of unimaginable grace has occurred! And it
has occurred in the most astonishing of all possible ways. God
became man! He became a man for our sakes! But more wonderful yet — he died for us. He died the most wretched, the
most humiliating, of all deaths! Against every canon of human

reason, against all sensible human expectation, against what all religious experience might lead us to believe — God died for our sakes!

What, then, is there for us to do? Are we to undertake to bridge the gap between ourselves and God by moral deeds, pure motives, and pious attitudes? Impossible! All such efforts are the expression of our foolish pride. By our petty achievements we blind ourselves to the wretchedness of our state and make light of the gift of God. God has done all, and there is nothing left for us to do — nothing except to acknowledge the truth, to believe, to trust, to give thanks and praise, to witness and to testify.

And even this, after all, is not our own achievement, as if some of us have the virtue to acknowledge the truth and can boast of our superiority over those who do not. Nay, even here it is God who gives faith and we who receive, humbly, gratefully, and in amazement at its transforming power.

Luther and Calvin and the spiritual descendants of both are, here in their central religious understanding, in complete agreement. The Christian life is one of testimony and response to what God has done. To proclaim God's work is the task of the church and of its members. All else in life and thought must stand judgment by this norm.

Doctrinally, there are few points of complete disagreement between Lutheranism and Calvinism. Even with regard to the sacraments, where historically the most heated disputes have arisen, the differences in formulation appear minor from the perspective of many in the twentieth century.

Yet as we read the works of Luther and Calvin, we cannot help feeling that there is much in the spirit of each quite alien to the other. And as we trace the history of the peoples whose life and thought have been marked by their separate influences, the impression of difference is greatly strengthened.

Lutheranism centers in the grateful apprehension of the gift of God, rejoicing in the inward assurance and peace that the gospel brings, accepting with resignation the sorrows of this life and the tyranny of wicked rulers, expressing at home and at work the spirit of Christian love in service for others.

Calvinism centers in the confident affirmation of the truth contained in God's Word, the application of this truth to all of life, and the continual struggle to discipline man's sinful nature to conform to the standards of the divine law.

Lutheranism leads inward to the world of poetry and music and philosophy. Calvinism leads outward to the remaking of the world according to the commands of God. The greatest intellectual achievements of Protestantism have been in lands where Lutheran influence has been strong. The greatest practical achievements of Protestantism have been produced by Calvinist cultures.

Lutheranism centers in public worship and private prayer. Calvinism expresses itself most characteristically in a disciplined life dedicated to upholding the moral and spiritual standards found in God's Word, both in personal life and in the life of the community. The heresy into which the Lutheran is most likely to fall is quietistic passivity, whereas the Calvinist, for all his talk of predestination, is far more inclined to legalistic moralism.

The history of the Lutheran and Calvinist churches is complex indeed. If it is read in terms of the ideas of the leading theologians, it reflects every current of cultural and intellectual change in the Western world. However, Lutheranism has tended to retain an amazing continuity of life and spirit to which its vigorous theological tradition has repeatedly been recalled. It has on the one hand guarded with great success its central understanding of the Christian experience and faith, while on the other hand dealing in modern times with remarkable flexibility with the findings of Biblical and historical scholarship and with the new sciences of nature and man.

Calvinism, on the contrary, has viewed the new intellectual developments less flexibly, clinging tenaciously to the details

of its faith and its stricter view of Biblical authority. Partly
for this reason it has been more deeply and painfully affected
by the shifting tides of cultural development and the conclusions of critical Biblical studies. The Calvinist has often seemed
to face the painful choice between loyalty to his heritage and
intellectual integrity. Such a choice is never so simple as that,
for intellectual integrity is an essential ingredient in the Calvinist heritage. Hence, many gradually moderated the convictions of their fathers and developed new patterns for understanding the Christian faith — such as those called below
the " experientialist" and the " social gospel."

Even more commonly, Calvinists almost insensibly moved
from their emphasis upon God's objective work of grace to the
emphasis upon the steps that men must take to receive the
benefits of Christ's work. This shift, scarcely recognized, gave
rise to great new denominations, such as the Baptist, and
gradually articulated its inner logic in their full development.
This form of Protestantism is discussed in Chapter IV as " Biblicism."

Those who remained loyal to the teachings of Calvin seemed
for many years to do so at the cost of losing his openness to
new truth. To outsiders, at least, they appeared to be characterized by a narrow dogmatism and a cultural isolation alien to
the dynamic spirit of primitive Calvinism. Yet, by their rigidity,
these groups have kept alive precious elements in the Calvinist heritage that would otherwise have been lost.

Now at last the painful dilemma of Calvinism seems re-
solved. Calvinists have come to believe that the greatest intellectual honesty, the most perceptive interpretation of history, the fullest recognition of the most reliable findings of
Biblical scholarship and natural science, all these are compatible with the ringing affirmations of the central doctrines
of Calvinist faith. By this conviction the spirit of Calvinism
has been revitalized, and once again in our century Calvinism
states its case with unsurpassed vigor and persuasiveness.

The two sections that follow present the convictions and attitudes of Lutheranism and Calvinism. The remarkable continuity of Lutheranism makes it possible to depict simultaneously the ideal spirit of primitive and contemporary Lutheranism, following the teachings of Luther himself as a norm. The revival of Calvinism points to the importance for contemporary Protestantism of many aspects of the spirit of Calvin also, but to a greater extent than in the treatment of Lutheranism the material is selected and the emphases are made in terms of the historical development of Calvinist ideas as well as in loyalty to the explicit teachings of Calvin.

LUTHERANISM

The deepest need of the human soul is to be at peace. The peace it needs is not freedom from danger and from the hatred and opposition of others. There are persons who have known peace in the midst of strife and persecution. There are others who have been favored in worldly comfort and security, those even who have basked in the esteem and affection of their neighbors, yet who have nevertheless been restless and dissatisfied in the depths of their souls. There seems to be a dimension of the human spirit whose needs cannot be readily expressed in words, but whose disquietude disturbs the whole tenor of life. Even in the midst of success, even when every conscious goal is realized, this uneasiness remains to taint man's happiness with an ultimate doubt — the strange doubt of himself, the feeling that ultimately he does not belong, that he is not in harmony with what is most real in the world.

Man's doubt of himself is not the recognition of specific violations of the moral code — though it is relevant to that. It is not the insight that there is an inborn tendency to assert himself continuously against reason and righteousness — though it is relevant to that too. It is rather the restless uncertainty of the spirit hungry for assurance that it is at one with God.

Man's feverish busyness in the work of the world and his

passionate desire to succeed in all things and to be praised by his fellow man on the one hand, and man's licentious self-abandon and cruel lust for power on the other, are but twin expressions of his need to satisfy or to forget his deepest hunger. But sensitive spirits throughout the ages have learned the lesson that in these paths there lies no hope, and men have been driven to acknowledge their need and to seek in religion for the fulfillment they cannot find in the world.

Religion, also, as a human creation has failed them. Some have sought by spiritual and ascetic practices to lose themselves in unity with that reality with which they need harmony. By denying self, by ultimately ceasing to exist as a separate self at all, by being wholly possessed by divine reality, surely that harmony can be attained without which there can be no true peace! But despite the profundity of the insights of many of the mystics into man's needs and God's power, despite even the apparent achievement by some of extraordinary states of spiritual life, the path of mysticism is an illusion.

For each one who climbs the ladder to the top and there finds ecstasy, a hundred self-deluded pretenders shout their wares, and a thousand, more honest, fall despairing along the way. The tiny spiritual elite who do seem to succeed pay too high a price for their success — the price of separation from the world, of depreciation of the value of the human self, and of the ever-present and even inevitable danger of the delusion that the self is really transcended, really lost in God, so that all that they feel and think is now God's truth and God's reality.

Others have believed that harmony with divine reality must come, not by mystical identity, but by moral obedience. They believe wrongly that the inner lack of peace must be due entirely to some thought or act against the divine will, some failure to behave as God directs. If a man conforms all action to the highest laws of righteousness, if he searches out in his soul every impure motive and licentious thought, if in utter self-denial he struggles unendingly to discipline his flesh, then surely he will find himself at total harmony with the divine righteousness, and peace will come to satisfy the hidden hunger of the soul.

But, once again, for every moral giant who does attain in wonderful measure the superhuman righteousness that is his goal, a hundred pretenders fill the air with the stench of their hypocrisy, and a thousand, more honest, are left in despair. Even the one who does succeed does so only in terms of a rare approximation to the ideals of human righteousness — not in his deeper quest for peace. Some pride he may indeed take in his great achievement, some self-righteous joy he may feel in his superiority over his fellows, but if he is as supremely honest as he is heroically virtuous, he will know in spite of himself that he has failed. The self-centeredness of inner motive, which alienates him from the deeper reality without and beyond, is not transcended.

Even religion thus fails to meet man's deepest needs. No spiritual exercise or moral discipline can quiet the ultimate anxiety of the soul, and out of this anxiety there flows a constant stream of rottenness to corrupt all that is best and noblest in human achievement. Man's lot seems hopeless, doomed to wretchedness even in the midst of plenty, to failure even in the midst of success.

But man's feverish and futile struggle to attain peace is only one side of the total situation. God has been at work. Eternally self-sufficient as God is, without need of man's praise or love, he has nevertheless been mindful of his creature's needs. In order that we may find the peace for which we yearn and may taste the joy that flows therefrom, God not only has accepted us, rebellious sinners though we are, but has revealed his acceptance to us, and has paid that price through which alone we can accept his acceptance! He has taken upon himself the form of man! He has emptied himself utterly of his majesty and power, has abased himself to our human level, has taken upon himself the full wretchedness of our human lot — even

temptation, suffering, and death! That divine reality to the
level of which we have striven so hard and so uselessly to rise,
from which we have attempted to claim acceptance by righteous obedience — that reality has condescended to our estate.
God's grace, utterly free, wholly unconditioned by anything
we have done or can ever do, gives to us what we must forever fail to achieve for ourselves.

It was the discovery of this great truth which rescued Luther
from spiritual torment, brought him to inward assurance of
the forgiveness of God, and hence gave to him the peace he
had sought so desperately so long. God has done everything
for us; we need only give thanks. God has forgiven us already;
we need only accept his forgiveness. God has promised to us
all that we need and desire; we need only trust and receive.
God has already come to us — we need not go to him, but only
believe the glorious good news. God has reconciled us to himself, and nothing that can happen in life or death can separate
us from the riches of his grace.

All that is required of us is that we trust him. Such trust is
utterly simple, yet for us in our rebellious pride, utterly impossible. We are determined to solve our own problems, to rely
on our own capacities, to triumph in our own power. We may
be willing to accept the help of others, even the *help* of God.
With our lips we may confess our inability to save ourselves
and ask God to save us. But in the depths of our hearts we
stubbornly buttress our pride, our pretense to deserve good at
God's hand, and we refuse to throw ourselves unreservedly at
his feet in desperate supplication.

Human life, therefore, is the life of self-justification. We
must at all costs maintain in our own eyes an image of ourselves that we can respect. So long as we can believe in our
own respectability we demand of God that he accept us in
terms of our desert. At least, we persuade ourselves, we are
better than our fellows, and God must acknowledge our superior merit.

But human life as the life of self-justification hangs pre-
cariously over the abyss, for it rests ultimately upon a self-
delusion. The restlessness of our souls is not stilled, the consciousness of our alienation from God is not wholly stifled, and
the knowledge that we are deceiving ourselves is not quite
successfully repressed. There are moments when we feel the
judgment of God upon us and when all pretense is impossible.
We glimpse ourselves as we really are and know both our
sinfulness and our misery. We endeavor to regain our blindness, but for a time it will not return. In these moments we
despair, and if our despair is great enough, if we despair also of
ever restoring our blindness, then there is hope. Only the man
who has despaired utterly of justifying himself will accept in
total humility the free unconditioned gift of God's total forgiveness. Only in the valley of utter darkness will man abandon
himself to the sheer simplicity of faith.

Since God has done all for us, given all, and promised all,
it is wrong for us to doubt. He would have us trust him utterly,
believe him completely, throw ourselves entirely on his mercy
— and there find the total peace for which we yearn. But so
long as we continue to live in the flesh we are never wholly
free from tormenting doubts. The inner restlessness, though
stilled in principle, yet makes itself felt from time to time. We
become conscious that our faith wanes, our trust diminishes,
the promises of our God elude our confidence. Our subjective
uncertainty and the coldness of our faith themselves appear to
us as signs that we have not received from God his gifts, and
we are tempted to despair.

This is indeed the supreme temptation. To despair is to fail
to believe in God's promises, to deny his grace. Hence, we
must at all costs refuse to yield to the dark moods of doubt.
Our momentary psychological attitude is not a sign that God's
promises are not for us. It is indeed a manifestation of the
weakness of our faith and of the power that evil still exercises
over us. But the weakness of our faith and of our resistance to

evil suggestion is not the measure of the power of God. God
wills our salvation! Believe *that* even in the midst of doubt,
and slowly, reluctantly, but surely, the darkness will be lifted
from the heart, and once again the inner confidence can match
the outward truth.

When we are assailed by doubts we must not dwell upon
them. Rather, we must refuse to give them a hearing. We must
seize upon God's Word, immersing our minds in its gracious
promises until they drive out the tempting doubts. We may
offer our doubts and temptations to God, praising him that he
has paid the price to ransom us from them as well, thanking
him for the promises of forgiveness, and indeed that our sins
are forgiven already even before we ask. Thus gradually, by
faith, faith grows within us; doubts, though they always
threaten, lose their sway, and a blessed peace settles ever
deeper upon our spirits.

Just as doubt is overcome in principle by faith but still remains to tempt us throughout our earthly pilgrimage, so also
sin, though its power is broken in principle by forgiveness,
still remains a part of the Christian's life. Justification is an act
of God by which he accepts us, sinners though we are, an act
by which he gives us freely that relationship with himself
which only the ideally righteous might justly claim as their
due. It does not involve any infusion into us of actual righteousness. It does not give us a new moral character. It does
not make the Christian ethically superior to the pagan.

Indeed, outward morality is not a matter of God's grace but
of human discipline. Whether or not men are Christian, for
the sake even of natural society they must be trained in self-
discipline. They must learn to subordinate their outward actions
to the control of their will, not yielding to momentary impulse,
but ruthlessly suppressing those inclinations which lead away
from the intelligent direction of life. A society that cannot
attain to even this level of righteousness will be torn to pieces
by its willfulness. It is the function of rulers, whether they are

Christian or pagan, to punish those who cannot or will not restrain themselves from gross violations of the moral code. To this end their office is ordained by God.

Some persons apart from Christ may attain to a very high degree of self-discipline. Self-discipline is not a distinctively Christian virtue at all, and some who have been blessed by the gift of faith may still be seriously lacking in discipline. The lack of self-discipline does not prevent us from being truly redeemed by the grace of God, and our possession of this virtue gives us no assurance that we are justified. Indeed, so great is the ever-present danger that the moral man may seek to substitute his moral attainments for the grace of Christ that he may actually be farther from the Kingdom of God than the person whose sinfulness is obvious to all. We can never forget that it was sinners and not Pharisees who heard Christ gladly. The gospel is the proclamation of freedom from all law, from all duties and obligations!

But when we have said that justification is not a moral change in man, that moral self-discipline is independent of Christian faith, and that the Christian life is one free from all bondage to law, we have expressed only one side of the whole truth. Better perhaps to exaggerate this separateness, yes, even this enmity, of faith and morality than to minimize it, for common sense forever strives to identify the two to the destruction of the gospel. Nevertheless, if anyone claiming to be a Christian should seize upon the divorce of faith and law as an excuse for moral laxity, then indeed must God's word of judgment be proclaimed against him in all its power and awfulness.

True, the practice of self-control is a natural virtue, and our lack of this discipline need not cause us to question that God's grace is sufficient even for us. But the joyous confidence that we may find inwardly in Christ will not cause us to be indifferent to our outward behavior. On the contrary, we will now for the first time have real reason to control our behavior and conform it to the law. Whereas for others the reason for self-discipline is merely the enhancement of self-esteem, the Christian desires to discipline his actions in the service of God. Shall the Christian do less for God than the pagan does for self?

Whatever, therefore, may be the degree of self-control possessed by the individual at that time when God grants him the gift of faith, from that moment he will strive more diligently to increase his control of his outward actions. The bad habits of youth are not easily overcome, and the Christian with lax training may never attain to the degree of outward morality exemplified by many righteous pagans. He will not for that reason despair. He knows he is forgiven, accepted by God, and for this his heart is filled with joyous gratitude. But he will not for that reason excuse himself. On the contrary, his faith will lead him to a far more sensitive awareness of the scope and depth of his moral wickedness, a wickedness he will confess to God with shame and sadness.

Therefore, though discipline saves no one, it must not be neglected. Long before the child can understand the human situation or the meaning of faith, he must learn the hard lessons of self-control. True, he will control himself for motives that are prideful and selfish. Even this is better than self-indulgence. But beyond this we can believe that God will vouchsafe to him also the joy of Christian faith. When that time comes he will be ready. The habit of self-control will then enable him to conform the acts of his outer man to the new inward determination to serve God.

Thus, although justification is not a moral change in us, it is not barren of empirical consequences. Faith brings peace to our inmost soul, joyous gratitude for God's forgiveness, and a heightened consciousness of our moral guiltiness. These issue in their turn in an intensified determination to live for God and to conform all outward actions to his will. But this is not all, for the peace that comes from faith in God's acceptance transforms all the possibilities of human experience. Ethical determination is but a part of a larger whole, and in this larger whole it is remade into something quite different.

When we have achieved the profound inward security of assurance that God has graciously accepted us despite our enmity toward him, we are free from the terrible need to justify ourselves or to drown our anxiety in self-indulgence. Since we do not need to justify ourselves, we no longer calculate the consequences of all our actions in terms of the prestige they will gain for us in the eyes of others. We no longer need to believe ill of others in order to think well of ourselves. We no longer resent the outward success of others or bemoan the lack of fortune that prevents us from excelling them.

All this is replaced by love — not the love of desire, the love that drives us to possess and control, but the selfless love of one who needs to give and not to receive. Our life is touched by that love which is truly of God — forgiving, accepting, self-giving, suffering, redemptive love — that love which is manifest in Christ Jesus and which we have only from him.

This love does not seek to dramatize itself. It does not demand large fields of action and restlessly seek for greater opportunities for heroic self-denial. Rather, it accepts the lot that God has given, insignificant as it may seem, as its sphere of action. In home and family it manifests itself most perfectly in the self-giving of each to the other. Husband lives for wife, and wife for husband. Parents live for children, and children for parents. The family gives itself unstintingly to the neighbor who is in need, and the neighbor in love ministers in his turn.

Beyond the calling to family and community responsibility, each man is called also to serve his fellow man in some useful employment. We are not led by love to question our calling, to demand some greater responsibility or some more obviously fruitful work. To demand this is to assert oneself — not to love. To any calling, however humble, we may give ourselves diligently, conscientiously, self-forgetfully — doing more than is expected, serving beyond the call of duty, and demanding nothing in return. Love does not demand justice for itself, though it may protest injustice against another. It does not insist upon recognition or praise, though it bestows them freely on others. Cheerful obedience to those whom God has placed above us, careful workmanship without thought of recompense — thus love expresses itself in work.

The new life of faith frees us from all bondage to law. But this can never mean that it carries us back to the licentiousness of the undisciplined. Rather, it means that without the love that flows from faith men are motivated at best by obligations. They feel they should, they ought, and they must. Life consists at its highest in joyless obedience to commands from without and from within.

But when love comes, the law is superseded. All that before we did under obligation, now we do from desire — and more than this we will do. What once seemed an unbearable burden now seems a happy occasion for service. Even painful sacrifice seems but a glorious opportunity to participate in the fellowship of the suffering Christ.

Christianity does not, therefore, add rules and further restrictions to those demanded by the interests of secular society. The rules of social living it accepts and transmutes into expressions of love, but beyond these there is no need to go. One need not prescribe the course of love. One need not seek to predetermine the personal habits that Christians will find appropriate for the redeemed life.

Neither can one propound patterns of social reform or reconstruction as distinctive requirements of Christianity upon the body politic. Human sinfulness will pervert any order, and Christian love can express itself through all. Of the state we can demand only the maintenance of order and the freedom of the Word of God. To the state that gives this, the Christian owes earnest loyalty and wholehearted obedience.

It may be that those persons in positions of authority are

not worthy of their positions. Indeed, most persons who have worldly power are corrupted by that power and wield it unjustly. The greatest men are likely to be the most outrageous sinners, for they have the greatest opportunity for rebellion against God. But we are not called to stand in judgment upon our rulers. To do so is presumptuous. Our task is to express love in service and to obey in true humility the persons who are placed in positions of command. Some, it is true, may be called by God to proclaim his word of judgment against the iniquities of the rich and strong. All may be called to pray earnestly for relief from their tyranny. But love does not express itself in angry words and violent resistance. It prefers to suffer rather than to inflict suffering, to yield to evil rather than to rebel against it.

In the midst of a world corrupted by sin and filled with the suffering that men inflict upon one another, we may still live in inner serenity, lightening in loving service the burdens of others. We may still testify to the glorious good news of Jesus Christ. Each may still be a Christ to his neighbor.

The supreme reality is the good news that God has already given us the peace we seek. God has descended to us; we need not futilely attempt to climb up to him. This message has come to us through the Bible, the church, and the sacraments, and all these like the Christian life itself are to be understood in their connection with its truth.

It was in the Bible, especially in the letters of Paul, that Luther found the teaching of God's grace as free forgiveness. To speak more precisely, it was as Luther opened his mind to the real meaning of these Scripture passages that God spoke his comforting Word in Luther's heart. This Word had been concealed to generations of Christians because of a habit of interpretation that read into the Scriptures the ideas to which men had become gradually accustomed through tradition. When men cease to read their ideas into the Bible and listen instead to what God would say to them through the Bible, then, and only then, can they encounter the living Word.

This Word, which God spoke to Luther and which he speaks ever anew to us, is none other than the one Word that he spoke in Christ. Indeed, the Word is ultimately and in its fullness Christ, and in him and in him alone is the meaning of all Scripture made plain. When all is read through Christ, and is judged and understood in the light of Christ, then alone the truth of all Scripture can be grasped.

The earnest seeker may read the Bible in confidence that in and through it he will find the incarnate Word. God's Word is not the mere written letters on the page, but it is the promises they contain made effective in our hearts by the grace of God. God has promised that he who seeks will find and that to him who knocks the door will be opened. Take, therefore, and read with confidence.

We find in Scripture not only the glorious assurances of redemption but also the commandments or law. Wherever we turn, in New Testament or Old these two ingredients of God's Word confront us, and although it is to the promises above all that we must cling, we will not thereby escape the demand of the law. Part of the law is indeed superseded. The ceremonial law, especially, belongs to a day long past. But the basic moral law, brought to its final perfection in the exalted commandments of Christ himself, remains to judge and condemn us as well as to challenge and inspire us. In so far as we are transformed by love we are freed from the commandments of righteousness, but the commandments remain to guide our conduct, to check our pretense, and to bring us ever anew to repentance.

The redemptive Word found in the Bible is proclaimed also in the sacraments instituted by Christ for this purpose. Nor are these sacraments mere memorials, mere reminders of an event long past, or outward symbols of a merely supposed event within. The sacraments are God's chosen channel by which and through which he communicates his Word to men.

They are constituted by the promises that they embody. Yet in a very profound sense they are not promises only but also the fulfillment of promises.

In Baptism, through the words of institution, the enactment according to the commands of Christ, and the faith of the recipient, God's Word is truly mediated into the life of the baptized. If the one baptized is an infant brought by believing parents, God is not handicapped by the lack of reason in the child. The parents' faith affords the channel for the justifying Word. Indeed, faith itself, whether of child or parent, is not to be understood as a precondition of God's Word, as if God were impotent to use his sacraments until man provided the proper attitude. Faith is not ultimately an independent contribution of man which he can make or withhold at his pleasure. Faith is the gift of the Word made efficacious in the heart of man. Through baptism the Word of God works its miracle in our hearts, not in accordance with our attitudes but in accordance with his will and promise. Seize with faith upon that truth, and it will be to you a source of comforting assurance.

It is at the Table of our Lord that the greatest and most beautiful assurance is vouchsafed. There Christ gives himself to us anew. He empties himself again of glory and majesty and takes upon himself the lowly forms of bread and wine. He does not offer himself to us at the behest of a priest endowed with supernatural powers for transforming bread and wine into the body of the Crucified. It is the height of presumption for priests thus to pretend to manipulate by their incantations the body of their Lord. When anyone speaks of man's offering his Lord to God in sacrifice, he has added madness to his presumption. *He* offers himself to us, we do not offer him to God. He offers himself, not in accordance with our power, but in accordance with his promises and his incredible compassion. He gives himself to us just as truly as once upon the cross of Calvary he died for us. His giving is not conditioned by our faith, but when in truth we do believe, how gloriously does this consummate gift work within us to strengthen our belief, our love, our joy, our gratitude! How unpardonable is our indifference, our faithlessness to such a Lord — who yet pardons even these!

The authority of the church, also, rests in the Word of God. Indeed, its very existence is constituted by the proclamation of that Word. No man can pass on to other men divine authority or power, but the Word can ever anew awaken man's response. The church, therefore, is not constituted by a continuity of institutions or personnel. The church is found wherever the Word is proclaimed; and wherever the Word is silenced, no directness of descent from great Christians of the past, no vaunted ordination, even if it were by Christ himself, would suffice to sustain its existence.

This does not mean that where the Bible is incorrectly interpreted and the sacraments improperly administered there is no church. When the Bible is read at all and where the words of sacramental institution are pronounced, however confusedly the truth is perceived, God's Word is not powerless to perform its redemptive work. Some heart will be awakened to true faith, true trust in Christ, however little it may understand its own response.

Thus it is through the visible church, the institution that accepts the responsibility for proclaiming the Word through Scripture, preaching, and sacraments, that God calls men into the fellowship of his invisible church. This invisible church cannot exist without the visible, but it is for the sake of the invisible church that the visible exists. One must not, therefore, sneer at the visible church for its manifold failures and its appalling unworthiness of its allotted task, but, equally, one must not falsely glorify it by pretending that it possesses authority over the Word. It exists to serve the Word, and it exists truly only as it fulfills this function.

God's Word is not thwarted by the human corruption of his chosen instrument, but this does not justify complacency in that corruption. An institution with so lofty a function must be purified to the uttermost of all that prevents it from fulfilling its true purpose. Its leaders must ever be alert and vigilant against the infiltration of falsehood and corruption. But this does not mean that there is only one form that the church may take, or that the services of worship must conform to some archetypal pattern. In organization, in architecture, in aids to worship, and in liturgy there are a thousand matters irrelevant to the great purpose of the church. In these matters men have freedom to act as they wish in accordance with temperament, tradition, and religious need.

It is the function of the church not only to proclaim the Word in preaching and sacrament, but also to protect it from error of interpretation. To do this, men of learning and intellectual ability must formulate the true doctrines with utmost care and precision. Never again can we allow the Word to be obscured as in the days before Luther. The blessed peace of assurance which depends upon a clear grasp of the gospel must be always available. Hence, doctrine is important, not incidentally, not because it is desirable to preserve sectarian opinion, but because right doctrine is the basis of right faith, because without it we lose the grounds of certainty that in neither death nor life is there any power capable of separating us from the love of Christ.

Doctrine cannot be based on reason, if by reason we mean those intellectual faculties shared by the unbeliever. It may be that the unbeliever will form arguments for the existence of God and will attribute to God many high and lofty qualities. It may be that he will even be led by his reason to posit a doctrine of rewards and punishments after death. Probably he will advocate a moral life similar in many ways to the life of the Christian. But all this is not a natural theology to which a few revealed truths may be added to complete the Christian system.

So long as men rely upon their reason in their quest for ultimate truth they will forever make God in their own image.

They will project their ideals and their prejudices and invent arguments for their objective existence. They will believe ultimately what they want to believe in order that they may justify themselves, and they will buttress this self-delusion by the pretense that they are led only by the unbiased norm of pure rationality. Superficial resemblances there may be between the wish-fulfilling projections of man's prideful imaginings and the truth that God has graciously revealed, but at their center they are utterly opposed. God's truth destroys the pretense of righteousness that is the source of our vain speculations and confronts us with the living God at whose Word all the idols of our hearts melt away.

There is nothing elaborate or complex about true doctrine. It may be found by any open and honest mind that searches the Scriptures. However, even when we acknowledge Scripture as the final source of all truth about God, we are prone to use reason so as to obscure the living Word. In the name of reason one makes modifications here or there. These changes are so slight that it seems a mere cavil to object, but they introduce into the pure gospel a principle of doubt. Perhaps he tells us only that we must co-operate with God's grace in the development of our faith. And is this not surely reasonable? Is it not desirable to give advice and encouragement to those who wrestle with doubt? Does this not assume that men can do their part and must do so?

But note: If the theologian yields here, what follows? It follows that there is something *I* must do — and do rightly — in order to receive God's gift. And if I do it not rightly, if my motives are impure, if I do not try hard enough, then I do not receive the gift. And how can I be sure? How can I be certain of the purity of my motives, of the adequacy of my effort? Indeed, when we know ourselves fully and deeply as the sinners that we are, how can we ever really believe that we have done anything rightly? If it depends on us, if anything whatsoever depends on us, then there is for us again only doubt and despair.

If the alternative to this is predestination with all the intellectual problems that this doctrine raises, then predestination must be accepted. But there is no need to draw from such a doctrine any conclusion that places in question the universality of God's love or the universal efficacy of the work of Christ. The need is not that problems be avoided or that common sense be pleased. The need is that the gospel truth be preserved in all its purity. If in our testimony to what God has done for us we contradict ourselves, even so let us remain faithful to our testimony. If thereby logic and metaphysics are rejected, very well, they have their sphere, but we are beyond reason here, dealing with ultimate reality and man's most basic need.

There is great diversity of doctrine even among those who recognize the historical importance of Luther for their special traditions. Many seem to have missed the real significance of his great spiritual insight. Some have based their faith upon principles that seem almost antithetical to Luther's teaching and that tend to weaken the redemptive power of the gospel. Toward those who seek sincerely, the only Christian attitude is hopeful love. All who name the name of Christ, all who seek salvation through him, should be united in common endeavor. But union cannot be accepted at the cost of compromise with error. Purity of doctrine is far more important than inclusiveness of institution or even co-operation among institutions.

Luther was not infallible, and no person or group today possesses all truth or a monopoly upon the truth that it has succeeded in grasping. Fresh insights are always to be joyfully acknowledged, and old truths can be expressed more clearly in new ways. Scholarship can throw new light upon the meaning of Scripture, and scientists and historians can contribute to intellectual growth. But openness to growth is not willingness to surrender. Rather than endanger pure doctrine, it is better to appear narrow, rigid, and exclusivist, trusting that in time all Christians will grasp the meaning of the gospel in its fullness and its purity, so that all may join together in outward expression of their inner oneness in Christ. Only through the gospel of God's pure grace can we find the peace of the assurance of the forgiveness of sins and live the life of love for our sinful fellows.

CALVINISM

Christianity is service of God. It is not a means of gaining gifts and favors, even the gift of salvation from sin and death. To place man at the center of religion — either as the subject of religious acts or as the object to be benefited by them is to pervert the true faith. Christianity is the recognition in thought, in motive, and in deed of the majesty, the sovereignty, the indescribable glory of God.

Beside the infinite greatness of the Creator, what importance has the finite created world? As we vainly strive to contemplate the vast reaches of eternity, what meaning can we assign to our ephemeral existence? When we consider the timeless and limitless knowledge that God has of all things, what value can we find in our feeble and partial understanding? When we pause to marvel how all creation from the smallest grain of sand to the largest star, from the humblest amoeba to the angelic hosts — all lives and moves according to the dictates of God's sovereign will — we cannot but be overwhelmed by the thought of his ineffable majesty. God is indeed utterly, incomprehensibly greater and more glorious than we and all our dreams.

Yet, though we are overwhelmed, we are not annihilated. Though we perceive our own utter insignificance before God, we are not left purposeless and empty. Though we must see and acknowledge that God is all in all, we are not thereby made nothing. For ours is the sacred opportunity to give to God the praise, the honor, the glory that is his due, and in that act our lives take on meaning and seriousness.

Indeed, it is not the acknowledgment of the glory of God but its denial that empties man of value and purpose. When

we boast of our importance and look upon ourselves as the
end of all endeavor, then the endeavor loses significance. The
happiness of the self is too trivial and transitory an end to
justify either heroic sacrifice or sober work, and without sacrifice and work the self loses dignity even in its own eyes. Whenever we turn from the glory of God to the admiration and enhancement of ourselves, we lose that which we seek to gain.
He who would save his life shall lose it.

When, instead, we look upon reality as it is, when we give
to each part its due, then life, though not easy or comfortable
or pleasant, is profoundly worth the living. It is true that for
us to give to each part of reality its due is to give all praise
and glory to God and to reserve nothing for ourselves, but
when by this fundamental act of self-denial we accept our
proper place in the ultimate order of things, life becomes infinitely meaningful. Suffering and work may not be pleasant,
but they can be endured with a fortitude born of confidence
in the supreme worth-whileness of our existence.

In the eyes of those who are blinded to God's glory the negation of all in life incompatible with that glory may seem mor-
bidly ascetic. But to those who are intoxicated by the vision
of God's majesty, the abandonment of the frivolous is pure
gain. We do not deny ourselves in order to improve our standing before God. Such a motive is perverse. We deny ourselves
in order that we may affirm what is infinitely better than ourselves — the glory of God. We do not avoid the pleasures of
the world because they are pleasures or because they belong to
an evil order. The world and all its pleasures are in themselves
good, given to us for our enjoyment. But when such enjoyment becomes our end, when it comes between us and the
enjoyment of God, then it is to be renounced. Enjoy the world
and all its fruits, but enjoy them to the glory of God!

Not only are we free to enjoy the world in which we find
ourselves in so far as we can do so to the glory of God, but our
lives are suffused by a great hope and expectation. This

world is not our final home and resting place; we are transients, pilgrims here. Our real home is with God, and to that home in God's good time we will be called. How unimportant, then, that for the present we forego some amusement or suffer ridicule and persecution! Let us praise God that he counts us worthy to suffer for his sake.

To perceive the truth that God is utterly glorious and that the end of man's life is to glorify him is surely open to everyone born with the natural light of intelligence. Do not the heavens declare his glory, and does not the firmament show forth his handiwork? Does not conscience direct that we should give glory where glory is due? Certainly all this is so. Yet through all the ages of human history men have universally rejected the truth so plainly visible to reason and conscience. For our sovereign Lord and Creator we have substituted the idols of our evil imaginations. Even these idols we have worshiped to glorify ourselves rather than them. The reason given to us to perceive the greatness of God we have used instead to excuse our guilty consciences. We have enthroned appetite and placed intellect in its service, thus destroying the natural harmony in which God created us. Surely we who have rejected so high a calling with such vicious perversity are worthy of nothing but to be left to the wretchedness of self-destruction!

But God has not dealt with us according to our deserts. In his infinite compassion he has come to us with new light. He has revealed himself in a way that even our willful blindness cannot finally conceal from us. He has condescended to our low estate in covenants suited to our sinful condition. He has spoken to us through his prophets, and finally he has revealed himself in the person of his only Son. He has caused the record of his self-giving to man to be set down in a book through which he speaks his Word to every age and every human need.

But God's revelation of himself did not overcome our rebellion against him. The very openness and clarity with which

God spoke only caused our fevered minds to seek further ex-
cuses for our disobedience. The truth that God revealed to us
we tried to conceal from ourselves lest we be compelled to
acknowledge the depths of our wanton sinfulness. Finally, we
crucified God's Son!

Even so, God did not leave us to our misery. The very act by
which we proclaimed our utter shamelessness, the very act in
which we tried to destroy our Lord was, in the mysterious
counsels of God, the event through which he worked our redemption. Christ, given to us by God and nailed to the cross
by our guilty hate, so satisfied the righteous judgments of the
Father that he in his boundless mercy has chosen to attribute
to those who trust him the righteousness of his Son! If by the
light of reason we ought already to have acknowledged the
glory of God, how much more should we who live by grace
under the shadow of the cross of Christ give ourselves wholly
in praise and thanksgiving to the glory of him who both made
us and restored us!

When the scales of our self-imposed blindness have fallen
from our eyes, we can see the glory of God revealed in nature,
but we can understand him there only because we have found
him first in Scripture. This Word, the record of our redemption and God's self-disclosure, must be for us always our most
precious possession.

The Bible is not an object to be reverenced from without.
It is not a book to be read once and put away. It is a living
Word through which God addresses us, illumines our minds,
opens our hearts, and directs our lives. No problem of personal
living is so small that in this vast storehouse of God's truth we
cannot find direction for its solution. No issue of international
affairs is so great that we cannot learn to view it in the light of
God's total dealing with man through history recorded for all
time in Scripture.

Knowledge of the Scriptures must never be the private possession of the scholar. The scholar may serve a useful function

in explaining difficult passages and in throwing light upon the historic situation in relation to which God spoke. But God has not used an esoteric language open only to the highly trained. He has spoken to us all in the language of chronicle and song, which each of us can grasp. The meaning we are to seek is not to be found in the allegories of human imagination by which the plain truth of the account is so often obscured. The Scripture speaks openly and distinctly to all who read with minds eager to learn and hearts willing to obey.

The readiness with which Scriptural truth is available to the common man does not mean that he grasps in a single reading its full import. The Biblical truth is a living truth vitally related to the condition of the reader. What we seek when we seek aright is a truth for ourselves as we exist in the moment we read. We return again and again to the same passages, not because we misunderstood before, but because we bring to them a new situation, a new concern, a new self. To each new moment of encounter between ourselves and the Bible, the living Word yields a new and ever deeper truth.

Thus it is that the Christian knows in faith that all truth, all, that is, that matters ultimately, is available for him in Holy Writ. This does not mean that he who has read the Bible knows all that is to be known about God. No man has exhausted the riches of God's Word. Furthermore, the serious Christian should study other writings and expositions and interpretations of the Scriptures. But these are true finally only as they help us find truth in God's own Word.

The Bible is the focus of the most personal and individual moments of life. Each of us must find God for himself in the pages of sacred lore. Each must bare his own soul before God, confess his own sins, receive his own forgiveness. But the Bible does not function only in this most intimate and private role.

The Bible is also the focus of the life of the family. Gathered together in the home, the family reads the ancient stories, each member contributing his special insight into their meaning. In common reverence for God's Word, in common quest for its significance for the common life, the Christian family is bound into an unbreakable fellowship. Because the family, too, exists for the glory of God, because each member comes to feel this common purpose as his own, the natural bonds uniting husband, wife, and children are undergirded by the supernatural bonds of the Christian spirit. Into the very bone and marrow of the child who grows up in such a home is poured a strength of conviction that enables him to stand alone against the world for the glory of God.

The Bible is the focus, finally, of the life of the Christian community; indeed, the witness to the Biblical message is the essential function of that community. The church is the product of God's redeeming act, and it exists for the purpose of proclaiming that act. It possesses the Word of God, but only in the sense that its very being is constituted by that possession. Where God's Word is preached, *there* is the church.

As there is only one Word there can, in truth, be only one church constituted by that Word and thereby rendered apostolic, holy, and universal. The divisions among those who profess the faith are a heartbreaking denial of that unity. If all would fully submit their total thought to the sovereignty of the Word of God plainly recorded in Scripture, the visible church could once again witness to the unity of the invisible church. But until that day comes, loyalty to the Scriptural Word must be maintained, whatever the sacrifice to the secondary goal of hastening church unity.

The church does not depend upon any liturgy or any organization. Its power does not rest in a treasury of grace over which it has control or in a mysterious capacity communicated from generation to generation by the laying on of hands. Its clergy possess no power other than that which all Christians share. The church needs to make no such pretense to the possession of special power, for it embodies the only power that is real and enduring — the power of the Word of God.

To say that organization and liturgy are inessential is not to say that they are unimportant. It is inexcusable to organize that institution which exists as proclaimer of the Word by any pattern other than that contained in the Word. The church should search the Scriptures to discover what orders are sanctioned and should conform itself with all diligence to what it learns.

The service of worship should be cleansed of all that is merely human, of all that points to itself and man's achievements, of all that might seem to suggest that the finite symbol, created by the human mind, can participate in the absolute glory of God. God's Word alone is adequate to the praise of God.

Since the church is no merely human institution established to serve natural ends, it does not depend upon the moral character or correct beliefs either of its ministers or of its membership. But this independence is no excuse for laxity. The standards of the clergy especially must be guarded with care. They must be trained in doctrine and disciplined in life, and little tolerance can be shown toward those who fail. Lay people, too, should be watched and encouraged to struggle after the highest standards. But their failures do not reduce the concern of the church to minister to them. It is within the church that the hearts of the weak and sinful can be touched and healed. Only those who blatantly proclaim by word and act their indifference to the things of God must be excluded.

The proclamation of the Word is not only a matter of reading and expounding the Biblical texts. Important as these means are, they cannot stand alone without the sacraments. In the sacraments, even more clearly than in the spoken word, is dramatized the ultimate truth upon which all faith rests — God's gift of salvation through Christ. Here we enter into the promise, not as listeners only, but as participants in an act established by Christ himself.

Acts are constituted sacraments only by their establishment

by Christ. To add to their number on the basis of human custom and tradition is seriously to confuse the Word of God and the words of man. There are and can be only two true sacraments, Baptism and the Lord's Supper. These sacraments are the outward and visible signs of an inward and spiritual grace. In themselves, simply as outward acts, they can do nothing, but as the chosen instruments of God and conjoined with the inward activity of his Spirit, they work faith and repentance in our hearts.

Thus the sacrament becomes much more than a sign of God's grace. It is also the seal of his promise. He has promised to incorporate us in Christ's body and to impart to us Christ's righteousness that we may be heirs of Christ's inheritance. In the sacraments, God gives us what he has promised in a form adapted to our weakness. In receiving the sacraments we are united with Christ, our understanding of God's promises becomes clear, and our confidence in his gift grows sure.

Baptism is the sign and effectual seal of our being in the church, both visible and invisible. In this act the church and the baptized individual or his parents profess their confidence that in the providence of God this person is of the elect. God's eternal decree is here temporally affirmed. The faith that brings one to Baptism is, in and through the sacrament, strengthened and deepened.

The lack of faith on the part of the infant brought for Baptism does not hinder the efficacy of the sacrament. Indeed, we have in infant Baptism a vivid portrayal of the truth that it is God who acts in the sacrament and not man. The consciousness of faith may not come to the child for many years, but when it comes he will experience it as God's gift to him, and he will recall the sacrament through which God has chosen to act. The sacrament of Baptism will be for him a source of awakening and strengthening of faith as he daily acknowledges his total dependence upon the gift of God continually renewed.

In the Lord's Supper we find the very body and blood of

Christ given to us spiritually for our comfort. Through it we
are engrafted into our Lord to become ourselves truly a part
of his body. As we receive the elements to his glory we are
lifted up to share in that glory as fully as the conditions of this
life permit. We receive from him that faith in which alone we
can have life.

We do not offer Christ in the Supper as a sacrifice to God.
Once for all Christ gave himself on Calvary, an all-sufficient
sacrifice for our sins. But in dependence upon that sacrifice
and as united by faith with Christ who is our entire righteousness, we do offer to God our thanksgiving, our praise, and
finally, our very selves.

To take these supremely precious spiritual truths of the
sacrament and crudely translate them into statements about
the physical elements is to corrupt the sacraments and degrade
our faith. Surely we cannot seriously suppose that in eating
the bread we are actually chewing with our teeth the physical
body of Christ! The glorified body of Christ is risen from the
grave and ascended into heaven. To suppose it cut up into an
infinitude of tiny pieces that are mysteriously associated with
bits of bread is ridiculous and disgusting. What we need is
not physical food but spiritual sustenance, and such sustenance
in richest measure God gives us by his Holy Spirit as we com-
mune with Christ in his Supper.

If we are truly to give God the glory that is due his name,
we must do more than study and proclaim his Word. Above
all we must live in obedience to that Word. The Christian life
must be one of glorifying God by progressive conformity of
thought, word, and deed to his will as revealed in Holy Scripture. This is a lifelong and never completed process of morti-
fication of the sinful nature. Our study of Scripture clearly
reveals norms for conduct and for motive that we *must* obey
and yet constantly *fail* to obey. Earnest effort combined with
complete honesty in the recognition of our failure marks our
lives as Christians.

As Christians we are humble, however, not only because of our continuous failure, but also because we know that even our success is not our own. Subjectively we have felt that we have been struggling against sin, and we know that we must continue unrelentingly to do so. But we know at the same time that the battle against sin has really been waged, not by ourselves, but by God's Word and God's Spirit. Only as we hear God's Word in faith do we repent of our sins and struggle to overcome them, and only as God's Spirit opens our hearts can we hear his Word in faith. It is the sin and not the battle against it that represents our own wills.

To believe otherwise is to detract from the glory of God, and since the glory of God is the only true end of action, to claim credit for ourselves renders all that has been achieved tainted, corrupted, and evil.

But to attribute all good to God and all evil to ourselves is not to excuse any indifference, negligence, or laxity on our own part. When we suppose that it does so, when we accept our incapacity to glorify God as an excuse for not earnestly striving to do so, we express to ourselves and to the world that the Spirit of God dwells not in us. He in whom God's Spirit dwells *does* seek to glorify God in deed and in word, all the more so because he knows that his very desire to glorify God is itself God's free gift. Apart from this combination of earnest moral effort and total personal humility there is no real Christianity.

What, then, if we find that we are not striving to the uttermost, or that strive though we may we do not grow in conquest of sin, or that we claim to ourselves the glory of victory? Are we then utterly lost? Must we completely despair? Are we to probe more and more into the recesses of our own consciousness only to be the more appalled at the depths of pride, lust, and selfishness there revealed? Are we to beg God endlessly for the gift of his salvation and yet never to know whether it is given?

No! By no means! Do not search within yourself. There you

will never find aught but sin and evil. Your search will lead inevitably to despair. Look outward to the promises of God that cluster about the cross of Christ. Those promises are true. Believe them, not merely that they are true for others, but that they are true for you as well. Do not ask yourself whether you believe, meditating upon your doubts and uncertainties. Forget the weakness of your faith as you experience it within your heart. Certainty lies in the objective truth. Believe it in spite of your doubts — believe even because of your doubts! Your concern, your anxiety, your very doubt, are already marks of faith, but do not begin with them. God has chosen you from the foundations of the world and predestined you to share his glory! Comfort yourself with the assurance that your salvation is God's work, not yours; it depends upon the surety of his will, not upon the ever-uncertain sinful will you find within you. Believe! — and all is sure. And believing, go forth in confidence, in gratitude to God for his certain gift, to do all that may be done for his glory. The acts that you do for his glory will themselves be the seal of your election. In denying yourself for his sake, you will know yourself as eternally his.

We do not grow morally and spiritually by concentrating directly upon our own improvement. We grow by performing deeds that bring glory to God. We grow by doing the work into which he has called us, however menial it may be, for his glory, seriously, diligently, to the very best of our ability. We grow by making our homes as Christian as we can, building upon the bedrock of God's Word. We grow by serving our neighbor in time of need and exhorting one another to more diligent obedience to God's will.

We cannot rest content merely to make over our own lives and those of our relations and neighbors to the glory of God. All society must give him honor. God is Lord of history as well as of nature, of nations as well as of individuals. His Word is addressed to society as a whole as well as to private persons, and until the whole people yield him obedience, he is dishonored. It is intolerable that we should live in a community that owes ultimate allegiance to merely human leaders and ignores the plain teaching of the Word of God. Not the individual alone, but the commonwealth as well, must be holy.

We cannot endure the claim of any man who would oppose the transformation of society into a holy commonwealth. Whatever his human dignity, whatever his rank or ancestry, he is merely a sinful man like ourselves. If he is our rightful ruler, we serve him gladly for the glory of God, but in so far as he places himself against the Word of God, he cannot stand.

The success of God's plan for the world does not depend on us. His purposes are steadfast and sure. What he wills, he executes. But this is a reason, not for standing aside to let others carry out God's purposes, but for rejoicing in the glorious opportunity to share in the victorious work of God. God calls us to the high privilege of serving as his instruments in the fulfillment of his eternal plan. Proudly and joyfully we respond to his will.

At best the holy commonwealth, brought about by the power of men of faith, is no utopia. Sin remains to corrupt alike the rich and the powerful, the poor and the weak. To fail to recognize in the organization of society the continuous power of sin even among Christians is to be blind and foolish. Society must be so structured that temptation to pride and to the seizure of power will be minimized, while at the same time every force of social pressure shall be mobilized to the development of morally disciplined men and women. Liberty from arbitrary despotism there must be, but not license to allow the sinful nature to develop and freely express itself. Mere freedom to express *oneself* is nothing. True freedom is freedom to live to the glory of God, and for the achievement of this freedom Christian men may strive to the uttermost, unafraid of anything that life or death may bring.

Christianity consists first of all in a living relationship with God, an apprehension of his glory, and a life disciplined in accordance with that glory. But the emphasis on life must never be understood as implying the depreciation of doctrine. God's saving Word must be accurately formulated and vigorously defended; its statement and defense are an essential part of the propagation of the Christian faith.

Sound doctrine consists in the Biblical teaching ordered and arranged so as to bring out its true meaning to the glory of God. Since the Bible speaks plainly to the open mind, the formulation of doctrine as such is not difficult. But all too often the critic takes those doctrines which are believed to be to God's glory and twists them to give the appearance of damaging God's honor. These objections to the true Biblical faith center in the assertion that, if God is absolutely sovereign, the blame for evil must be placed upon him rather than upon men.

Any honest man must immediately recognize that none of the faithful has ever understood his beliefs in so blasphemous a light. Nevertheless, the specious arguments by which this criticism is supported must forever be silenced by clear reasoning. How, then, can God escape the imputation of cruelty in damning to eternal torment the majority of his helpless creatures? If God is the sole ultimate cause of all that occurs, how can man be held responsible for sin? Is not God, in punishing sin, inexcusably inflicting suffering upon men for deeds that are God's own responsibility?

The explanation of the true relationship between man and God begins with an analysis of the human situation, which reveals man in the fullness of his guilty responsibility for his sins. When man's reason operates according to its own principles, unhindered by the will, it is capable of discovering through nature the reality and the glory of God as creator and preserver of the universe. It can perceive that the sovereign will of this creative Power rightfully lays upon man a demand for perfect obedience. It can even discern sufficiently for man's needs the character of the obedience demanded. In so far as man's will, therefore, plays its rightful role in subordination to and dependence upon the intellect, man obeys God and lives righteously. Objectively, therefore, man has the capacity to live righteously and to believe truly about his God. But he does not do so. He does not allow his mind to point out to him the way of obedience because he does not desire to know it. Even in so far as his mind does show him the truth, he refuses to be guided thereby.

Man's will, instead of choosing its natural and proper role of docile obedience to truth, chooses that of the tyrannous ruler. Voluntarily, and therefore with full responsibility for what he does, man overthrows continually the rightful ruler of his nature in favor of selfish and perverse desires. Rather than the freedom in God which is objectively available to him, man chooses slavery to his passions. Rather than recognize his true place in the universe and in relation to God, man places himself at the center, remakes God after the image of his appetites, and worships the projection of his sins.

The common objection to this Biblical faith is that, if all men find themselves inescapably in this wrong relationship to God, they cannot, therefore, be individually blamed. But one man is not innocent before God simply because others are equally guilty. We do not need to believe that righteousness is as easily available to us as sin in order to perceive that we are truly responsible for our sin. What a man does according to his will, that is, voluntarily, he does responsibly. What is justly to be rewarded or punished is the will. If the will is bad, it deserves punishment, and if every will is bad, every will deserves punishment. It is meaningless to ask about the responsibility for the badness of the will, for the will is simply what it wills to be.

Since all human wills are utterly bad, since none, that is, recognizes and accepts the truth of God and yields obedience to it, since all mankind is in revolt against its rightful Lord, God's justice can be expressed only in the universal condemnation of all mankind. No suffering could be incommensurate with man's desert, for his sin is total and wholly inexcusable. The charge that God's condemnation of men to eternal torment is unjust, therefore, is wholly without foundation, and reflects only the ignorance and perverse pride of those who make it.

For the critic to point out that there are many persons outside the church who live in conformity with relatively high ideals is beside the point. Certainly such may be the case. Certainly there are some who accept civic responsibilities and fulfill them admirably, whereas others lie, murder, and steal, and in every way attack the foundations of all human society. Certainly from the human perspective the former deserve honor and praise, the latter, disgrace and punishment. Facts so self-evident as these should scarcely require noting down at all.

But even at this level of virtue, it would be easy to live under an illusion. There is far more pretense to civil righteousness than there is actual righteousness. It would be naïve to be taken in and thrown off guard by the appearance of honesty and generosity. Almost everyone has his price. Power corrupts the best of men, and each of us is more likely than he himself knows to express in his own life that sort of conduct which he condemns in others.

However, the case for universal guiltiness does not depend on cynicism with regard to the integrity of one's neighbor. It allows for the utmost realism, and such realism is not likely to lead to a high estimate of man's natural righteousness. But suppose such realism also leads us in all honesty to the recognition that some great souls outside the Christian church are truly unimpeachable in their conduct. What then? Does this mean that before God they can stand upon their own feet and lay claim to his reward?

No indeed! The integrity of the good citizen is rooted still in selfishness and pride just as completely as is the corruptness of the thief or murderer. We will certainly prefer the virtuous man and appreciate his contribution to the stability of human society and the justice of its institutions; but we must pity him as well, for, like the Pharisee of Jesus' day, by his very right-eousness he will be blinded to his sin, and he of all men will prove least able to receive the redeeming grace of God.

An ambiguity in the meaning of justice has created consid-erable confusion. Justice may be thought of, not only as ap-propriateness of reward or punishment to desert, but also as impartiality — that is, as treating equally persons who are equally deserving. In the former sense we have already seen that all men are justly condemned, but in the latter sense, certainly, God is not just. This does not mean that he is less than just; but rather, more than just. God is not only just, but also merciful — wonderfully, incredibly merciful — in that he chooses some from among sinful mankind to be objects of his grace and to enjoy fellowship with him forever.

Who, then, is to complain of this partiality? The elect? But they have no room in their hearts for aught but praise and gratitude. The nonelect? But they, by their blasphemies against God, by their willful refusal to recognize the utter justice of their condemnation, do but proclaim anew how fully they deserve their suffering.

The remaining question is that of God's responsibility in creating a being doomed eternally to deserve his wrath. Was God ignorant of what would transpire? Was he incapable of creating a better world?

In answering these questions, some have attributed to Adam a freedom *not* to sin that his Fall has denied to his successors, but few have been content to say that God created Adam in ignorance of what he would choose or of the inevitable conse-quences of his choice for his descendants.

Some have placed the real Fall in heaven where Lucifer re-volted against God and introduced into the universe that principle of disobedience which inevitably corrupted God's pure creation. But this explanation does not avoid the acknowl-edgment either of the limitation of God's power or of some responsibility on his part for the evil that exists.

It must be maintained, therefore, that in the mysterious wis-

dom of God what *is* is what ought to be. What man wills sin-
fully for his own selfish, prideful ends God wills simultaneously
for the greater good. Just as Pharaoh stubbornly refused obedience to God's will, while God willed and caused his disobedience so that he might be more greatly glorified, so through all
time God's good and gracious will has employed man's sin for
good.

God is indeed the cause of all that is and all that occurs. To
claim that anything has being apart from his will is to detract
from his infinite majesty. But God's causal efficacy does not
free his creatures from the responsibility for those acts of
which in another sphere they are causal agents. Hence, sin
and guilt belong to man, and all glory and power belong to
God.

If the critic still persists in his complaints, if he still raises
against God the standard and ideal invented by his own mind,
there remains one last answer, final and decisive. What God
wills *is* good. There is not and can never be any other standard
of good and bad or right and wrong save that of God's im-
mutable will. To set ourselves up against him, to chide him
for failing to measure up to our standards, is unutterable vanity
and folly. However far we may go in explanation and justification of the ways of God, we must ultimately acknowledge that
no human mind can grasp his counsels. The finite cannot comprehend the infinite, nor the creature his Creator. Our task is to
accept our finitude, rejoice in God's mercy, and give to him
the glory that is his due.

SELECTED READINGS FOR FURTHER STUDY

LUTHERANISM

I. *Primary Sources*

Luther's writings are available in many forms. An important
English translation, in fifty-five volumes, began appearing in

1955 under the general editorship of Jaroslav Pelikan, published by Concordia Publishing House. Previously, the best English edition had been the six volumes published by A. J. Holman from 1915–1932. In addition, Volumes XV through XVIII of The Library of Christian Classics, published by The Westminster Press, contain valuable selections of Luther's works in readily accessible form. Important selections from Luther are being translated by Bertram Lee Woolf, entitled *Reformation Writings of Martin Luther*, and published by Philosophical Library, Inc. The following selections may be useful as an introduction:

Luther, Martin, *A Treatise on Christian Liberty*. Found in several selections of Luther's writings and also published separately. Muhlenberg Press, 1943. The clearest and most persuasive brief description by Luther of the Christian experience and life.

Kerr, Hugh T., Jr., editor, *A Compend of Luther's Theology*. The Westminster Press, 1943. A convenient selection of key passages from Luther's writings arranged according to major theological subjects.

Plass, Ewald M., compiler, *What Luther Says: An Anthology*, 3 vols. Concordia Publishing House, 1959. A very extensive selection of passages from Luther arranged alphabetically by topics, carefully documented, and systematically organized.

Tappert, Theodore G., editor, *Book of Concord: The Confessional Writings of the Evangelical Lutheran Church*. Muhlenberg Press, 1959. The authoritative confessions of Lutheranism made newly accessible to the modern reader.

II. *Studies of Luther's Life and Thought*
Bainton, Roland H., *Here I Stand*. Abingdon Press, 1950. A widely read and reliable account of Luther's life and religious development.

Bornkamm, Heinrich, *Luther's World of Thought,* translated by Martin H. Bertram. Concordia Publishing House, 1958. A series of essays which jointly constitute a fresh and vigorous reconstruction of the spirit and thought of Luther for our day.

Watson, Philip S., *Let God Be God.* Muhlenberg Press, 1949. An enthusiastic interpretation of Luther's spirit and thought which shows the influence of modern German and Scandinavian scholarship.

III. *Histories and Expositions of Lutheranism*

Allbeck, Willard Dow, *Studies in the Lutheran Confessions.* Muhlenberg Press, 1952. Provides a running account of the argument of the basic confessions.

Kantonen, T. A., *Resurgence of the Gospel.* Muhlenberg Press, 1948. A statement of Lutheran faith as it is relevant for contemporary life and thought, designed for pastors and intelligent laymen.

Lutheran Churches of the World. Foreword by Carl E. Lund-Quist. Augsburg Publishing House, 1957. A survey by seven Lutheran leaders of the history and present situation of Lutheranism in seven geographical areas of the world.

Traver, Amos John, *A Lutheran Handbook.* Muhlenberg Press, 1956. A popular survey of Lutheran history, practice, and thought.

Wentz, Abdel Ross, *A Basic History of Lutheranism in America.* Muhlenberg Press, 1955. An authoritative account of American Lutheranism from colonial times to the present.

CALVINISM

I. *Primary Sources*

A fifty-one-volume set of Calvin's works which includes Commentaries, Institutes, and Letters is published by Wm. B. Eerdmans Publishing Company. Volumes XX through XXIII of The Library of Christian Classics, published by The Westminster Press, are devoted to Calvin's works. The first complete edition of Jonathan Edwards' works is being published by the Yale University Press under the editorship of Perry Miller. Convenient selections from the writings of Calvin and Edwards are listed below.

Ferm, Vergilius, editor, *Puritan Sage: Collected Writings of Jonathan Edwards.* Library Publishers, Inc., 1953. One of several useful selections from the writings of America's greatest Calvinist.

Kerr, Hugh T., Jr., editor, *A Compend of the Institutes of the Christian Religion by John Calvin.* The Westminster Press, 1939. A skillful selection of the essential material in Calvin's Institutes which makes the systematic argument of the work more readily accessible to the ordinary reader.

Heppe, Heinrich, *Reformed Dogmatics*, revised by Ernst Bizer and translated by G. T. Thompson. George Allen & Unwin, Ltd., London, 1950. The orthodox Reformed tradition painstakingly formulated by the author as it has developed up to recent times.

Schaff, Philip, editor, *Creeds of Christendom*, Vol. III. Harper & Brothers, 1877. Among relevant materials in this volume: The Heidelberg Catechism, The Westminster Confession, and The Larger and Shorter Catechisms.

II. *Studies in Calvin's Thought*

Dakin, A., *Calvinism.* The Westminster Press, 1956. A summary of Calvin's doctrine, based chiefly upon the Institutes, followed by discussions of the organization of the Calvinist churches.

Hunter, A. Mitchell, *The Teaching of Calvin: A Modern Interpretation*, revised edition. James Clarke & Company, Ltd., London, 1950. A Scotch Calvinist's account of Calvin's thought and influence de-emphasizing, though not denying, those features of his thought which provoke the hostility of liberals.

Niesel, Wilhelm, *The Theology of Calvin*, translated by Harold Knight. The Westminster Press, 1956. A scholarly interpretation of Calvin's intellectual system as expressive of his religious apprehension of the living God in Christ; includes a survey of Calvin studies as of 1938, the date of the German publication, with an added note on later publications.

Torrance, T. F., *Calvin's Doctrine of Man*. Lutterworth Press, London, 1949. A careful statement of Calvin's doctrine on this crucial question, based on full use of Calvin's sermons and Commentaries as well as the Institutes.

III. *Histories and Expositions of Calvinism*

Berkouwer, G. C., *Studies in Dogmatics*. English translations of some twenty volumes being published by Wm. B. Eerdmans Publishing Company. A vast theological undertaking symptomatic of the remarkable scholarly vitality of the contemporary Calvinist revival.

Bratt, John H., editor, *The Rise and Development of Calvinism*. Wm. B. Eerdmans Publishing Company, 1959. Five essays by four conservative Calvinist scholars on Calvin and the development of Calvinism on the Continent, in the British Isles, and in America.

McNeill, John T., *The History and Character of Calvinism*. Oxford University Press, 1954. A thoroughly reliable historical account of the development of Calvinism, both doctrinally and institutionally, and an assessment of its present situation.

Warburton, Ben A., *Calvinism: Its History and Basic Principles, Its Fruits and Its Future, and Its Practical Application to Life*. Wm. B. Eerdmans Publishing Company, 1955. A very conservative defense of the intellectual and spiritual value of the famous "five points" of Calvinism.

CHAPTER III

Churchly Protestantism

A LTHOUGH Protestantism began in the Reformation, there are persons within Protestantism whose spirit stands in almost complete continuity with the pre-Reformation church. They have broken with Rome. They have purged their churches of the abuses of the later medieval system. They have adopted a friendlier spirit toward the Reformation churches than has characterized Roman Catholicism. But their life and thought reflect neither the special emphases of Luther and Calvin nor the individualistic tendencies of modern Protestantism.

When we speak in terms of Protestant institutions, it is within the Church of England and its offspring in other lands that we find this spirit most frequently. But elsewhere too there are many sensitive souls hungry for the beauty of the traditional liturgy, longing for the authoritative guidance that only a catholic church can give, discouraged and depressed by the seeming provincialism of the Protestant groups in which they find themselves. Such persons may call themselves "catholic" but only with an uncapitalized *c*. If we expand our horizons to the ecumenical movement as a whole, the Orthodox Churches of the East provide a still stronger emphasis of this kind.

The churchly Protestant deplores the deep rift caused, on the one hand, by Reformation radicalism and, on the other hand, by the uncompromising spirit of the Jesuits who finally had their way with the Roman Catholic Church. He desires to serve as a bridge through which someday the great Christian bodies may be brought together again.

A number of factors in the modern situation have converged to strengthen the churchly position even outside the Roman Catholic communion. The romantic movement beginning in the late eighteenth century gave Western man a new appreciation of history and of traditions and institutions with great antiquity and continuity. Men under the influence of romanticism have cared more that they belong to something great and enduring than that they be able to form new groups in which all members hold the same opinions. Those who felt this influence but remained in the churches of the Reformation preferred to interpret the Reformation as merely one step among many in the continuous development of the faith rather than as a radical break with tradition and an unmediated return to Biblical authority.

Modern Biblical scholarship, by interpreting the Bible in large part as the literary expression of a religious community, has seemed to corroborate the churchly interpretation of authority. The Bible is the Word of God because it is the expression of his Spirit, alive in the Christian community. If so, it cannot be put in opposition, as by the Reformation, to tradition and ecclesiastical authority. These too are expressions of God's Spirit guiding and energizing the communal life of all Christians.

The vigor with which the radical Reformation emphasis upon discontinuity has been propounded in recent years has driven some to a more catholic view. The extreme teachings as to the worthlessness of human efforts, the total depravity of man's spirit, the utter impossibility of man's rising to God in religious experience or of attaining true knowledge of him through the use of reason, have caused some to realize that their deepest convictions do not stem from the Reformation, but rather from a much wider tradition within which the Reformation is only one element — an element that needs to be balanced by others.

The decline of Protestant culture in northern Europe and especially the rise of pagan nationalism have caused some to feel that Protestantism alone is insufficient. Although the Reformation has been an important and needed corrective to the idolatries of Roman Catholicism, the Protestant witness can exist fruitfully only where it can be sustained in the larger context of the total Christian church.

Others have been troubled by the identification of Protestant denominations with the middle class and their tendency to identify Christianity itself with the ideals of this group — sobriety, thrift, industry, sexual morality, community spirit, and patriotism. They have been distressed to find that certain aspects of traditional Christianity have been silenced. And they have felt that only a truly catholic spirit can be commensurate with the Christian witness.

Dissatisfaction with the barrenness of Protestant worship, the sentimentality of much of its music, the ugliness and bad taste of many of its buildings, the commonplaceness of its preachers and their preaching — all these also have contributed to that growing dissatisfaction with Protestantism which is found within Protestantism. And out of this dissatisfaction many turn with longing to more catholic ways and ideas.

Churchly Protestantism is characterized by a rejection of individualism in favor of an exalted view of the church. It seeks the meaning and fulfillment of life in a church that is not an institution formed by like-minded men to further their common aims but a creation of God embodying his power and authority.

The emphasis on the church need not contradict the Reformation teaching of the immediacy of God's relationship to man. As Christians we may pray to God for ourselves, we may confess our sins directly to him, we may worship him in private, we may study for ourselves God's Word. No representative of the church can determine the destiny of our immortal souls.

Nevertheless, what is supremely important is not what we can do in our unmediated relationship to God, but rather

what God does for us in the church. Certainly we may pray
and worship in private, but how much better and more bene-
ficial is the communal service where all the riches of an ancient tradition, selected through the centuries for their permanent value, are provided in an atmosphere of fellowship with
other worshipers and with the saints of all ages! One may indeed study God's Word alone and unaided, but how much
better to benefit from the cumulative learning of the past embodied in the wisdom of the church, its creeds, its confessions,
and its liturgy!

Within the context of this unity in basic belief in the spiritual
authority and power of the church there are two forms that
churchly Protestantism may take. The one regards the corporate
worship of the faithful as the essence of the Christian life and
seeks to retain and develop those forms of worship which most
fully satisfy all the needs of the Christian. Because of its emphasis upon the traditional liturgy of worship it will be called
" liturgical." The other regards the essential Christian act as
the renunciation of private will and judgment in favor of the
authority of the body of Christ with its incomparably greater
right to determine all questions of faith and morals. It will be
called " authoritarian."

These labels are more arbitrary and less adequate than those
used in the preceding chapters. Luther and Calvin have individually exercised such profound influence on millions of
Protestants that many rejoice in proclaiming themselves Luther*ans* and Calvin*ists*. They recognize proudly that these names
distinguish them from each other and from other Protestants.
But those who plead for a recovery of worship or for a return
to the authority of the church appeal to the authority of no
individual and minimize the ecclesiastical divisions that have
denominational names. They believe that Roman Catholic,
Lutheran, and Calvinist alike need to restore the church as the
vital center of the Christian life, and that such a restoration involves no *ism*, no special theological position, but only that we

take seriously what all Christians necessarily believe.

Nevertheless, despite the apparent inappropriateness of any label, some such terms as "liturgical" and "authoritarian" must be used. These terms must be used for convenience' sake to avoid cumbersome explanatory phrases. But they must be used also because these points of view are, after all, two perspectives among others. Whether they wish to do so or not, they do constitute parties or *isms*. They are not alone in their dislike of this situation. Other Protestants with widely different approaches have even more vigorously claimed that they simply desire to recall all Christians to true faith and vital Christian experience — not to establish new sects or new parties within sects. Sometimes the very vigor of the rejection of party spirit has been the special hallmark of a party.

Those who are here called "liturgical Protestants" may properly object that in fact they have functioned within the separate denominations rather than tending to develop as a parallel or alternative movement. Lutherans have sought to restore and deepen Lutheran worship, and Anglicans have worked within their somewhat different tradition. Similar if less fully developed movements have occurred within the Reformed and Free Churches. In each case the peculiar doctrinal and institutional principles of the church involved have been accepted, so that one remains a Lutheran or a Calvinist, simply adding the special emphasis on worship and its forms.

Nevertheless, this emphasis does have its own inner logic. The Lutheran who is also committed to the development of liturgical worship as the central Christian act may find a greater congeniality of spirit with an Anglican who strives for the same ends in his separate communion than with a Lutheran whose special concern is with the maintenance and promulgation of pure doctrine. In so far as he progressively emphasizes liturgical worship, he is likely to become aware of his spiritual unity with catholic Christianity as he understands it. This will not cause him to leave the Lutheran Church, but rather to interpret Lutheranism as one part of the family of Christian institutions with whose unity rather than differences he is primarily concerned. Thus the more he develops his special liturgical interest the less he remains *distinctively* Lutheran if being Lutheran means not merely being loyal to an institution but also viewing in a particular way the world of life and thought, God and man.

What is said of the Lutheran may be even more true of the Anglican, but it is in any case sufficient to indicate that liturgical Protestantism as such does have its own distinctive character. However harmoniously this movement may find its place in a wide variety of institutions, it remains within them an alternative to other basic Christian orientations.

The position of authoritarian Protestantism is more difficult, for it stands in sharpest conflict with other tendencies in most churches. Indeed, many Protestant groups have provided but little soil for the development of such a point of view, and many both within and without the authoritarian orientation regard it as alien to the spirit of Protestantism generally. Authoritarian Protestantism is included in this volume because of the importance that it has had in the Anglican churches especially since the rise of the Oxford Movement under Newman and Pusey.

Liturgical and authoritarian orientations may be combined easily and harmoniously. Yet they may also be rather sharply distinguished. The liturgical Protestant understands the church as the corporate life of Christendom at worship. The authoritarian stresses the institutional integrity and objectivity of the church. The former may be much more liberal in his attitude toward dissident groups, much less insistent on determining precisely the marks of the true church. The latter may be much less concerned with the forms of worship and the subjective experiences of the worshiper.

Therefore, despite the ease with which these two emphases may be conjoined, they are presented in the following pages rather as they tend to develop when separated than in the form that each takes in union with the other. The presentation in both cases is guided largely by the situation in the Anglican churches, for both forms are most fully developed there. But most of what is said in the treatment of liturgical Protestantism is equally applicable to its other expressions, especially to that in Lutheran churches.

AUTHORITARIAN PROTESTANTISM

The conscientious man seeking to live as he should and believe as he ought has never had an easy time. Baffling problems of daily living and perplexities of belief have always confronted the thoughtful. In the face of such problems men turn for guidance to those who are older and more experienced, and through much of history most men have been able to find in parental and community wisdom a solution, inadequate no doubt to silence all uncertainty, but adequate to give direction and meaning to life.

In the modern world, however, there can be no such easy solution of man's perplexity. The Protestant Reformation destroyed the homogeneity of European faith and paved the way for endless variety of opinion and practice. The rise of science has heaped further doubt upon traditional ways and thrown the ranks of Protestantism into seemingly hopeless confusion. The Enlightenment brought to the European man an introverted confidence in his individual reason, and we are still reaping the bitter fruits of this abortive optimism.

So desperate is man's need for certainty that in our own twentieth century we find the masses of people in some of our most advanced countries willing to believe the most fantastic ideas and practice the most villainous immorality if only some leader free them from the unbearable responsibility of personal choice. Others among modern men simply abandon the effort to know any ultimate truth or to conform their lives to any ultimate principle. They adjust placidly to the life about them, indifferent to any deeper significance of human existence. What can we do when we are confronted by a thousand conflicting claims of truth and loyalty except tolerate all and have faith in none?

Such a course is not restricted to the unlearned and unintelligent. Indeed, their problem is less acute because they are aware of a far less extensive range of seemingly plausible alternatives. They may even suppose that greater intelligence or wider learning would resolve their uncertainties. But the man who has been favored by nature and by opportunity knows that in the world of the spirit all hope of rational certainty is illusion, that even the claim to probability is suspect as soon as it transcends the phenomenal flux within which man moves.

Religious experience does not help. On the contrary, the endless variety of such experiences, each with its divergent claim on loyalty and belief, contributes to the final undermining of all hope of certitude. It is the religious man, the earnest seeker after truth at the deepest levels of life, who is most frustrated by what he finds. A less sensitive spirit may find partial satisfaction by immersing himself in the wealth of information that the scientist provides for his study, or he may largely forget his spiritual uncertainty in the practical affairs of business or profession. But for the deeply religious man there can be no rest. The unanswered questions will not allow themselves to be forgotten, for they pose the problem of existence itself.

One solution is for man to accept ignorance with courage and in ignorance to assert himself as a man, a free moral agent, responsible for his deeds though without a standard by which to measure them. But this is the solution of despair, heroic despair perhaps, but despair nonetheless. It does not satisfy our need; it rejects all hope of answer. Surely we are made for some better end than this! Surely there is in this world some guide to which we may turn when reason and experience fail — some guide that can with more than human authority lead the perplexed to truth!

The first answer to such a plea might be the Bible. But this answer is little more than a restatement of the problem. True, no doubt, the Bible is God's Word, but a hundred mutually exclusive interpretations are hurled at the hungry seeker, each demanding acceptance on the authority of Scripture. How can we decide among them? Should we accept the one we *like* the best, or the one to which our first studies of Scripture seem best to correspond? Should we weigh the training and intelligence of the interpreter, or should we accept the claims to immediate divine guidance of one less highly educated? Must we ourselves spend a lifetime trying to learn the truth for ourselves? For such an end will one lifetime suffice? And if it does, if at the end of life we can find some assurance with respect to the principles by which life should be lived, will it not be for us too late? Or will some young seekers like ourselves be guided by our new-found knowledge? Can someone else accept on our authority the truth we have at length discovered, or must each generation begin again where we began?

In any case, is the Christian really to claim that all truth is to be found in the Bible? What of the relation of Biblical teaching to the sciences — geology, biology, and psychology? Even if we should say that what we seek in the Bible transcends the realm of science entirely, what of philosophy and of the profound insights of the mystics? Do we not owe almost as much to Athens as to Jerusalem?

Furthermore, we cannot seriously maintain that the Bible is the simple and direct expression of God's wisdom unmediated by faltering human minds. It is a library containing the most varied ideas and reflecting the widest variety of historical situations. Certainly it is inspired, but it is inspired by the Spirit alive in the faithful community, not for the most part by private disclosures of new facts and ideas to a favored writer.

The Bible cannot settle the perplexing issues of life and thought with clarity and certainty except as it is authoritatively interpreted. It cannot be authoritatively interpreted except collectively by the Christian community. Moreover, our reasonable acceptance of its authority depends upon the prior acceptance of the authority of the community. On the testimony of the community that the Bible is a normative expression of the common faith we accept its teaching as truth.

Not only are we dependent upon the living community for our basis of accepting and interpreting the Bible, but also we are dependent on the primitive community for the very existence of the Bible. The writings sprang from and expressed the life of the community, and the community selected from among the wealth of writings those which held most closely to the norm embodied in its faith and practice. These writings, produced by the community and tested by the community, were gathered by the community into the canon. Thus at every step the authority of the Bible depends upon that of the community.

The assertion that the authority of Scripture rests upon that of the community does not imply that the Bible is a "merely human" document; on the contrary, this assertion assumes that the community is moved by a more than human Spirit. The community is not authoritative by virtue of its human components; indeed its very nature as community cannot be understood at the level of human association. The community is called into being by God through his incarnate Son and is preserved and enlarged by the Holy Spirit. Private human opinions do not determine its faith and life. Each individual finds himself drawn by his participation in the community into the stream of the common life. The multiplicity of individual differences tends to cancel one another out, so that the common reality of the divine life becomes increasingly manifest as the essence of the community.

The supernatural character of the Christian community is manifest to all who participate in its life. The believer understands the community as the continuation of the work and purpose of Jesus Christ and, as such, an extension of the incarnation. Even to those outside its boundaries its supernatural character must be manifest in its survival and growth despite all that men have done against it and within it.

The community is misunderstood if it is regarded as merely the formless collection of the faithful. From earliest times, indeed in the plan of Christ himself, the community is also a church — an institution with structure, unity, and continuity. The institutionalization of the community is not an unfortunate imposition of human machinery. It is the natural and necessary expression of the element of discipline in the Christian spirit itself. Only through structural organization can the spirit of the community find itself and articulate its inchoate unity. Without it the individuals within the community would misunderstand the principle of its unity, would identify private opinions with the universal truth, and would create endless sects and divisions.

However, ecclesiastical organization has another and higher justification than the pragmatic one of expressing and maintaining the unity of the community. It also embodies, according to the divine plan, the channel of God's grace by which he creates the community. The Christian spirit does not first well up in isolated individuals. It comes to us from above — from God through Christ, and is mediated to the individual by the organized church. Although in one sense, therefore, the community produces the ecclesiastical institution, in another and ultimately truer sense the institution as God's chosen channel of grace creates the community anew in every generation.

The recognition of the divine authority of the church not only supports the authority of the Bible but also resolves the difficulty as to its interpretation. The church that produced the Bible has also the power to interpret the Bible. The endless debates as to the Bible's meaning can be settled, not by arbitrary pronouncements or private guesses, but by the official agencies of the church which can crystallize and articulate

the judgments of the whole community with divine authority.
Each new problem that arises with the ever-changing historical
situation and the ever-expanding knowledge of history and
nature can be settled in this manner. The individual Christian
need not wrestle in endless uncertainty with problems too
great for a single mind. The church speaks and its members
gladly hear and obey.

Perhaps we cannot prove in strictly logical form the divine
authority of the church, for the evidence of history and faith
does not lend itself to such use. But what alternative have we
to such a faith? What competitor presents itself with a reasonable demand upon our loyalty?

Are we to set against the church the convictions of a single
man or the conclusions of an individual philosopher? To do so
is really only to assert against the whole body of the faithful
our private judgment as to who has found truth. And is this
self-assertion not in essence prideful, even insanely so? Do we
really claim as isolated individuals to treat ourselves as authorities in matters of the spirit? Is it not infinitely wiser, humbler,
and more Christian to be guided and controlled by the church,
the body of Christ, rather than to insist upon our own private
and often willful judgment? Does not the whole history of
Christianity confirm that those who insist upon their own way
have torn to shreds the body of Christ and in addition have
destroyed themselves in confusion and disunity? When each
seeks to emphasize that aspect of the truth which he privately
grasps, to isolate this and raise it to the level of a universal
principle, then the whole is torn apart by dissension and strife.
But when each accepts the authority of the whole, acquiesces
even when by limitations of training or temperament he cannot understand, then the church endures, and the full truth,
adequate for all men, is preserved.

The very heart of the Christian faith, then, is to surrender
our individual determination and to accept the authority of
the church as God's instrument for our salvation. By this great

act of renunciation, the pride of intellect and the selfishness of will are broken. Humble obedience replaces willfulness, harmony and mutual love replace division and resentment, inward peace and purpose replace the restless emptiness of the self-directed life. By losing our lives we find them. By giving up our freedom to believe and to do what we please, we find security and happiness in the community of the obedient.

But the final reason for accepting the authority of the church is not that we thereby find a solution to our problems. The final reason is that the church really possesses truth. Outside the church, men live and think in a world of shadows. The reality by which they live eludes the grasp of their minds. Some speculate feebly but proudly about it, contemptuous of the one possible source of knowledge. Others regard it as the height of realism to deny that there is any reality except the shadows. They suppose that the more profoundly men alienate themselves from the thought of God, and the more successfully they secularize their institutions, the more they have progressed. Such " progress " is bringing the world to spiritual bankruptcy, to the ultimate exposure of its nothingness. Only the church that is constituted by the Spirit of God holds fast to reality, and about that reality — the reality of God — only the church has knowledge. Only the church has truth, for only in and through the church does God speak; and only the truth of God is truth indeed.

The demands that are placed upon us by the church are surprisingly easy to bear once the fundamental step of self-surrender is made. The church has learned through the centuries to deal with the great variety of needs and capacities that we bring to it. To those who are ready simply to accept its teaching with little understanding, it offers its truth gladly and in the simplest forms. Of those with restless minds eager to understand as well as to believe, it demands no abatement of intellectual curiosity. Rather, it guides the inquirer step by step through all the complexities of its doctrine, explaining, justifying, proving as it proceeds. Nor does the church seek to prevent further inquiry. There are, indeed, the great mysteries of the faith that must be accepted by an act of obedience. But there is always also a growing edge of investigation in which one may participate, enjoying to the full the excitement of disciplined debate. Indeed, the debate within the church is far more satisfying than that without. For within there is a common ground of faith and a common context of doctrine, and without there is not enough mutual understanding for intelligibility, much less for the resolution of difficulties.

The church demands no abandonment of science and philosophy. It does not fear the findings of secular reason. In the ample scope of its accumulated understanding it has itself drawn heavily upon the best of Greek and of modern thinking, bringing their treasures into synthesis with the revelation in Christ. Study what you will, participate freely in the learning of the day — only be careful not to be swept away by every mood and fad of the intellectual world. Be guided in your conclusions by the broader and deeper perspective of the centuries as it is maintained and interpreted by the church. Thus you will not only be loyal to the church but you will also communicate a stability and freshness of insight to the world of secular and sectarian thought.

In ethics as in doctrine, the church provides ways for all. Heroic morality and extreme asceticism are unattractive and unnecessary for the ordinary Christian. Hence, he is guided by the church into a sober but normal life. Avenues of wholesome recreation and ordinary social intercourse are open to him, but he is warned against excesses and guarded from too severe temptation.

The church knows that moderation is often better than absolute prohibitions, that flexibility and resilience are often better than rigid restrictiveness. It has learned also that the weak and sinful men and women with whom it deals need above all else to know that even when they are disobedient and rebellious the church endures, giving meaning to life and healing to the soul.

Life in the world involves family responsibility and the necessity of spending much of one's time in the procuring of material goods. It involves degrees of wealth and poverty. It involves bargaining and restless planning for the future. In short, it involves the rejection of that way of life which Christ proclaimed as highest.

To judge merchants and farmers by Christ's teaching of perfection is entirely unfair. It is their duty to rear children, to support them, and to insure their future security. The responsible head of a household cannot give to all who ask or abandon wholly his concern for material possessions. The church recognizes this and adapts its demands to the realities of life. But it cannot acquiesce in simply ignoring the teaching of Jesus as impractical. The absolute ideals of the Sermon on the Mount must forever be exemplified within the church as testimony to the truly Christian life and the church's wholehearted obedience to its Lord.

There have always been those in the church who have found within themselves a divine dissatisfaction with the kind of life possible for those who live in the world. They are determined to be unreservedly abandoned to God, totally obedient to the highest demands of the church. The church separates these sensitive and earnest spirits from the world so that they may be freed from its cares and responsibilities and spend their time wholly in the exercise of the religious life.

Those who are called out of the world must forever renounce both the pleasures and duties of family life. The church alone is their spouse. All merely natural desires, which compete with God for the attention of the mind, must be sublimated. All concern for the future and all desire to assert the self must be abandoned. In company with like-minded men or women who have joined in the vows of chastity, poverty, and obedience these loftiest Christian souls may grow to spiritual heights impossible in the outside world. For them the ordinary pleasures of physical comfort and pride in worldly success are replaced by the consummate blessedness of the contemplation of God.

Whether we live in the world or are called to the wholly religious life, obedience to the church is not to be understood as harsh and joyless slavery. It is, rather, a life of finding our own fulfillment in the relationship of dutiful sonship. We do not need to struggle incessantly to please God, always uncertain as to the way. Obedience to the church is obedience to God, and since the way in which the church directs us is one within our powers to follow, the burden of a strained and painful conscience is lifted from us. We know that we often fail to follow the way we are shown, but if in contrite humility we confess our sins to God as the church directs, it can mediate to us the forgiveness of God. When we have done what we can to make amends, we begin again with untroubled conscience to follow the precepts of the church.

The church has known from the first that, in addition to its responsibility for doctrine and morality, it has also the task of providing for its people those opportunities for worship which they need for inner spiritual sustenance. Therefore, one of its central demands even upon its weaker children is that they come regularly to the services of worship. Worship is the supreme act of obedience. Through worship all obedience is consummated and made easier and more joyful.

Worship is not primarily a matter of moods, attitudes, and emotions, however reverent they may be. These have their place and add to the total richness of the Christian life. But the worship that is essential to the Christian life is that in which we receive the sacraments. The church knows that for our salvation we require not only to believe its doctrines and obey its moral demands but also to be spiritually and supernaturally fed upon grace. Without grace we cannot believe and obey as we ought, and such belief and obedience as we offer will not save us. God saves us through the church by giving to us that food on which alone our spirits can grow toward him. What is supremely important, therefore, is that we receive the grace which is objectively offered to us by the church in the mystery of the sacraments, regardless of how we feel subjectively.

The culminating power of the church lies in its ability to mediate grace from Christ to his people. It is this power above all else which explains and necessitates the form of institutionalization of the Christian community. It is unthinkable that supernatural power to communicate grace could be the prerogative of anyone who happens to call himself a Christian. Under such an order the sacraments would be endlessly desecrated and wholly despised. But it will not do to relate the prerogative to the private faith or moral standards of the administrator. If this were done, the recipient would be endlessly uncertain as to whether he had or had not received grace. The objectivity of the sacrament can be preserved only as it depends upon the official capacity of the administrator.

Still, this is not enough. The objectivity of the grace that is in question is not a matter of human opinion or human designation. It is a supernatural fact for which the words of Christ and the divine faith of the church are warranty. It must rest, therefore, upon a supernatural source, a source that can be only Christ himself.

Christ communicated the divine authority that was his own, not to all who believed in him, but to his apostles. They, by the laying on of hands, communicated authority to the chosen leaders who succeeded them. These in turn from generation to generation in unbroken succession through nineteen centuries have transmitted the awesome power that they received from Christ through his apostles. It is this power, rather than any human excellence, which stands guaranty for the objectivity of sacramental grace.

Since not only the authority over belief and action but also the power to communicate grace to its members belong to the true church, the one theological question that must be of greatest concern to us is that of the marks of the true church. Christendom seems to be torn with endless divisions. Which of the many contending groups is really the church? Not all, certainly, for their teachings contradict one another. To fail to distinguish true churches from false churches would place us again in the impossible situation of setting ourselves up as judges of every question in our own wisdom. We must make one decision, not a thousand, and having made this, the rest are settled.

Even this decision is not really our own, a matter of private whim or inclination. Many a group of Christians manifests in the most obvious manner that it is not a church with supernatural power but only a human association for religious purposes. Many so glory in the right of private judgment as to refuse explicitly to function as God's spokesmen. Many make no claim to mediate grace to their members, but place the whole stress upon private spiritual or moral exercises. Many readily acknowledge their recent origins and make no effort to show their continuity with the early church. Many are so small in membership and so limited geographically that to regard their tenets as true would be to condemn the vast body of Christendom to serious error.

Such groups as these, whatever they may be, cannot be seriously regarded as the church. The church today must be the same church as that which was founded by Christ and the apostles. It must have transmitted the power of the apostles to the present clergy through the episcopal laying on of hands. It must be universal or catholic, embodying the traditions of Christendom generally and capable of being found throughout the Christian world.

There are a number of churches that do seem in general to meet these requirements: the Eastern Orthodox and Coptic Churches, the Roman Catholic Church, the Old Catholic,

Jansenist, and national Catholic Churches, the Anglican Churches, and a few churches of the Reformation such as those Lutheran churches which have maintained unbroken the episcopal succession. These churches still contain the great majority of the Christian peoples of the world, and all retain a deep loyalty to the ancient traditions of Christianity.

Yet a problem still remains. Though all these churches have much in common, there is also diversity among them. They do not all recognize one another as parts of the true church. Though in part separation is geographical rather than theological, nevertheless their separate developments have led to differences that mar the unity of the church and confuse its teaching. Hence, though each partially embodies the authority of the church, some reservation as to the wholeness of the truth of any one remains to mar the perfectness of self-surrender.

One further test may be objectively applied. The validity of sacraments depends only on the official capacity of the administrator, but the authority of the church in matters of doctrine and moral teaching depends upon the unity with which it speaks. Only as the special views of the parts of the true church cancel one another out can the divine truth which they all share stand clearly revealed.

Today the unity of Christendom is ideal rather than actual, but in the early centuries of our era it was real. Christians of East and West, united in one church, together formulated in the great creeds the fundamental principles of the church. Wise teachers gave expression to these principles in extensive theological and ethical treatises that were widely approved by the whole church. There in the early creeds and the great fathers of the church we find clearly expressed, before the tragic schisms, the purest formulations of the most authoritative teaching.

That church, therefore, whose development is truest to the faith of the early church, that church which has been least affected in its teaching by the special circumstances of time and place or which is most willing to correct its peculiarities in the light of truly catholic teaching, that church is the purest embodiment of the true church.

The claim of Rome to be the true church is imperious, and it demands serious attention. Certainly it is *a* true church, apostolic in both order and doctrine. Yet Rome has been guilty of exaggerating its catholicity, and of claiming to speak authoritatively for all Christendom, while ignoring the belief and practice of sister catholic churches. It has claimed for itself an infallibility that rightfully belongs only to the whole church and as a result has tended in both doctrine and practice to absolutize what should be relative.

Therefore, although Rome is a true church, an important part of the church universal, it speaks less purely and with less willingness to be corrected than do other catholic churches. However strongly the earnest Christian is drawn by the dignity, the unity, the certainty of Rome and the great wisdom of most of its teaching, he does better to remain outside its borders where he may be more open to the total spiritual development of Christendom and work more freely for the ultimate institutional reunion of the whole Christian church.

The church as the body of Christ far transcends in dignity and importance the secular state. It possesses a wisdom needed by the state, and the noblest function of the state is to serve the interests of the church. There is nothing wrong with the legal establishment of the church. On the contrary, the whole principle of radical separation of church and state rests upon an erroneous conception. There is and can be only one true church represented in each geographical area by a single institution. Schismatics and heretics have their sects, it is true, but they do not by virtue of their institutional separateness constitute ecclesiastical bodies that should be recognized by political authorities as coequal with the church. Where they are strong and numerous, the political establishment of the true church may be impossible. But to exalt into a principle the compromise necessitated by the unhappy proliferation of the sects is altogether foolish. The true church has room for all. Within it every person, whatever his special temperament or spiritual need, may find rest, if only he will give up his willful assertiveness and yield the church the obedience that is its due. There is no need for multiplicity and division. The goal must remain steadfastly that of bringing back to the church all who through circumstance or willful error have been separated from it. The church must seek, yes, when opportunity offers, demand the recognition, support, and obedience of the secular authorities.

The Protestant groups that have separated themselves from the church have thereby denied themselves divine authority and deprived themselves of the fullness of the wealth of the catholic tradition. Their departure is a judgment upon the men who have had positions of authority in the church for their shortsightedness and even selfishness and immorality. The church as a human institution is indeed in constant need of reform. But the fact that men may have left the church for reasons that were partly good does not prevent the consequences of their departure from being bad. The church must reassert itself as truly catholic, bringing its blessings richly to all. Each of us must yield himself in complete obedience to the church, finding there the truth and direction in which alone our minds and consciences can find rest.

LITURGICAL PROTESTANTISM

In the modern world, religion has often been identified with opinions and actions. The opinions frequently appear outdated or even harmful, and the actions seem either unimportant or capable of being sustained independently of religion. Many have rejected religion quite sincerely in the name of intellectual honesty and moral righteousness.

Indeed, if religion is really nothing but a system of metaphysics and morals, there seems little justification for its continued existence. Metaphysics should be the special province of the trained philosopher, and right can be successfully distinguished from wrong without benefit of revelation. The modern psychological and social sciences are at least as adequate in the practical guidance that they offer for our mid-twentieth-century situations as are the moral teachings of the first-century church.

But religion is *not* doctrine and morality! In recent years intellectuals have learned what the religious man has always known — that religion is man's encounter with the Holy. When we experience the Holy, we do not ask whether God exists or how we ought to behave. We know ourselves as in God's presence, and we find that we cannot help responding to that Presence with adoration and praise. Such response is worship, and such worship is the very heart of all genuine religion.

When worship is absent, beliefs, however pious, actions, however virtuous, and emotions, however intense, are not truly religious. Beliefs are religious rather than philosophical when they are intertwined with worship. Actions are religious rather than merely moral when they are inspired and sustained by worship. Emotions are religious rather than sentimenal when they are formed in worship.

Christianity claims to be, not merely one religion among others, but the culmination of all religion in an ultimate life that is more than religion. But a partial or fragmentary worship can neither nurture nor express such a life. To be true to itself Christian worship must grasp the whole richness of man's encounter with God, giving full scope to every proper element in man's response and synthesizing it all according to the incarnate truth in Jesus Christ.

Alas, it must be confessed with shame that Protestant worship has often been a travesty of true Christian worship. The Holy God has been replaced by the overconfident preacher, and adoration has been neglected in the interest of producing pleasing sentiments in worshipers. Instruction, exhortation, even emotional engineering, have all too often occupied the central place in the service.

The Protestant has found his experience in the church service remote from the reality of day-to-day life and even more remote from his more truly spiritual experiences — his private intuitions into reality, his personal confrontation with the Holy. As a result religion has become increasingly divorced from life; the bridges built between the two have grown weaker; religion has come to appear optional. The less vitally religion has really been related to life, the more vehemently the preacher has proclaimed the importance of being religious. If religion seems to afford no dynamic for this life, the preacher may urge the terrors of hell and the joys of heaven. If he cannot make the life after death seem real to his people, he may turn instead to discussion of the current social scene or the latest theories of modern psychology.

These shifting emphases of the Protestant pulpit are both the cause and the result of the loss of worship. Redeeming moments of praise and adoration are still to be found in all but the worst of Protestant services, but they often stand anomalously unrelated to the central note of the sermon. Often they are regarded as little more than a time-consuming introduction to the main business of the morning. Still, they are there, bearing witness to the fact that the service *should* be one in which God is worshiped.

If Protestantism is to be faithful to its calling to embody Christianity both purely and fully, if it is to restore wholeness of work, of thought, and of worship to its members, if it is to undergird its tremendous outward activity with spiritual power, it *must* rediscover its heritage of worship.

The poverty of corporate services of worship has led many earnest Protestants to develop a rich variety of private worship. Often the Protestant, alone in his bedroom or with his intimate friends or family, may achieve a sense of reality in

prayer and meditation that is painfully lacking for him at his
church. Youth groups have learned to use " the great out of
doors " as a cathedral in which worship becomes deeply meaningful. Some Protestants may learn to pray in crowded stores
and subways and to praise God for every experience of the
day.

These achievements testify to personal spiritual strength informed by the Spirit of God, but they are at the same time
both pathetic and dangerous when they are cut off from the
historic liturgy of the universal church. The self-invented
forms of worship unchecked by the cumulative wisdom of the
Christian heritage will inevitably express and accentuate peculiarities of temperament and limitations of grasp of Christian truth. Only miraculously can they be saved from some
imbalance between praise and petition, adoration and dedication. Only a spiritual genius can avoid endless repetition of a
narrow circle of ideas that gradually grow stale. Outdoor worship is all too easily tinged with a sub-Christian nature-mysti-
cism.

Even at best nonchurchly worship becomes a principle of
separation rather than of communion with fellow Christians.
Almost inescapably the man who practices such worship develops some sense of superiority toward others who do not so
richly cultivate the life of the spirit. The awareness of the
division between true Christianity and mere church membership becomes a source of pharisaic pride. This pride, not admitted, corrupts the ripest fruits of Christian devotion.

We would not condemn the earnest Protestants who have
sought in private devotions the reality of worship, but we
would — indeed we must — reform the churches that have
failed to provide them out of the riches of the Christian heritage with the experience of corporate worship that alone can
finally fulfill and express their deepest needs. We must recall
the church to its distinctively religious task — the task of confronting its people with the holiness of God and of leading

them in the expression of the adoration that is their Christian response. Where this is done, where worship is again truly worship, religion regains reality and relevance to all of life. When the ultimate reality of all life is made central, the deepest reality of the individual's life is creatively involved in his worship. When the Lord of all life is adored, the life of every day is inspired by new purpose and meaning.

Sometimes critics affirm that the return to traditional worship is led by snobbish aesthetes and antiquarians who would substitute " good taste " and esoteric symbolism for moral earnestness and spiritual sincerity. Nothing could be farther from the truth. Any movement may have some superficial supporters who misunderstand and misrepresent its purpose. But the liturgical movement as a whole repudiates sensuous beauty as an end in itself and seeks the ancient only as it is justified by intrinsic spiritual superiority. Indeed, the attachment to that which is sensuously and emotionally satisfying at a superficial level, and the insistence on retaining what has become locally traditional, frequently operate as the greatest obstacle to the recovery of true worship.

It may be that a great deal of training is required to develop in the typical Protestant congregation a genuine appreciation of the traditional Christian liturgy, but this is not because the liturgy is esoteric. The liturgy expresses in the simplest symbols the deepest truths of Christian experience. Education is necessary only where Christian experience has been stunted by lack of worship and where Biblical symbolism has been forgotten through neglect. True, the symbolism may be elaborated almost endlessly, but its detailed understanding, whatever richness it may add for the experienced few, is not necessary to the full act of worship.

Corporate worship is the summation and intensification of the moods and acts of the Christian life as a whole. It takes the feeble, fragmentary, chaotic responses to God of every day and deepens, synthesizes, and reinterprets them. Thereby it

heightens the capacity for response to God and gradually develops in the worshiper the ability to live all of life as worship
— a living sacrifice to God.

It is not necessary that all corporate Christian worship conform to one pattern. A variety of services may be appropriate
to special days. But stemming from the command of Jesus himself, universal in the early church, and continuing unbroken
to the present time, is the liturgical observance of the Eucharist as the fundamental pattern of Christian worship. Where it
has been abandoned, no adequate substitute has been discovered. And, indeed, in principle we can say with confidence
that no adequate substitute can ever be found, for in this liturgy alone all that is most sacred in our Christian heritage is
enacted and commemorated. In it every proper response of
the Christian to his God finds adequate scope, and from it,
all that is unworthy is excluded.

The Eucharistic liturgies are themselves diverse. The theory
and practice of worship has been affected by the shifting tides
of popular sentiment and official dogma. But through all the
varieties of detail there runs a common pattern, which each
people and each age may enrich according to its special needs.

We enter the sanctuary to find God and adore him. Whether
it be the smallest chapel or the greatest cathedral, the worship
of God that has occurred within its walls for decades, perhaps
for centuries, lends it an atmosphere that speaks of his presence. Every symbol points to him and the very structure of
the sanctuary uplifts our hearts toward him. God is here! The
ground on which we stand is holy ground.

Thus God comes to us, overshadows us with his vital presence. If he did not come to us, we could not come to him. If
we did not confront the Holy God, we could at best seek for
ourselves peace of heart and moral inspiration. But because
God *is* here, we forget ourselves, and in simple adoration
praise his holy name.

In the presence of God we know ourselves as utterly un-

worthy of his visitation. We confess with shame our lovelessness, our weakness, and our unfaithfulness. We beseech him
to have mercy upon us, to forgive us, not because of our worship, not because we have aught with which to repay him, but
simply because of his infinite graciousness. Thus our hearts are
prepared for the hearing of God's Word, the record of his
merciful dealing with sinful man. The amazing simplicity and
startling realism of the Biblical stories speak to us again in our
present condition. The Word exhorts and condemns, but it also
comforts and reassures.

As in life, so in worship, which is the epitome of life, we must
not stop with contrition and reassurance. We must give ourselves to God, a living sacrifice. Without this inner response
to his love, true Christian worship is impossible. The offerings
of bread and wine and our separate offerings of money are but
tokens of this total offering of ourselves. As such, they are rich
with meaning, for only by turning completely from self to God
in utter self-surrender can we enter finally into communion
with him.

Yet even this is not enough. The God to whom we come is
not our God only. He is the God of all men everywhere, of
those who acknowledge him, but of those who reject him as
well. We cannot come alone to such a God, bringing only our
private selves. We must seek to lift all mankind with us to the
throne of his grace in prayerful intercession. Only thus can we
express the profound truth that it is the God of all who draws
us to himself, not ourselves who seek our own in him.

All that we have done in worship of God is God's own act
in and through us. It was his coming to us that enabled us to
come to him, and our spirits have been lifted to him by his
Spirit working in us. But the climactic moment of worship is
something still more wonderful, more mysterious than this,
for God descends to us to make us over into what we must be
for him. As the sacred drama is performed in memory of how
God once gave himself for man in Palestine, as the bread and

wine offered to him are imbued by his presence with redemptive power, we also are consecrated by him for his service.

Finally, the whole movement of adoration and renewal is consummated in Communion. Kneeling around the altar, consecrated by his grace, we find ourselves in the deepest inner unity with him that is possible in this life. We are stripped of all that separates us from him and feed upon him to the nourishment and renewal of our souls. And because we are here one with our Lord, we are one also with those who kneel with us, and with the faithful of all ages and lands who have been nurtured at his Table. From such Communion we rise in peace to go forth in the unity of love to give ourselves to God in the service of our fellows.

The liturgical observance of the Eucharist is thus an opportunity for the richest subjective experience on the part of the worshipers, but it is also much more than this. The Eucharist is not merely a means of reminding the worshiper of events long past. It *is* those events mysteriously made present, here and now. The atonement once made for all time in Palestine is re-enacted and relived. Christ is present just as truly, just as substantially, now in the sacred drama as then in an upper room and on Golgotha. Only as we believe this truth, only as we become participants in the reality of these events, can we know in its depths the ultimate meaning of Christian worship.

The achievement of the fullest Christian worship does not depend upon the artistic surroundings of the worshiper. The barest and ugliest of rooms may suffice. But even the most spiritual of us are prone to wanderings of mind and coldness of heart. We *may* worship truly despite poor surroundings, but in our weakness we are foolish to despise anything that may aid us to leave behind the selfish and material cares that so often occupy our minds. We are unwise and even prideful to insist that only " spiritual " means are appropriate, for we are creatures of sense and sensuous imagination as well. Sound, color, odor, as well as intellectual ideas, contribute to our total human state. We must adore God with our whole selves, and to do so we need to be led to God through our senses as well as through our minds.

Painting, sculpture, stained glass, architecture, and music are not, then, unimportant or merely incidental to worship. They can function either as obstacles or aids, and how they function should be of great concern to the church. They are obstacles to worship if by either their ugliness or their intrinsic interest they call attention to themselves, or if they create moods alien to that of true worship. But if the artist subordinates himself to his end, if he accepts the instrumental role of his art and dedicates his talents to the glory of God, then his work may help many a weary heart to find its peace in God. Only art that is transparent to reality, that points beyond itself to the spiritual ground of all life and art, can take its place properly as the environment of worship.

Not only the visual and auditory arts, but the priests as well, must point beyond and away from themselves. The worshiper's attention must not be fixed upon the personality and peculiar mannerisms of the men who lead the worship; attention must be directed only to the significance of their acts and words as representatives of the church. Hence, priests should not stand as the focus of attention, but rather guide the attention of the worshipers to the altar. They may preach if it seems appropriate, but only as spokesmen for the church, not as expressing private opinion, however wise or instructive it may be.

For both priest and people, worship is truncated if it is not properly expressed in gesture and posture. Psychology is rediscovering the truth that the church has always known, that mood and attitude are developed as well as expressed by bodily movement and position. The bending of the knee and the bowing of the head are not unnecessary concessions to the physical; they are a part of the total human experience of humility before the Holy God. The direction in which the worshiper looks determines to a large extent the focus of his attention. Along with the verbal participation in the service of worship, these bodily movements enable each worshiper to appropriate to himself the sacred meaning of the moment.

Concentration of attention upon the liturgy of worship does not detract from the proper emphasis upon the moral life of the Christian. The communion with God that is achieved in worship can be preserved only in a life of love. Excessive attachment to worldly things and even to persons can interfere with the spirit's achievement of peace in God. But rigid moral legalism, ascetic rejection of pleasures simply because they are pleasurable, insensitivity to the beauty of the world and men's artistic creations, even absorption in humanitarian and reform programs — these may prove as damaging to the true Christian spirit as are occasional indulgences in what the narrow-minded call " sins." Moderation in all things, a generous and sensitive spirit, a mature awareness of the limitations of man's ability to remake the world, and a sense of humor are the weapons that best prepare the Christian to live in the world and yet not become worldly.

If we truly find God in worship, there is little danger that we will seek to justify ourselves in works righteousness. We will know and freely confess our incapacity. The overzealous determination individually to achieve moral perfection hampers and impedes the work of God. It replaces the spirit of charity toward all by self-righteousness and censoriousness, or it leads to despair. The constant refreshment of the spirit in worship enables us to live free of these blights and to find inner peace and strength in the midst of turmoil. Holiness we must and do seek, but holiness is found only in a union with God, given by him in worship.

The life of worship makes of us far more useful instruments of God than we can make of ourselves by straining after righteousness. But worship is not to be understood as a means to becoming useful in some other activity. Worship is not truly worship at all when it is chosen as a means to something else.

Worship is itself the supreme act of life, the communion with God that is the purpose and fulfillment of life.

Apart from the worship of God nothing is more important to the Christian than that he comprehend truly the nature of the church. Despite the care with which the Protestant Reformers tried to safeguard the doctrine of the church, tens of millions of Protestants have lost all sense of its supernatural character. This has led many of them to seek within themselves what they can never find except in the church.

The church is the body of Christ. It is the consummation of his life and ministry, his death and resurrection. It is no creation of man, and it cannot be changed by man. Man can misunderstand it, reject it, or ignore it. Even those who understand and accept it may sin against it. But the reality and ultimate victory of the church are independent of human weakness and vileness. They depend only upon God. As worshipers we may become a part of the body of Christ, filled with his Spirit and united through him with all who call reverently on his name.

The divine power at work in the church is manifest above all in the sacraments. In Communion at the Lord's Table the worshiper knows that Christ is truly present. The bread and the wine are not merely symbols of that presence, they convey it. We are not ascending to God by our memories and mental associations with the elements; rather, the consecrated bread and wine are imbued with a supernatural power to minister to our spiritual needs.

In the moment of Communion we know Christ's living presence. Outside that moment we find in theological debate a score of theories as to how he is present, each with its intellectual difficulties. Communion with God is far more important than theological opinion, but because some opinions have tended to destroy the supreme significance of Communion, the theological debate on this subject is of utmost practical importance. The objectivity of Christ's presence, its independence of the mood or thought of the worshiper, its intimate and essential association with the consecrated bread and wine, these principles must be maintained. That they cannot be fully rationalized does not matter. Certainly the worshiper knows that he confronts here a mystery beyond all human reason. The promise of Christ himself and the experience of the worshiping community through nineteen centuries are more than ample warrant for unshakable conviction.

Both the divine power and the true nature of the church manifest themselves also in the sacrament of Baptism. Through Baptism we are ingrafted into the body of Christ. We do not first become Christians and then present ourselves for church membership. We are Christians only as a part of the corporate body of Christ, and into this body we are brought by Baptism. In true Baptism we are cleansed of our guilt and redeemed in Christ.

A man who has grown up outside the church may at any time present himself for Christian Baptism, but it is to be deeply regretted that anyone should have grown to maturity without the ministrations of the church. It is far better that the church surround each one of us from infancy with its wisdom and power. The baby is baptized into the fellowship of the church and while still in the cradle he becomes the object of God's redemptive work. As the child grows older he comes to understand and appreciate what God is already doing for him. When he is old enough to act by his own will he receives the symbolic confirmation of what is already true.

Christian faith involves the mind and the will, but it need not originate with them. In every area of life we receive from parents and from society gifts that we could never make our own if they were not bestowed upon us before we knew or cared about them. So also in the church. Men are not to be understood as utterly autonomous individuals — self-made and self-determined. We are communal beings, each of whom brings into a new focus what he receives consciously and unconsciously from the past. There is nothing incongruous, therefore, that in the area of the spirit the community should bestow upon its children its greatest and most precious gifts. But the church's nurture, even its Baptism, cannot guarantee that all of us will use constructively what we receive. Many neglect and even abuse the church's help. Nevertheless, freely and gladly the church gives to all.

The full appreciation of the divine greatness of the church causes us to adopt toward all its historic teachings an attitude of reverence and acceptance, but we need not condemn Christians who seek other doctrinal expressions for their faith. Fellow worshipers, even when they differ in explicit teachings, do not differ as greatly as they themselves suppose. If their worship is real, they all seek expression in doctrine for the same ultimate reality that must forever elude the grasp of human thought. The full truth of the creeds is known only to the Christian worshiper in the moment of his closest approach to God.

Scientific knowledge and modern points of view pose difficulties for the traditional formulations of orthodoxy, so that there often seems to be good reason to give the old truths more modern dress. But the need for modernization is more superficial and less urgent than many believe. The new style of today will become just as outmoded tomorrow as is that of the fourth century now. Indeed, it will prove less able to stand the test of time, for in our individualistic age it is less likely to reflect so well that corporate experience of the church which endures through all external change.

The real meaning of all Christian doctrines can be grasped only from the point of view of worship. The creeds speak truly of the Trinity, but their truth is grasped only as they are understood to speak, not of a metaphysical entity, but of the reality to which the worshiper is related in prayer and sacrament. In the life of worship, God is encountered in a threefold way — as transcendent mystery, as incarnate in history and sacrament, and as indwelling the soul of the worshiper. This encounter and that which is there encountered are reality. Verbal formulations are never more than approximations, limited by man's capacity for conceptualization. The ancient formulations of Trinitarian dogma have never been surpassed and are least guilty of taking the doctrines out of the realm of religious truth and into that of philosophical speculation. Contradiction and confusion are to be expected, but they are not disturbing, for the reality experienced in worship is certain.

In Christology, too, the classical formulations are best for much the same reason. The creeds affirm that Christ is both man and God. They do so without explanation, and indeed preclude the possibility of any explanation by simultaneously insisting upon the otherness of God and refusing to compromise in any way the completeness of both natures in Christ. This is done precisely because such a God-man is needed to account for and justify Christian worship. For the worshiper knows that it is only because God became man without ceasing to be God that he can now become united in fellowship with God. Only a God-man can atone for man's guilt and bring God into the very presence of the worshiper. Only a God-man can institute the church and give it the authority and power with which the sacraments invest it. The worshiper does not understand the Christological doctrine intellectually or conceptually; he understands it only as worshiper. As thinker, the doctrines may perplex him, but because he has known their truth in worship he is content to reaffirm them, aware within himself of an understanding which he cannot communicate but which others also can find in worship.

More authoritative even than the creeds is the Bible. It is the first and greatest creation of the church and remains eternally its most valuable possession. The greatest worship is filled with the language of the Bible, and the whole movement of worship is determined by the revelation of God recorded in the Bible.

The Bible may indeed be read and studied even outside the

church. The findings of objective scholarship, with respect to Biblical dates and authorship, the history of the Jews, or even the life of Jesus, are not to be despised or rejected out of hand. But the Bible cannot really be understood from such a point of view. It is a product of the church, and it can be understood only within the church. Private study of the Bible is wholesome and profitable so long as the student does not pretend to set his understanding of Scripture over against the wisdom of the church. The Bible is a perplexing and baffling book. It contains a thousand sayings, which, when taken in themselves, are likely to prove misleading. The Bible should, therefore, be studied in the light of its interpretation by the church, for the church can bring to bear upon it the wisdom of the ages of Christian life.

Important as the intellectual study of the Bible may be, the highest and noblest use of Scripture is in public worship. Through it God speaks again to the hearts of his people, assembled to adore him and open to receive his Word.

SELECTED READINGS FOR FURTHER STUDY

AUTHORITARIAN PROTESTANTISM

I. *Expressions of the Movement*

Newman, John Henry, *Apologia Pro Vita Sua*. Everyman's Library, No. 636. E. P. Dutton & Co., Inc., 1942. Although a spiritual autobiography written by Newman after he had become a Roman Catholic, this still remains the classic account of the revival of the authoritarian principle in the Church of England.

Przywara, Erich, editor, *A Newman Synthesis*. Sheed & Ward, Inc., 1945. A systematic presentation of Newman's thought in selections from his own writing, with extensive use of his sermons.

Abbott, E. S., and others, *Catholicity*. The Dacre Press, London, 1947. A report to the Archbishop of Canterbury by a group of leading thinkers of the "catholic" party of the Church of England which explains their view of Christian faith and institutions.

Hebert, A. G., *The Form of the Church*. Faber & Faber, Ltd., London, 1944. A careful formulation of the doctrine of the church by a leading Anglo-Catholic scholar.

Hebert, A. G., *Liturgy and Society: the Function of the Church in the Modern World*. Faber & Faber, Ltd., London, 1935. A profound treatment of the significance of the order and liturgy of the church for the life of the world today, urging the superiority of the catholic movement to noncatholic forms of Protestantism.

More, Paul Elmer, and Cross, Frank Leslie, editors, *Anglicanism*. Society for Promoting Christian Knowledge, London, 1951. An extensive compilation of seventeenth-century Anglican writings, relevant here because of the honor in which they are held in the modern "authoritarian" tradition.

Moss, Claude B., *The Christian Faith: An Introduction to Dogmatic Theology*. Society for Promoting Christian Knowledge, London, 1943. A clear, well-organized, comprehensive statement of doctrine by an Anglo-Catholic theologian.

Pittenger, W. Norman, *His Body the Church*. Morehouse-Gorham Co., Inc., 1945. A vigorous and highly readable statement of the catholic doctrine of the church by one who combines devotion to the teaching of the church with acceptance of radical critical views on the New Testament.

II. *Histories*

Dawley, Powell Mills, *The Episcopal Church and Its Work*. The Seabury Press, Inc., 1955. Sixth and last in the "Church's Teaching" series. A brief history of the Episcopal Church and its English heritage that, while it does not stress the "authoritarian " tradition in Episcopalianism, is a useful introduction to the denomination as a whole.

Simpson, W. J. Sparrow, *The History of the Anglo-Catholic Revival from 1845.* George Allen & Unwin, Ltd., London, 1932. An enthusiastic account of the doctrines and practices of the catholic revival in England and their reception by the church and the nation.

Stewart, H. L., *A Century of Anglo-Catholicism.* Oxford University Press, 1929. A thorough and critical history of the catholic revival in England from 1827 on.

LITURGICAL PROTESTANTISM

I. *General Studies of Worship*

Heiler, Friedrich, *The Spirit of Worship: Its Forms and Manifestations in the Christian Churches.* Hodder & Stoughton, Ltd., London, 1926. A brief but appreciative survey of the diversity of Christian worship, which points to its underlying unity of meaning.

Jones, Ilion T., *A Historical Approach to Evangelical Worship.* Abingdon Press, 1954. An evaluation of the contributions of the liturgical movement to Protestantism and a reconsideration of the Evangelical cultus.

Maxwell, William D., *An Outline of Christian Worship,* revised edition. Oxford University Press, London, 1949. A concise outline of the forms of Christian worship in Eastern and Western Catholicism and the Reformation Churches.

Underhill, Evelyn, *Worship.* Harper & Brothers, 1936. A scholarly study of worship in the world religions generally as well as specifically in several forms of Christianity. Now available in a Harper Torchbook edition, 1957.

II. *Typical Interpretations of the Eucharist*

Brilioth, Yngve, *Eucharistic Faith and Practice, Evangelical and Catholic,* translated by A. G. Hebert. Society for Promoting Christian Knowledge, London, 1953. A scholarly and influential treatise on the history and present practice of Christian worship from the point of view of a Lutheran sympathetic with the liturgical revival.

Dix, Dom Gregory, *The Shape of the Liturgy*. The Dacre Press, London, 1945. A detailed and authoritative study of the Anglican liturgy. Accepted as generally definitive by Lowry and Pittenger, as well as by most other Anglican and Episcopalian scholars.

Lowry, Walter, *Action in the Liturgy, Essential and Unessential*. Philosophical Library, Inc., 1953. A collection of essays and addresses by one very independent Episcopalian scholar on the history and present understanding of the Lord's Supper as this understanding has developed out of the act of worship itself. Includes an appendix that attacks the Pittenger book listed below for its one-sided emphasis on sacrifice and its Christology.

MacDonald, A. J., editor, *The Evangelical Doctrine of Holy Communion*. W. Heffer & Sons, Ltd., Cambridge, 1930. An expression of the revived interest in the Eucharist on the part of leaders of Calvinist churches.

Pittenger, W. Norman, *The Christian Sacrifice: A Study of the Eucharist in the Life of the Christian Church*. Oxford University Press, 1951. A doctrine of the Lord's Supper that is in most respects harmonious with that of Roman Catholicism. Presented by the leading American writer of the catholic party in the Episcopal Church.

Underhill, Evelyn, *The Mystery of Sacrifice: A Meditation on the Liturgy*. Longmans, Green & Co., Inc., 1938. A rather subjective account of the worshiper's experience in the observance of the Eucharist. Written from the viewpoint of a mystically inclined Anglican.

CHAPTER IV

Individualistic Protestantism

IN GREAT BRITAIN the catholic revival is now more than a century old. In Continental Europe, neo-Reformation theology was revitalized in the period following World War I. Both movements were reactions against individualism in favor of emphases on the church and the Word as the objective sources or instruments of authority and grace. The profound influence that both movements have had in the Protestant world cannot be denied.

Nevertheless, any candid observer must recognize that neither the churchly nor the Reformation spirit provides the dynamic of American Protestantism. Each has ardent supporters and has produced an impressive literature. But neither has affected deeply the religious life of the Protestant masses. Even in those churches most conscious of their historical ties to the churchly or Reformation traditions, the traditional emphases on the objective efficacy of the Word or the church are more often the subjects of education and exhortation than the natural expressions of the common religious experience.

For the vast majority of earnest Protestants in America the decisive question is, What shall *I do* to be saved? The answer to this question determines the spiritual quest. If a preacher refuses to accept as his primary task the answering of this question for his people, his sermons are likely to be regarded as academic and irrelevant.

107

Central concern with the means that each one of us can personally employ to receive our salvation is the special mark of what is here called "individualistic" Protestantism. Posing the problem in this way does not minimize the importance of what God has done for us in Christ or what he now does for us in the church. But it does recognize that the area of our greatest concern must be where we are free to act. It is true that God offers us a salvation we could never have attained by our own efforts, but he does not force his gift upon us. We must willingly accept, and it is upon the "how" of such acceptance that attention must be turned.

Individualistic Protestantism, marked by this deeply personal concern, dominates the religious life of many lands, and it is in those lands where its dominance is most marked that the Protestant churches are enjoying the greatest vitality and growth. The vast sums of money lavished upon church buildings, the large number of persons attending church services, the great amount of time and energy given to the church schools and to lay organizations, the crowded theological seminaries, and the impressive benevolence programs all witness to the dynamic vigor of individualistic Protestantism. They demonstrate conclusively that, whatever critics may say of it, such piety continues to exercise a powerful appeal for the multitudes and to call forth magnificent dedication of time, talent, and treasure.

Part, at least, of the great strength of individualistic piety lies in the simplicity of its message. Perhaps this simplicity alienates a few sophisticates, but it makes available to ordinary men and women a vital gospel that is often obscured by the learned discourses of the professional theologians. It recalls for them beliefs that they have ignored rather than rejected; it draws out the simple, inescapable implications of these beliefs for their lives; and it challenges them to respond immediately.

Where this simplicity and directness are lost, the churches

begin to decline. Where attention is focused primarily upon social issues or theological problems, whatever interest these may have in their proper sphere, the church ceases to win souls for God's Kingdom. But when the fundamentals of the gospel are proclaimed without embarrassment or hesitation, ordinary men and women respond, and the church grows in numbers and in spirit.

This simple message of the gospel rests upon the profound conviction that this life is not the end, but is rather the preparation for another life beyond. Some Christians believe that this further life begins with the resurrection of the dead on the Day of Judgment. More expect to enter into it at the moment when our earthly life ends. This difference matters little, for in either case the new life is understood to be unending, and by virtue of its infinite duration incomparably more important than this life in the world of time and space.

Most Protestants further believe that their life consists in an absolute either-or. On the one hand, there is heaven, understood by some almost spatially as a place of beauty and pleasure, by others purely spiritually as the absolute presence of God, but in either case as the final fulfillment of all right desire. On the other hand, there is hell, understood again in many ways, but agreed to be an everlasting existence deprived of all joy, all love, and all meaning. Not only is the difference between heaven and hell absolute, but according to the overwhelmingly preponderant view, there is no second chance in hell, no further opportunity to escape from the doom once sealed, no faint glimmer of hope, but only utter and unending despair.

Finally, the great majority of Protestants today, however sympathetic they may be to the doctrine of predestination, still firmly believe that God offers to all men in Christ the gift of salvation. It is man who refuses the gift or accepts it ultimately by his own individual decisions. No church, no parent, no friend, can make that decision for him, however much they may help. Even God will not compel the right decision, though his help is always available to us.

This decision, therefore, made by each individual in his own solitude before God, is of ultimate significance. Beside it every other act of life is trivial. No other way to salvation is possible. In the absolute freedom of the moment of choice, the eternal destiny of the soul is sealed — for eternal joy or everlasting wretchedness.

Long before Kierkegaard, therefore, Protestant Pietists knew that life is decision, and that decision is solitary and ultimate. And the masses of simple people know it still. They need only to be vividly reminded, to be compelled to remember what they prefer to forget, to be brought sharply up against the urgency of decision, and year after year they will come by the millions to give their allegiance to Christ and his church.

The spiritual dynamic produced by the emphasis upon individual responsibility and personal experience has expressed itself in ardent support of the world missionary movement. Both the amazing missionary activity of the Moravians in the eighteenth century and the great world-wide programs of the nineteenth century were nurtured in the churches in which the concern for individual salvation was uppermost. Even today, whenever this passion for the redemption of souls is superseded by social idealism or by ecclesiasticism, the missionary program becomes weak and ineffective.

An equally great contribution of individualistic Protestantism has been made in the sphere of religious and political freedom. When Lutheranism, Calvinism, and Anglicanism were content to form state churches and to use the power of the secular government to compel religious conformity, tens of thousands protested. In the name of liberty of conscience under God, and often at the cost of their lives, these true Protestants refused to bow to political coercion in the affairs of the spirit.

Through the centuries their testimony to individual freedom

gradually prevailed. Persecution gave way to toleration, and toleration to freedom. In the New World, church has been separated from state, and within the churches there prevails a spirit of freedom.

The intense training in democracy that the common man has received in the individualistic churches has prepared him to accept and caused him to demand a share also in political affairs. Where individualistic Protestantism has prepared the way, where it has inculcated both self-respect and the sense of personal responsibility, political democracy has flourished.

Historically, individualistic piety seems to have arisen quite spontaneously in the most diverse cultural environments. Often, it is true, its clearest manifestations have appeared among groups that the church has declared heretical — the Montanists, the Donatists, the Waldenses, and the Anabaptists. But within the dominant churches as well, individualistic piety has maintained its hold and has been a source of renewed vitality for the whole — among the second-century apologists, the early Franciscans, the Brethren of the Common Life, and the Pietists and Evangelicals of the eighteenth century. Wherever men have found that the emphasis upon the objectivity of God's Word or Christ's church has operated as an excuse for individuals to deny, in practice if not in theory, their ultimate personal responsibility for what they are and do, and whenever they have responded to this situation in terms of an intensified demand upon individuals to appropriate to themselves the proffered truth and grace and to conform their lives without reserve to the demands of God — there we find the individualistic piety of which we speak.

But though this piety has flourished wherever Christians have taken their faith with deepest seriousness, only within the past two centuries has it been free from the harassing restrictions of ecclesiastical authority. Catholic hierarchical theory and practice have always been suspicious of a vital personal religion that finds in the Bible an adequate guide to salvation.

Lutherans and Calvinists, for all their talk of the immediacy of God's relationship to man, have regarded with disdain the earnest souls who practiced what *they* preached. They have clung instead to political authority and economic support by the state and often suppressed those who preferred to trust God to provide for the needs of his church.

Not unnaturally, during the centuries of persecution, the victims sometimes developed practices and attitudes that do not appear entirely defensible from our standpoint today. But finally, with the decline of official religion in Europe and especially in the free air of new continents in America and Australia, the long-suppressed spirit of individualism found full and wholesome expression. Institutions have appeared adapted to the deeper, more personal character of individualistic piety, sanely directed and loyally supported.

In many matters, effectiveness is more important than custom or taste. What matters is not that hallowed traditions be observed, that particular organizational patterns be maintained, or that subtle theological distinctions be understood. What matters is that men and women be saved. What facilitates this end is good; what hinders it, whatever its other values may be, must be pushed aside.

Perhaps the aesthetic sensitivity of a few may be offended by the music in the revivalist's tent, but that music draws needy souls who would never be attracted by Bach. Perhaps some temperaments are revolted by the emotional and sentimental appeal of the common evangelist. But far more men are moved to decide for Christ and his Kingdom by the fears and longings that such a speaker stirs in their hearts than are won by the arguments of the intellectualist. To quibble over method when souls are daily descending into hell because of our failure to reach them with the gospel of salvation is a travesty on all that is truly high and holy. If a leaf from the showman's book or a page from the propagandist's manual will enable the preacher to reach lost souls, then for him to reject such aid as secular or unbecoming is to place personal taste above the eternal welfare of God's children.

Thus far, for the most part, much of popular individualism stands united. But when the question is raised as to how one achieves salvation and as to the character of the redeemed life, differences begin to emerge. These differences are subtle and easily blurred, but in their fuller development they are far-reaching in their consequences.

Since individualistic Protestantism is genuinely individualistic, its forms are innumerable. It has no classical spokesmen whose positions have authority for myriads of followers. Each earnest spirit must seek for himself as God gives him to see the truth.

For most individualistic Protestants today the Christian faith may be represented as an ellipse, the two foci of which are the objective authority of the Bible as the guide to salvation and the subjective decisiveness of religious experience as the appropriation of salvation. These foci need not be contradictory, but they do stand in dynamic tension. Each focus tends to produce a circle of which it is the center and for which the other focus becomes only a point on the circumference. Although the full realization of these perfect circles is rare, most of the ellipses do tend to become egg-shaped as environment, experience, temperament, or dogmatic conviction encourage the placing of more emphasis on one or another of the foci.

It is, of course, impossible to describe separately the multitudinous forms of ellipses that are to be found in the contemporary scene. Hence, it is clearer and more helpful to discuss the two circles that tend to appear as one or the other of the foci achieves dominance in the life of an individual or a group and freely expresses its inner logic in a characteristic pattern of Protesant faith.

No generally accepted terms are available by which these two patterns may be conveniently distinguished, and none can be proposed that simply and accurately suggests the essence of each. However, since any labels are better than the confusion that follows from their absence, the terms "Biblicism" and "experientialism" will be used.

The Biblicist understands the Christian life primarily as one of belief and obedience. Our minds must assent to the truths of Scripture, and our action must conform to its teaching. When we believe and obey we can safely trust God for our salvation.

The experientialist insists that Christianity is a matter of the heart even more than of the head and hand. It must be felt as well as believed. God grants to those who truly trust him an inward assurance of their salvation — a sense of joy and peace that man can find here and now, a foreshadowing of the still richer life beyond the grave. Without this, we have the outward appearance of Christianity, but not the full inner reality.

These differences lead the two groups to develop in rather different directions. Biblicism maintains a simpler witness to the path of salvation. It is preoccupied continually with the addition of new converts and with the moral character of all, but it has a less-developed emphasis on spiritual growth after conversion. The chief task of the convert is to convert others.

Experientialism, on the contrary, easily develops mystical tendencies, and in any case places heavy emphasis on the inner life of the Christian. It tends to define the truly Christian life in such exalted terms that the initial act of conversion is thought of more as the starting point of a process than as itself completing that process. The emphasis on joy and peace in the present life of Christians also forms a natural transition to a preoccupation with the this-worldly effects of Christian experience and to an integration of the insights of Christianity with those of clinical psychology.

Thus Biblicism tends to be more stable or static than experientialism. This more rigid character has caused it to have the greatest difficulty of any Protestant tradition with the changing intellectual outlook of modern man. Its churches have been those most sharply divided by the controversies over evolution and Biblical criticism, and it is within them that the extremes of modernism and fundamentalism are still found in their most pronounced forms.

Experientialism, on the contrary, has been less divided by scientific thought than by conceptions of, and emphases upon, religious experience. Some have drifted gradually toward an emphasis on moral and spiritual growth through the normal channels of an institutionalized program, whereas others have insisted upon sharply distinctive experiences without which the process of growth is not regarded as Christian at all. Those emphasizing development have tended to modify their standards of Christian attainment in terms of the practical exigencies of modern life. Those stressing supernatural experiences have cultivated a holiness that stands aloof from the world and have regarded all adjustments as compromises with worldliness. The former regard the latter as narrow, legalistic, and impractical. The latter regard the former as lax and secularized, and in serious danger of replacing the distinctive Christian message with emotional good feeling and " do-goodism." But the great majority find their place somewhere between the two extremes, preferring harmony and brotherly affection to definiteness and factionalism.

The Baptists as a whole come closest to exemplifying the moderate Biblicist position, but the two can by no means be identified. The English Baptists of Cromwell's day were deeply imbued with the essential spirit of Calvinism. Only gradually did the consequences of their own special emphases lead to the fuller development of a more distinctive character. In the eighteenth and nineteenth centuries, Baptists were profoundly affected by the Methodist revivals both in England and America, and much of the life of the present-day Baptist movement seems to have been deeply modified.

The correlation of the Baptist churches with Biblicism as a type of Protestantism must not be pressed too far. Not only do

Baptists emphasize many ideas derived from other traditions than Biblicism, but also the logic of Biblicism has expressed itself in many other churches. Most obviously and in its most extreme form it has determined the life of the Christian and Disciple groups which sprang from the work of Alexander Campbell and his associates. With relatively minor differences, it is found among the scattered remnants of the earlier Anabaptist movement, especially in the Mennonite churches. Many of the same elements, though moderately expressed and tempered with great openness to the changing cultural and intellectual scene, are to be found in the Congregational churches.

But the influence of Biblicism is far more extensive than this sort of listing of groups could suggest. It possesses a strong appeal in all the Calvinist churches, especially where the original ties between church and state have been severed. It has permeated much of the thought and life of the Wesleyan churches. Even Anglicans and Lutherans, under the influence of the individualistic spirit of the age, have not proved immune to Biblicism.

The chief institutional embodiments of experientialism are the Wesleyan churches, but here too identification of a spiritual tradition with any group of denominations is misleading. From its inception the Wesleyan movement contained a diversity of emphases somewhat in tension with one another, and only a few groups that separated from the major Methodist bodies have seriously tried to preserve the more extreme implications of the experientialist aspect of Wesley's teaching.

Furthermore, the experientialist emphasis in the Wesleyan movement was not original. Continental Pietists and Moravians had long preceded Wesley, and their descendants retain much of the same spirit. Certain strands of Puritanism, which have developed their implications largely independently of Wesley, have come to a parallel understanding of the Christian faith. Wesley's own influence extended far beyond the Methodist denominations both within the Church of England and among the Dissenters. In the more intense atmosphere of the American frontier, aspects of experientialism proved infectious and in various modifications they have tinged the life of almost all of American Protestantism.

However, despite the lack of identity between Biblicism and experientialism, on the one hand, and the Baptist and Wesleyan churches on the other, the expressions of these two forms of Protestantism do seem to be found most purely and fully developed in these denominations. In actuality they are extensively interfused in both denominations. Yet it is possible to distinguish those aspects of each which are distinctive of the separate traditions. Hence, the following chapters attempt to present successively the inner logic of Biblicism and of experientialism as characteristically developed by moderately conservative Baptists and Wesleyans in so far as they remain relatively unaffected each by the other.

BIBLICISM

" What will it profit a man, if he gains the whole world and forfeits his life? " To such a question there is only one answer. Beside the endlessness of eternity our present mortal existence fades into insignificance. There can be no greater madness than to doom ourselves to eternity without God simply in order to satisfy our passing fancy or the passions of the flesh. Reason, prudence, and sanity demand that we seek promptly and at all costs the path of salvation.

But where shall we seek? Can any human mind penetrate into the mystery of the life beyond the grave? Can we turn to princes or philosophers for guidance? Certainly not. Only he who created man and implanted within him the privilege of eternal life, only he can know the plan of man's salvation. Only God can give salvation; hence, it must be God and not man who sets the conditions for receiving his gift. We know the way to salvation only as we are instructed by God. Without such instruction we remain inevitably floundering in the darkness of ignorance. If any of us are to be saved, God must not only provide the way but he must tell us the way, clearly and unmistakably.

God *has* told us the way. The Bible is his Holy Word. In sacred Scripture there is recounted for us the history of God's dealings with mankind from ancient times and especially the story of his incarnation and atonement in Jesus Christ. But most important of all, God has told us plainly how we individually can appropriate to ourselves the salvation for which he has paid the price.

The one supreme condition of salvation is that we believe. We must believe that God's Word is true and above all that Christ is really our Savior and Lord. We need not understand why belief is the appointed way to salvation. We can see dimly that no man is morally perfect and that God in his holiness could not set moral standards less than perfection as the requirement of salvation. We can see that belief is open to all and that on this condition even the weakest and poorest have an opportunity to receive the priceless gift. Since we know that God pities and loves us as a father, we can glimpse something of the reason for the simplicity of his demand.

But it is incomparably more important that we *exercise* faith than that we *understand why* faith is the way to salvation. God has only hinted at his reasons, but he has clearly told us the way. If we do not believe, we are hopelessly lost. If we do believe, however ignorant we may be, we are saved.

Belief is, to be sure, the assent of the mind to truths proclaimed by God. But belief is much more than that. If we believe God's Word, we cannot help being ashamed of our own lives. If we are truly ashamed of our lives, we cannot help willing to be changed. There is no real belief without a contrite turning away from sin and a deep desire to be remade. Thus repentance is inextricable from belief.

It does not matter whether we speak of belief as the only re-

quirement for salvation or whether we conjoin repentance
with it as a second requirement. Sometimes the New Testament speaks of both and sometimes only of one. No one really
believes without repentance. In that one act by which we
accept God's way we also turn away from our own erring ways.

Belief and repentance do not result in salvation as if they in
themselves were its sufficient cause. Salvation is a gift of God
by which he freely and faithfully crowns our obedient act according to his promises. By his grace we are reborn into a new
life in Christ Jesus. The old man is put off and the new man is
put on. The old will, which asserted itself against God, is replaced by a new will which desires to live righteously in accordance with the divine plan for our lives. The spirit of rebel-
liousness is replaced by obedience. The divided self, at war
with itself, is replaced by a new wholeness and unity of purpose.

This total experience is likely to be accompanied by deep
emotional upheavals, by agony over sin and unutterable rejoicing in the assurance of new life. Indeed, one who claims
to move through these greatest experiences of life with un-
ruffled feelings must inevitably be suspected of being unaware
of the full meaning of repentance and rebirth. Nevertheless,
the emotion itself is neither a requirement nor a sign of salvation. It is a customary by-product which may add to the richness of the experience subjectively but cannot affect the deeper
spiritual reality which is the work of God alone.

Once we have met the conditions set by God, we *are* saved.
We need no longer doubt or be anxious. God has promised,
and God is faithful to keep his promises. Once we have truly
repented and believed, we will never lose our salvation. We
may live the rest of our lives in absolute confidence that we
have been accepted by God. Even in those times when our human frailty is most manifest in our lives, even when the memory of the moment of regeneration grows dim, even when we
wander for a while away from God, we may still know that

God has not abandoned his own. God has acted and what God has done man cannot undo. If God has given us new life, that life is ours forever. This assurance gives us a deep-seated peace and joy even though our lives here and now may be filled with sorrow and suffering.

This does not mean that the saved man never sins. On the contrary, there is no complete freedom in this life from the possibility of disobedience to God. Trial and temptation, weakness and imperfection, are the Christian's lot throughout his earthly pilgrimage. But he who has once decisively turned his back upon the life of sin will never again fundamentally surrender himself to its power.

If it is objected that some do seem to fall from grace, it must be remembered that no man truly knows the heart of any save himself. Certainly the outward appearance of repentance and belief may occur without permanent effect. A man may renounce temporarily certain outward sins without repenting of the whole life of disobedience. He may even partially deceive himself into believing that he has met the requirements because of confusion over what is really meant by repentance. But God *knows*. He does not give man salvation one moment and then take it away the next. He who is saved is saved indeed.

The primary consequence of faith and regeneration is a life of righteousness. The confidence that God has saved us does not lead to moral indifference. If we are really indifferent, it is clear that we have not yet been reborn. He who is redeemed desires above all else to live in grateful obedience to God.

The Christian life is a continual struggle to obey ever more completely the will of God declared in the Scriptures. Fundamentally, it is always a successful struggle, though the success of the outcome does not lessen the difficulty of the effort. We may sometimes be in situations in which even the wisest Christians are uncertain as to God's will. We may be so blind and so dull that we do not understand God's will even when it is clear to others. But once we do see it definitely, with no shadow of doubt, we *must* act upon it, and we will do so regardless of the cost to ourselves. We must not, we will not, as Christians we cannot willfully and persistently refuse to obey a clear call to obedient action.

This outward obedience is not, some may argue, all that is required, for God demands the motive of unselfish love just as clearly as he demands righteous conduct. This is true, but there is an important difference. We do not have absolute control over our motives. We cannot by an act of will wholly replace selfish desires with the love of God. But we *can act* in conformity with his will. To depreciate the action because the motive is not pure, or to suggest that we must first desire to do the good in order that the doing be truly virtuous, is dangerous and destructive of the best Christian morality.

Our feelings vary from hour to hour; our motives are hard to determine, shifty, and elusive; our capacity to attribute pure motives to dubious conduct is unlimited. But what God demands of us is not the inward purity we cannot give, but the outward obedience we can offer to him. Act rightly, however you feel. Obey God, however confused your motives may be. The habit of obedience is primary, the emotions that accompany it secondary.

The life of habitual obedience to God's will is not always, in human terms, a happy one. For some it offers tangible rewards, but for others it means primarily a renunciation of actions that would otherwise give pleasure and gain wealth and prestige. The Christian life this side of the grave may well be marked by suffering and sacrifice. Men may persecute and despise us, and we ourselves may often feel inner pain and hunger for what we cannot have.

But what is all this present sorrow in comparison with the glorious prize for which we labor — eternal bliss beyond the grave? This life is short; at best its pleasures are fleeting and tinged with pain. What we forgo is far less desirable than it seems, and even if this life should last ten thousand years and be filled with the greatest pleasures the world can offer, untainted by shame or remorse, even so, how would that compensate for eternity spent in hell?

God offers his gift of salvation to all. Whosoever will, may come. In his Word, God makes plain to all the way of salvation. Every open and honest mind is capable of finding the truth there. God deals with each individually, and each, individually, is free and able to respond. No church, no sacrament, no parental act can save us. Each is ultimately responsible for his own fate, and each is ultimately free to decide either to accept or reject God's proffered gift. The weight of eternity hangs in the balance.

Much as we might wish to do so, we cannot elude the awful responsibility for our own salvation. Friends and counselors may comfort and advise, preachers and evangelists may exhort, but no one can believe or repent for us. Each of us stands immediately before the God who is not mocked, who knows our hearts better than we ourselves, who lovingly but inexorably demands of us that we do what we are quite able to do if only we will — to repent and believe.

When we have believed and been reborn, our immediate, personal responsibility to God is intensified. He demands of us an obedience that we *can* render, an obedience that is to him and him alone. For such obedience he gives us the light that we need. When we pray for strength he answers our prayers more abundantly than we can hope.

God demands of us belief and obedience, and he graciously helps us to fulfill his demands, but he never compels. God has made us free moral agents, and it is only as such that he addresses us. Belief is not belief if it is not voluntary, and obedience is not obedience if it is not free. The Christian life is one of free acceptance of the truth of God's Word and free obedience to its teaching.

Since God's plan of salvation hinges upon voluntary personal belief, clearly we can be reborn only when we have reached the age of accountability. To claim that the church can save us as infants by the rite of water baptism is to contradict the clearest teaching of Scripture. If the practice of sprinkling water on the heads of infants is correctly recognized as quite divorced from regeneration, then it should not be regarded as satisfying the Scriptural demand for baptism.

Baptism is commanded of us. Next to belief and repentance it is the clearest of God's specific commands upon his children. But baptism is commanded as an outward expression and sign of an experience that has already occurred. In baptism we gratefully testify to others that by God's grace we have died to sin and have risen to new life.

If baptism were a magical ecclesiastical rite, or a humanly instituted service of the dedication of babies, its outward form might not be important. But since the true significance of baptism lies in its expression of the believer's experience of salvation in Christ, its form *is* important. Because baptism is a symbol of dying and rising, the only form of baptism that is fully adequate is that which was used in the New Testament church. The believer is wholly immersed in the water to signify the completeness of his dying to his old self and the spiritual cleansing that accompanies this death. He rises from the water as he has risen to a new life in Christ. His old nature is buried with Christ in order that he may also share in Christ's resurrection. What more meaningful or appropriate rite could be observed to symbolize the greatest experience of human life!

Baptism is not observed in a particular way just because we consider it suitable. We are baptized because Christ commands it. The substitution of the sprinkling of infants for the believers' baptism is not only an unwise human decision; it is also a serious violation of the plain teaching of God's Holy Word. Such disobedience may be pardoned when it is ignorantly practiced by those who do believe and obey according to their understanding. But when groups persist in the practice after the truth has been plainly shown to them, they cannot fail to do themselves spiritual harm.

Baptism is not only the symbol of regeneration practiced in obedience to the ordinance of God; it is also the rite by which we enter into the church — the fellowship of baptized believers. This church must be a *voluntary* association of believers dedicated to obedience to God's Word. Therefore, it must be organized according to the New Testament pattern. It must be radically and permanently cleansed of all the contrivances of men whereby priests have gained pomp and power at the expense of the purity of the gospel.

The New Testament church was the fellowship of all believers, but it was institutionally embodied only in the local associations of the faithful based upon a voluntary covenant. Each Christian individually believed and acted as he was led by God and associated with others for the common good and the promotion of God's work.

Local churches might exchange ideas, but they did not dictate to one another. They might follow the guidance of a leader from another congregation, but only when they were persuaded of the truth of his words. Only gradually and at terrible cost in Christian life and faith was the primitive Christian freedom replaced by a centralized authoritarian hierarchy.

The task of the convinced Christian is to help the churches return to the primitive freedom under God of the early Christian community. Every Christian is a priest, and every congregation a church. Because the congregation is composed of believers obedient to the Word of God, it is competent to determine its own life without direction from human superiors. It is competent to select its minister, to admit to membership and to exclude from membership, to determine to its own satisfaction the meaning of God's Word, and as it is led by sober deliberation, to co-operate freely with other like-minded churches.

For local churches to have their decisions made for them

by others is bad, but when the others are politicians the situation is far worse. The church must serve God according to the enlightened consciences of its members; it cannot serve political governors. Each man must believe and obey as he is led by loyalty to God's Word, not as he is instructed by the state. The state has its proper functions in the fulfillment of which the Christian will gladly co-operate. But the state must not and cannot determine spiritual truth or tamper with the Christian conscience. Rather than submit to commands of the state that contradict those of God, the Christian must be willing cheerfully to die.

Even if the state should seek only to aid the church, its assistance must be rejected. The church wants no support that is not wholly voluntary on the part of those who give it. It wants no members who come because of political pressures. When the state undertakes to select the true church and to give it preferred treatment, it has overstepped its bounds and sought to replace the authority of conscience by external compulsion.

The universal fellowship of believers has been divided by men into competing sects and denominations. Thereby the full Christian witness has been greatly weakened. The divisions result from men's insistence upon creeds, traditions, practices, and modes of organization not sanctioned in God's Holy Word. If only all Christians would realize the foolishness of employing man-made principles and insist upon accepting only God's Word and what is clearly taught therein, the curse of division could be speedily overcome! But the stubbornness of men is great. Not only do they insist upon ideas and practices of human origin and erect them into a wall of separation against all others, but they even refuse obedience to the clear commands of God. Especially with regard to baptism and the organization of the church many of them fail to carry out the practices clearly taught in Scripture. To call their attention to this serious failing is not narrow and sectarian, as is sometimes said, but an act of charity. It is our Christian duty to warn those who violate clear Scriptural teaching of the dangerous consequences to which they expose themselves.

The reunion of all of Christendom is a consummation devoutly to be desired, but only if it is effected according to God's will. God's will is revealed in the Bible, and among those who make the Bible their sole norm, who seek in every way to conform their teaching and practice to its prescriptions, union proves easy. But to seek union at the cost of abandoning obedience to God's expressed will would be to place human convenience above the divine command. We dare not even cooperate with those who ignore the Biblical pattern if by doing so we seem to treat our differences as unimportant. Better to maintain our present witness to the truth than to endanger that witness for the sake of harmony with other men.

Of all the acts of Christian obedience, one is clearly primary. As Christians our concern for others will be expressed in ceaseless efforts to save them from the fearful judgment to come. We will, of course, also do what we can to make their lot in this life as free as possible from pain and want. The Scriptures speak with uncompromising clarity of the importance of feeding the hungry, clothing the naked, and defending the rights of the helpless. But these acts of kindness, whatever the immediate value of the happiness they bring, take on their full significance only as means of leading others to Christ. To help men with the problems of this life and still allow them to go to their death without guiding them to their souls' salvation is a trivial and ephemeral aid. The greatest gift that one man can give to another, the noblest act of Christian love, is to lead a fellow human being to Christ.

The services of the church likewise must serve, most of all, this one great end. Education of the membership and exhortation to greater devotion are important. But the effectiveness of the church is judged in the end by its success in winning souls for Christ. Hence, the church must organize itself for outreach to the unsaved, must conduct evangelistic missions in the community in which it is located, and must give of its sons and of its treasure to send God's Word to the uttermost parts of the earth. Only in this passionate dedication to saving the lost can the church fulfill its mission.

To most of its services, therefore, the church welcomes the unbeliever with open arms, hoping that in the hearing of God's Word he will be won to accept God's way of salvation. But there are certain acts of the church that by their nature are properly limited to the membership. One of these is the business meeting. The practical decisions for the conduct of the affairs of the church must be conducted with perfect democracy. Every member is given full opportunity to speak as he is led in conscience by God. The church *is* its membership, and each individual must accept personal responsibility for the wisdom of its decisions and the effectiveness of its outreach. In the church meeting the seriousness of the equal privilege and responsibility of every individual member is brought home to the consciousness of all.

The observance of the Lord's Supper is also primarily, at least, an act of the membership, although there may be differences of opinion as to the propriety of admitting other Christians to its fellowship. We take the bread and the wine according to the example and ordinance of our Lord, to keep alive in our hearts the remembrance that Christ died for us. In this service we who benefit from Christ's Passion express our gratitude and thanksgiving and renew our vows of loyalty and obedience. This act of worship is also an opportunity for the deepening of our spiritual communion with God and with our fellow members in the church.

In addition to the ordinances of Baptism and the Lord's Supper some understand Jesus to have taught also the practice of foot washing. Certainly we are told that we should wash one another's feet, and those who regard this as a sacred rite to be performed in obedience to Jesus' command have reasonable

Scriptural ground for their position. Most believe, however, that in this instance Jesus was setting an example of humble service to be imitated, rather than instituting a specific practice to be strictly observed. If this latter interpretation is correct, then, with the changing of social customs the true following of Jesus' example would lead to different outward acts.

All Christians are equally responsible for the spiritual welfare of their neighbors, and all are equally responsible for studying and obeying God's Word. All are equally priests. But this does not mean that each must serve the church in exactly the same way. Each is called to dedicate his peculiar gifts, and some are called to proclaim and to interpret God's Word and to guide the congregation in its worship. Those who are called to preach are not set aside as having special spiritual prerogatives, but they are given special responsibilities. Only men endowed by God with the gifts of understanding and skill can meet the exacting requirements of the ministry.

There is no one pattern into which the ministry must always fit. Often it is best that the minister should serve without salary. Certainly he should not accept pay from political and ecclesiastical authorities. If he is in need, those whom he serves will help him. At other times the work of the church becomes so demanding that the preacher must abandon the effort to earn a living in secular work. Then the congregation will gladly provide his total support.

Sometimes God calls men whose understanding of Scripture comes only from deep personal experience. Others whom he calls have great advantages of formal education. These differences do not matter ultimately. The church will expect of its minister what it considers best and most effective in the time and place in which it finds itself. God's call and the willing response — these are essential. How the ministry is trained and how it is financed are matters for determination as experience shows best.

God's call must be confirmed by ordination by a church. We may be sure that God does not call the spiritually dull or the morally slothful. Hence, the church can judge in part whether the one who believes himself called is suited by spiritual and moral character to the Christian ministry. His personal qualities and these alone enable a man to serve faithfully and well, and no act of the church can confer upon him any spiritual authority that his individual relationship to God has not already given him.

It is natural that Christians generally prefer to continue the practices of their fathers and to employ their methods for winning souls to Christ. But the method is not really important; what counts is success. If new techniques and modern methods reach men and women not touched by time-tested approaches, then the church must adopt them. Its goal is the salvation of individual souls. It knows what each must do in order to be saved. It cannot stand by with complacency while a single soul goes down to eternal torment. It cannot allow human traditions or prejudices of taste to stand between the sinner and his Savior.

The Bible is the *only* source of reliable knowledge of God and of the way of salvation. In it, and in it alone, God speaks. Elsewhere we have the traditions of men, the records of human experience and opinion. But men are fallible, and human experience and thought cannot be the basis of that certain knowledge which men must have in regard to this one incomparably important matter. God's Word must not be conceived as merely better or truer than man's word. The contrast is absolute. God's Word is truth. Man's word, unless it is instructed by God's Word, is error.

The Bible is the source of our knowledge not only of God's promises but also of God's demands. Not all of these demands are understood to be of equal significance. Some applied only to the ancient Jews and are superseded in the new covenant. But much of the old law still stands, heightened, intensified, and supplemented by the new.

There may be many sayings in Scripture that have little if any direct reference to the Christian life. Some deal with matters of ancient history or give details of the architecture of the Temple. In such areas it might seem that there is no need to insist upon the absolute infallibility of the Biblical record. But such a concession is exceedingly dangerous. Once one allows the critical faculty to come to play upon Scripture, it is difficult indeed to draw the line. Once it is suggested that error may occur at one point, there seems little reason to suppose that other passages are immune. Soon the whole becomes doubtful, and vigorous Christian living is replaced by argument and confusion. Therefore the wise policy is to cultivate the spirit of humble acceptance even where one cannot understand, to assume the truth even of passages that appear to confute each other, to believe in inerrancy even where the well-authenticated conclusion of empirical science *seems* to contradict what is believed. In most of these instances what is really important is not the idea itself. Most of the difficult passages are only remotely relevant to the salvation of the soul. What is really important is that unquestioned faith in the authority of Scripture as a whole be preserved so that no doubt can be raised in regard to those matters which *are* at the center of the faith.

Even variety of translations and discussion of difficulties in establishing the original text are dangerous, though they may of necessity be tolerated. The untutored layman who cannot enter into the endless debates of scholars must be made to feel confidence that the text in his hand is truly God's sacred Word, to be implicitly believed and obeyed. If he cannot accept it as such, if he is left always worrying that perhaps God's Word has been tampered with or is here misrepresented, then he can never be sure that he has met the requirements for salvation fully and accurately. If, therefore, scholars will insist on new revisions and translations from time to time, let them at least always emphasize that new manuscript discoveries never cast doubt upon the essential accuracy for all practical purposes of the older translations.

Scripture alone is the Word of God; hence its authority can never be shared by creeds. But this does not mean that the contents of the major creeds are generally repudiated. On the contrary, the ideas of the Apostles' and Nicene Creeds may readily be recognized as generally harmonious with the Scriptures. What is rejected is the use of creed or tradition as an excuse for failure to conform unreservedly to the manifest teaching of Scripture.

Since Scripture speaks plainly, there should be no need for any human formulation of the faith. However, at times men feel the need to express their common understanding, and at times perverse interpretations of the Scripture must be refuted. For these reasons, local churches may state the principles of their covenant and groups of churches may jointly formulate confessions of their faith. Still, only the Bible itself is binding on the individual conscience, not covenants or confessions, however clearly others may be convinced of their Scriptural character.

On such vexing questions as free will and predestination, disagreement seems irresolvable. There are good Biblical texts for both points of view, and where this is the case doctrinal agreement is unnecessary. Only if the doctrine of election should be used as a justification for failure to expend all efforts for the salvation of sinners, or if the doctrine of freedom should be used to suggest that men may set up other conditions for salvation than those ordained by God, must the church rise up to oppose the offending teaching. For the rest, what matters is not that every aspect of Scripture be understood, that every doctrinal dispute be settled. What matters is that sinners be shown the way of salvation taught us by God, that they believe, repent, and obey.

EXPERIENTIALISM

Christianity is not a new belief, but a new life; not a new moral code, but a new heart and a new spirit! It involves, of course, new beliefs. It involves also the most exacting of moral codes. But he who sees Christianity in terms of doctrine and moral legalism fundamentally misunderstands it. There is no gospel there! The good news is not that God makes demands upon us. The good news is that God gives us in Christ Jesus new life, abundant life.

God does not merely strengthen our determination to do his will. He makes us *desire* to serve him. The old self-centeredness and greed he wipes away. In their place he gives us love — love of our neighbors and above all love of himself. We serve him, then, not from painful straining to do our duty, but because we want above all else to please God and give him glory. We serve our neighbor, not because we perceive an unpleasant obligation that we must fulfill to avoid guilt, but because our hearts overflow with tenderness and compassion when we become aware of human suffering and need.

Because we love God and our neighbors, because we fulfill the demands of righteousness easily and gladly, we are at peace with ourselves and are filled with holy joy. The peace and joy that are in our hearts irradiate our very countenances, so that others in seeing us may know the power of God. Thus by our expression, our manner, our actions, and our entire lives we witness to the transforming efficacy of the Spirit of God.

When Christianity is truly experienced and truly lived, there is no need for labored arguments as to its truth or superiority over other religions. When Christianity is not truly experienced and lived, such arguments are generally useless. Argument may change opinion, though it rarely does even this, but it leads no one to Christ. Jesus himself did not win followers by proofs of his divinity. He lived a divine life, and the Spirit of God dwelling in him shone through him into a dark world. Men and women were drawn by his righteousness, by his inner peace, and above all by his love.

It has always been so. Where argument repels, love attracts. Where dogmatism appalls, the radiance of the Christian spirit reflects itself in the darkest mind and the most evil heart. At home both among the cynical and rebellious and in pagan lands where idols are worshiped, the Christian spirit bears faithful witness where all efforts at logical reasoning are doomed to failure.

Our most important Christian duty is to grow in the experience of God's grace and to live as our new spirit leads us. When we do this we will want to tell others of what God has done for us. If we tell them only that the Bible teaches certain things, they will not believe. They will feel that the world is different now, that the age of miracles is past. But if we testify as to how these promises have been abundantly fulfilled in our own personal experience, they cannot help believing. Our very lives bear witness to God's truth. Thus others will be led to seek for themselves the life we have found in Christ, the life of love, power, and joy. What greater joy can life bring than the consciousness that God uses us to win others to his Kingdom?

What, then, must we do to be saved? Can we enumerate certain steps that we must take on the completion of which God forgives our sins? Perhaps so, but there are two serious dangers in such an approach. In noting these dangers, the deeper truth as to how we are saved can be placed in bold relief.

In the first place, the enumeration of steps to salvation almost suggests that salvation is a reward for a certain human attainment, and such a suggestion fundamentally fails to recognize the divine initiative and freedom. The forgiveness of sin is not simply a judicial act of God in heaven following mechanically upon a certain kind of human behavior. To interpret forgiveness in this purely objective fashion is to show a lack of faith in the effective power of God among us here and now. When we experience the forgiveness of sins as a vivid reality in our own lives, we know that what happens is the work of God, not of ourselves. Our part is no more than to ask for a gift in confidence that it will be bestowed — not because we have asked aright but because of the love of the One who gives. That the gift is received only by those who ask it in no way denies that it is simply a gift.

Furthermore, even the asking, even the desire, is not really our human achievement. It, too, is God's gift, though not in the sense that God arbitrarily gives to some a desire that he withholds from others. God loves all men and wills that none be lost. But he wills that we all be saved as *men* by our own free consent, not that we be hurled into heaven as one might throw a stone. Therefore, the Spirit of God works upon the spirit of every child born into this world, seeking to draw it to himself. Without that ever-present act of grace, our own nature — avaricious, prideful, and sensual — would lead us to nothing but willful rebellion. Even as it is, even under the gracious influence of God's Spirit, our will resists his will, and many finally reject entirely the gift that God has proffered. But others, though of themselves they do nothing but resist, gradually allow themselves to be won by his grace to a longing for full forgiveness and for a life of obedience to his will. Not our wills, therefore, but God's grace has worked in us the desire through which we have come to faith and repentance and so to full salvation.

In the second place, the question as to what steps are necessary to salvation must be answered only by determining which procedures actually lead to the felt experience of salvation, and not by selecting from Scripture a verse here and there and listing the acts therein mentioned. When one assures all those who have followed a recommended course of action that they are saved, one ignores the primary fact that whether or not they are truly saved is to be determined by their spiritual condition — not by what steps they have taken. Whatever steps do in fact lead men to the vital experience of God's grace are *the* steps, and the only steps, they need to take, and once this experience is attained no question need ever be raised as to whether the requirements of salvation have been met.

The means that are actually effective are all spiritual ones. They begin with the true desire for salvation and they include deep sorrow for sin and great confidence in the love of God and in his intention and power to save us as revealed in Jesus Christ. We may differ with each other somewhat in our language as we seek to describe to others how they must feel and what they must believe. Perhaps no two persons have come to Christ in exactly the same way. That matters little. Where the hunger is really present, where there is true shame for sin, and where Jesus Christ is known and trusted, there God will find his way.

When we have truly experienced the inwardly transforming power of forgiveness we do not feel anxious as to our soul's salvation. We *know* God's love here and now! How could we doubt that the gates of heaven are open to us? We know ourselves redeemed, for we find our lives changed, not superficially or merely in terms of greater moral zeal, but radically, in terms of our deepest feelings and desires. Our assurance that we are Christian is complete, for we know that only God can give the kind of spirit we now find within us.

But even this is not all that God does to assure us that we are his. We are not left to inspect our own motives and actions in order to determine our Christian status. Such introspection might lead us to a self-concern incompatible with the highest expression of Christian love. God gives us his Spirit to guide, inspire, and enlighten us, but above all to assure us. God's Spirit testifies to our spirit that we are God's children. In the depths of our hearts we *know* because God tells us. In the strength of that confidence our joy is fulfilled and our love of God ever deepened.

In the moment in which we accept God's forgiveness of our sins we experience also a victory over the power of sin. But although the victory is real and in a sense complete, it is not absolute. The newborn principle of love of God has risen to dominance in our hearts, but the old man, though overcome, is not destroyed. Over and over again in moments of weakness the sinful nature seeks to reassert itself. Old habits of greed and licentiousness still struggle to overpower their new master. The Christian's life is one of constant struggle to hold these sinful motives in subjection and steadfastly to keep all action controlled entirely by the dictates of a true Christian spirit.

The old sinful habits when constantly suppressed gradually lose their power. The element of moral struggle is superseded by inner serenity in total victory. The principle of love, once constantly threatened, becomes habitual and all-encompassing. The old man is not merely vanquished, but destroyed!

Such an attainment may be rare indeed. There may be far more who pretend to possess this consummate gift than there are those to whom it has really been granted. But to deny that it is possible for man to achieve this holy state, to question the ability of God to work even this miracle in the human heart, or to believe that God's purpose for us is fully satisfied by anything less than this perfection, is to fall short in faith in God's goodness and power. There is no limit to what God can do for that man who claims God's promises and yields himself wholly to God's will in perfect trust. The most serious mistake of many Christian churches is that they have taught men to believe that sin can never be wholly removed from their lives and have discouraged sincere Christians from asking of God the highest of all his gifts. Perhaps it is because so many of us have never vitally experienced the marvelous power of God in the forgiveness of sin that we doubt that this same power can complete within us the work so gloriously begun.

The progressive sanctification of our lives is a work of God's grace for which we praise him as the sole author. But the acknowledgment of the divine initiative must never be understood as implying the sheer passivity of man. God does not sanctify by compulsion. He encourages us by his love; he entices us by his promises; he aids us by his indwelling Spirit. But only as we are willing to grow can he give us new life beyond all our imagination out of the riches of his grace.

In the process of spiritual growth we must not so emphasize the sublime fruits of the spirit — joy, peace, and love — as to neglect the hard task of overcoming specific evil habits in our lives. We dare not ask for the exalted attainments of the saint without first willingly sacrificing whatever we know is contrary to God's will, whatever interferes with the effectiveness of our service to God. To repent of a general state of sinfulness supposed to be shared by all may well be easy, and mean but little. God calls us to turn our backs upon those specific obstacles to his love to which we are individually most strongly attached. For one man this may be sexual appetite or intemperance, for another, love of money or power, for another, laziness or slothfulness, for still another, pride of race or ancestry. When one obstacle is overcome, others become apparent. But there is progress, for as the more obvious impediments to our service to God are removed we can see more clearly how to deal with those subtler, more insidious temptations of the spirit.

We work with God by consciously striving to do his will, to develop our love of him, and to suppress our selfish and sensual nature. This moral effort must never be replaced by an attitude of mere waiting for God to act, of doing nothing until we are specially prompted or directed. Nevertheless, absolutely central to our voluntary co-operation with God in the sanctification of our lives is the disciplined practice of prayer.

Prayer is our opportunity to examine our lives as they lie open to God, to praise him for what he has done for us, to seek forgiveness of those areas of our heart which still resist his grace, to strengthen our trust in him, and to deepen our love of him. Prayer is also the avenue through which we can open ourselves to fresh inpourings of his Spirit, deepen our inward consciousness of his abiding presence, and become aware of his secret promptings. Without the spirit and attitude of prayer we gradually shut God out of our lives, our faith atrophies, and our moral endeavor grows weak and uninspired. The life of prayer undergirds the life of moral discipline, and together they constitute the human side of sanctification.

Finally, however, we must never forget that sanctification, like justification, is through faith. At every stage of Christian life our best prayer and moral effort is still not worthy of reward from God. Even as Christians we do not build up a claim against his justice. We grow toward perfection only as God empowers us to grow, and God empowers us only as we believe in him and trustingly accept the gifts of his love. By faith and faith alone are we justified. By faith and faith alone are we sanctified.

Honest observation of ourselves and of one another leads us to see that some who put their hands to the plow do look back. Some start the race well, turning away for a time from the old life, only to be overcome by temptation and to fall again into the old ways. What are we to say to them? Was the experience that they once enjoyed false and unreal? Who are we to judge it so? If an immediate personal consciousness of forgiveness may be false, who can be sure of his salvation? Surely it is clear that some who were once really Christian are Christian no more.

Should we tell those who have fallen from grace that their case is hopeless, that having once denied their Lord they can never again find forgiveness? Surely *this* is not the gospel! Surely the Master who taught us to forgive seventy times seven times will forgive again and again the man who returns to him to seek restoration in the Christian life.

As Christians, we have assurance that we are Christians, but we cannot have assurance that we will always remain Christian. We can be sure that God will never betray us, never cease to give us his gracious help. But we cannot be sure that we ourselves will never reject God's help and yield to the temptations of Mammon. Therefore, we must be ever alert, ever prayerful, ever obedient, and above all ever renewing our faith.

If we do fall, if we do once again willfully rebel against God's grace and knowingly do that which is against his will, still we must not despair. We must repent, sincerely, with truly broken hearts; and acknowledging in deepest humility the weakness and corruption of our nature, we must hasten to throw ourselves again upon the mercy of God. God's tender, pitying love is unchanging. As a shepherd seeking his lost sheep, he comes to us again where we have been ensnared by the brambles of sin and gently restores us to his bosom. Unfathomable are the oceans of his mercy!

The norm for all experience and for all belief is found finally in Holy Scripture. The Bible is a record of God's gracious acts in bringing men into an experience of himself. It is not primarily a book of doctrine; much less is it a historical or scientific text; it is, instead, an expression and description of man's experience of redemption through the grace of God. The ideas and beliefs of the writers arise out of their experience which is itself the work of the Holy Spirit in their hearts.

This is not to say that doctrines cannot be found in Scripture. Certainly they can. But we must not press the precise statement of every idea in every verse to formulate some supposedly literal truth. The church has always been cursed by literal-minded dogmaticians who have insisted upon the letter and have lost the spirit of the whole. The real value of the Bible is that it can communicate to us the spirit of the authors which grew out of their life with God. What is important is that we enter into this life, not that we intellectually accept every idea entertained in their minds.

Of course, we should not play fast and loose with clear Scriptural teaching. To be truly Biblical in belief is of supreme importance. But to be truly Biblical in belief we must have our convictions formed by the spirit of the whole, and test each idea that is suggested in a verse here or there by the principles that clearly permeate the whole even if they are rarely explicitly stated.

To illustrate, we may consider briefly the old stumbling block of predestination. True, Paul uses the term and speaks also of the elect. What, then, are we to say? That it is heresy to reject the harsh Calvinism of double predestination? Surely not! We must ask, rather, the simple question: Which is more compatible with the spirit of the New Testament, the belief that God from eternity has doomed most of his creatures to hell or the belief that God strives ceaselessly for the salvation of all, and that only the free and willful refusal to receive his gift can separate anyone from salvation? The question hardly requires an answer. Even if we speak only of the spirit of Paul, it is clear that Paul himself assumed in practice that Christ died for all men and that no man is excluded from the benefits of Christ's Passion except by that man's own free will. That God loves all men is far more basic to the spirit of Paul, not to speak of the New Testament as a whole, than is any idea of unconditional predestination. Only a person blinded by the letter could fail to perceive the true spirit of Scripture.

What, then, of Paul's teaching of divine election? Are we simply to ignore it? No, it too is an expression of an aspect of the true Christian spirit. The Christian knows that it is God who saves us and not we ourselves, and in the ardent desire to give God *all* the credit he may be excused for unguarded utterances that seem to make God's redemptive work arbitrary. But though we may accept such utterances in the context of this spirit, we must guard ourselves vigorously against those who would exaggerate their literal significance. Some would use a few hyperbolic statements about predestination to justify a system of theology that distorts in a hundred ways

the much deeper, clearer, and more basic principles of the
New Testament.

The task of Christian theology is primarily protective, even
negative. Where an over-all view of Christian truth is desired,
it must be offered. When intellectual difficulties arise, they
must be met.

But the authority of theology does not rest on the cogency
of its logic or its use of Scriptural proof texts. It lies in Christian experience, and by this norm it must be tested again and
again. The truth of experience does not depend on its conformity to the teaching of some systematic thinker. On the
contrary, the doctrines of the theologian are true only in so
far as they conform to the living experience. The theologian
may help to overcome intellectual barriers to faith; he cannot
by argument produce that faith.

Preaching, not theological systematization, is the characteristic act of the Christian, and preaching is first of all testimony.
If we know the reality of redemption in our own lives, we can
speak of it to others with convincing authority. Through our
testimony others can be led, not merely to believe what we believe, but to experience for themselves him whom we have
come to know. Merely doctrinal preaching, therefore, is inadequate. It may, of course, be interesting and of educational
value; and education, especially in religious truth, is not to be
deprecated. But as preaching it misses its mark. It may belong
in the Sunday school, but not in the pulpit. The overwhelming
responsibility of the minister is so to proclaim the gospel that
hearts will be touched and changed.

Even those who are already Christians primarily need exhortation and inspiration rather than mere academic instruction.
It may certainly be desirable and even necessary to clarify our
ideas about moral and spiritual principles, but the purpose
and context should be that of eliciting commitment to the
principles — not merely offering them for detached inspection.
The preacher must appeal primarily to the emotions rather

than to the intellect, for it is emotion and not cold logic that moves the will to action.

Not only is it through the emotions that the will is generally affected, but the ultimate significance of religion is found even more in inward experience than in outward obedience. Hence the congregation have the right to expect not only that they will be urged to greater righteousness but also that they will be filled anew with assurance, with peace, and with that inner glow which we call joy. No presentation of doctrine in labored argument can produce such results; only a warm, stirring appeal to the whole person, coupled with earnest testimony to the living power of God already at work in our midst.

Since religious experience must be caught rather than taught, Christian personality is of even greater importance than a trained mind. The minister who shows in his face, his manner, and in his daily walk with men the reality of his inward experience may accomplish far more for Christ, however slight his intellectual and oratorical powers, than the greatest speaker or scholar. This is not to undervalue the latter. Ideally, intelligence and training should be combined with personal experience. But Christian experience even without them is self-sufficient, whereas without Christian experience they are of little value.

The church is primarily the society of those who have experienced God's redeeming grace in their lives, but it is always open to all who earnestly seek. In the church we strengthen and renew our spiritual lives by fellowship with one another and with God. We seek to create a Christian fellowship so warm and contagious that the non-Christian may be drawn to it and awakened to his lack of what we, by God's grace, possess. In singing, prayer, testimony, and preaching we strive to stir to more vigorous life within our hearts our zeal and joy in the Lord.

Sometimes the intensity of the feeling aroused breaks through the boundaries of what may be regarded by outsiders as strict propriety. Sometimes our inner experience may be expressed in outward movements or the utterance of ecstatic words. These manifestations are not to be deplored, for they may be a sign of God's special favor, and as long as they arise spontaneously out of the depths of spiritual joy they are to be accepted with rejoicing. Often, indeed, these outward manifestations of religious emotion are instruments of arousing the hearts of the listless and apathetic, so that they too are finally brought to feel the power of God in their lives.

The Lord's Supper simply as a formal ritual may be of little or no value. No magical power attaches to it, and to go through the form merely out of obedience to a command of Christ is to fall victim to the legalism from which the gospel is designed to save us.

But the Lord's Supper can be a sacred moment, a mountaintop experience in the life of the church. As we kneel together around the altar we may be made to feel our kinship with one another with a new poignancy. As we are there vividly reminded that Jesus shed his blood that we might have the victory over sin, our eagerness to grow in grace is heightened. As we meditate again upon the price that God paid in Christ to restore fellowship with his children, our yearning to realize this fellowship in our own personal experience is intensified.

Not only can the Lord's Supper be in these ways a time of renewal of determination to seek greater heights of spiritual attainment, but it can also be a time when those heights are actually attained. The whole mood of the service can give us a consciousness of the immediate presence of God that we rarely find elsewhere, and as we are stirred to open our hearts to that presence we often find the experience of inward cleansing, of peace, and of joy, for which we seek.

Water baptism is a service that is misrepresented even more frequently than is the Lord's Supper. It must not be regarded as having any saving efficacy, lest man should place a false confidence in a merely external act. *When* and *how* it is performed are matters of little importance. The only baptism that really matters is the baptism of the Holy Spirit. We who have received *that* baptism are saved no matter how or when water baptism is administered to us, or even if it is never administered at all. And if we do not experience spiritual baptism, then no application of water to our bodies can be of any efficacy whatever.

Since the spiritual reality alone and not the outward ceremony is ultimately all-important, there seems to be no reason for deviating from the ancient custom of the church in bringing little children for baptism. Indeed, this service is one of the most beautiful and moving experiences in the life of the church. Here, the parents solemnly promise their God and his church that they will accept the awesome opportunity he has given them, and all the joyful responsibility that comes with it, to nurture their children and to lead them into true Christian experience. The hearts of all who see are touched. The entire congregation feels with new keenness its responsibility to live so as to inspire these infants as they grow and to lead them finally to accept Jesus Christ as their Savior. The minister, as he lays his hand upon the children's heads, feels with new poignancy the marvel of his high calling as the parents thus entrust the spiritual nurture of their children to him.

But if there are those of tender conscience who wish to delay the outward ceremony of baptism until after the baptism of the spirit, or who feel that there is some special value in one form more than in another, there is no need to argue or criticize. Their personal satisfaction, not the time and manner, is important, and the church may well allow for the widest range of differences in a matter so inessential.

The particular form of the organization of the church is not a matter of great importance. Probably there was no uniformity of church order even in the earliest days. The church is the society of those who have been reborn into the life with Christ. The experience is crucial. How Christians conduct their business and call their pastors makes little difference except as it affects the efficiency of the church in its work of saving souls and spreading holiness. Questions of ordination and polity should be decided, then, according to time, place, and circumstance. They are subjects on which Christians may well agree to differ without in any way regarding their differences as germane to the Christian faith as such.

It is extremely unfortunate that some groups have claimed unique divine sanction for a particular form of church government in such a way as to throw doubt upon the genuineness of the Christian experience of members of other churches. These persons by a new legalism or institutionalism are thwarting the efforts of sincere Christians of all denominations to unite for common action against the common enemy.

The truth is that God's Spirit works in all Christian churches, transforming and sanctifying individual lives. Those who share this experience know a unity far deeper than that of common loyalty to an organization. It is unfortunate, certainly, that the doctrines of some groups seem to deny the reality of the full Christian experience of victory over sin, but the lives of many of their own members belie their espoused doctrines.

The best church is that which least seeks to have distinctive doctrines. It is the church in which people are most open to the richest blessings that God has promised those who seek. It is the one which is most willing to subordinate form to spirit, to place life above doctrine, and to practice Christian love across all ecclesiastical boundaries.

SELECTED READINGS FOR FURTHER STUDY

BIBLICISM

I. *Anabaptists, Mennonites, and the " Free Churches "*
Hershberger, Guy F., editor, *The Recovery of the Anabaptist Vision.* Herald Press, 1957. Essays by leading scholars pub-

lished in honor of Harold S. Bender and representing the best contemporary understanding and evaluation of the Anabaptist movement.

Smith, C. Henry, *The Story of the Mennonites*, new revised edition. Mennonite Publication Office, 1950. A history of the Anabaptist movement and the Mennonites in Europe and America.

Wenger, J. C., editor, *The Complete Writings of Menno Simons*, translated by Leonard Verduin. Herald Press, 1956. The writings of a man who impressed the stamp of his thought upon the remnants of the Anabaptists and whose views are still accepted as generally normative by Mennonites today.

Westin, Gunnar, *The Free Church Through the Ages*, translated by Virgil A. Olson. The Broadman Press, 1958. A history of left-wing Protestantism from the Reformation era.

II. *Baptists*

McGlothlin, M. J., *Baptist Confessions of Faith*. American Baptist Publication Society, 1911. A collection of confessions of faith of Anabaptist and Baptist churches otherwise little known and inaccessible.

Robinson, H. Wheeler, *The Life and Faith of the Baptists*. Kingsgate Press, London, 1946. A perceptive and attractive presentation of Baptist belief and practice by a moderately liberal contemporary British Baptist.

Stealey, Sydnor L., editor, *A Baptist Treasury*. The Thomas Y. Crowell Co., 1958. Selections from the writings of Baptists, from John Smyth to the present.

Torbet, Robert S., *A History of the Baptists*. The Judson Press, 1950. A scholarly, critical, but deeply sympathetic account of the Baptist movement from its Anabaptist and Nonconformist antecedents to the present time.

Turner, J. Clyde, *Our Baptist Heritage.* The Sunday School Board of the Southern Baptist Convention, 1945. A statement of Baptist principles published as a textbook for Baptist young people by one of the more conservative Baptist bodies.

III. *The Disciples*

Campbell, Alexander, *The Christian System,* third edition. Forrester & Campbell, 1840. The most systematic statement of faith of the dominant figure among the founders of the Disciples of Christ and the Christian Church.

Garrison, Winfred E., and DeGroot, Alfred T., *The Disciples of Christ, A History.* Christian Board of Education, 1948. A competent and appreciative study of the history of the Disciples movement.

Lindley, D. Ray, *Apostle of Freedom.* The Bethany Press, 1957. An exposition of Campbell's thought about the structure and functioning of the local church and its ministry.

Walker, Granville T., *Preaching in the Thought of Alexander Campbell.* The Bethany Press, 1954. A modern exposition of the thought of Alexander Campbell presented in its historical setting and contemporary relevance.

West, Robert Frederick, *Alexander Campbell and Natural Religion.* Yale University Press, 1948. A discussion of Campbell's relation to the issue of natural and revealed religion on the American scene.

EXPERIENTIALISM

I. *Primary Sources*

A fourteen-volume set of Wesley's works is now being published by Zondervan Publishing House. Standard sets of letters, sermons, and journals are published by The Epworth Press, London.

Burtner, Robert W., and Chiles, Robert E., editors, *A Compend of Wesley's Theology*. Abingdon Press, 1954. Statements by Wesley on major theological topics which are conveniently arranged to give the essence of his thought.

Welch, Herbert, editor, *Selections from the Writings of John Wesley*, revised edition. Abingdon Press, 1942. A collection of the more extended writings of Wesley, especially his sermons, treatises, and letters.

II. *Studies of Wesley's Thought*
Cannon, William R., *The Theology of John Wesley*. Abingdon Press, 1946.

Lindstrom, Harold, *Wesley and Sanctification*, translated by H. S. Harvey. The Epworth Press, London, 1952.

Yates, Arthur S., *The Doctrine of Assurance*. The Epworth Press, London, 1952.
Three studies in Wesley's theology written by critical but highly appreciative scholars, each focusing respectively on one of the three central doctrines of Wesley's ministry: justification, sanctification, and assurance.

Piette, Maximin, *John Wesley in the Evolution of Protestantism*, translated by J. B. Howard. Sheed & Ward, Inc., London, 1937. An excellent account of Wesley's work and influence set against the background of the whole history of Protestantism. Sympathetically presented by a Roman Catholic scholar.

III. *Modern Histories and Expositions of Wesleyanism and Allied Movements*
Anderson, William K., editor, *Methodism*. The Methodist Publishing House, 1947. A symposium on Methodist origins, history, distinctive emphases, and present situation and prospects.

Conn, Charles W., *Like a Mighty Army Moves the Church of God, 1886–1955*. Church of God Publishing House, 1955. A competent history of an increasingly important branch of the Wesleyan movement.

Lee, Umphrey, *Our Fathers and Us: The Heritage of the Methodists*. Southern Methodist University Press, 1958. A historian's effort to characterize the distinctive genius of Methodism in terms of its history.

Luccock, Halford E., Hutchinson, Paul, and Goodloe, Robert W., *The Story of Methodism*. Abingdon Press, 1949. A history of Methodism written in a very readable style and especially for American Methodists.

Peters, John L., *Christian Perfection and American Methodism*. Abingdon Press, 1956. A history of the fortunes of the doctrine of perfection in Methodism until 1900, with comments on current developments.

Redford, M. E., *The Rise of the Church of the Nazarene*. Nazarene Publishing House, 1948. A work that traces the holiness principle briefly through the history of Christianity and tells more fully the story of the organization of the Nazarene Church and its development.

CHAPTER V

Liberal Protestantism

MUCH OF WHAT is put forward today as Christianity is irrelevant to the actual needs of men. Old creeds and dogmas once vibrant with life are today remote and empty of real significance. No amount of eloquence or dialectical skill can recall the past, and no effort of the will can bring a man once freed from its shackles to bow to it again.

There was a time when the other world of heaven and hell was oppressively near and real, in constant interaction with this one. The mysterious forces of nature were readily interpreted as expressing the moral purposes of the sovereign Being. The daily manifestations of his absolute power in acts of grace and judgment created an intense consciousness of the awful imminence of the end of this brief sojourn on earth, and hopes and fears centered upon the life beyond.

Today all this is changed. The doctrines are not disproved; they have suffered a far worse fate. They have become mere speculations, impractical concerns for idle minds. They are not disbelieved; they are simply ignored. Life here and now has become the focus of interest. Men believe life can and should be good, and they are impatient of those who would direct them to other ends than its improvement. Nature is understood in terms of efficient causation, and man is learning to control it and to direct its powers for his own ends. Astronomy has banished heaven and hell to some other sphere of reality

150

utterly different from our own, incomprehensible to the imagination, and hence lacking in vividness and relevance.

If Christianity cannot adjust to a changing world, its days are numbered. Only the unenlightened, the naïve, and the immature will listen to it. The world of serious thought and action will look elsewhere for spiritual direction. Some new religion will arise to meet the needs of a new day.

But neglect need not be the fate of Christianity. Many times before it has adjusted to new environments, finding in its own rich heritage resources that it had almost forgotten. Such resources it has now in abundance. In so far as the spirit of the new age cleanses the Christian faith of its superstitious accretions and overzealous preoccupation with another world, it does Christianity inestimable service in helping it discover its own deeper meaning.

Emphasis on the importance of life here and now does not involve denial that life continues beyond the grave. Few would have the temerity to affirm outright that this is not so, and most believe that the hope of continued life is reasonable and proper. But we can no longer believe that God will judge us at death by strange and arbitrary standards remote from those by which daily we judge ourselves. We cannot believe that men and women who have found rich spiritual meaning in this life may be doomed to eternal punishment for failure to agree in detail with some creed or to follow the prescribed forms of some sect. We cannot believe that God would impose upon any soul punishments that its own nature did not force upon itself, or deny to any soul such happiness as it is capable of enjoying.

We know little of the life beyond the grave, but of this much we may feel confident: that life will not be worse than the one we now experience. If we here and now overcome the hell that is within our hearts, if we here and now make our contribution to the realization of a little more of heaven upon earth for others as well as for ourselves, we may go to our death with perfect confidence that there is no capricious or vindictive deity who will take from us such of heaven as we have found.

The contrary of this may, sadly enough, also be true. He who nurses in his heart his own wretchedness and makes those about him also miserable, whatever the creed he professes or the rigor of his moral code, is not likely to find at death that all is drastically changed. The rigidity and hardness of his heart belie his pretended hope, and the misery that throughout life he heaps upon himself and others by his false piety may well continue to be his lot through eternity.

Hence, it is clear that the Christian will profit greatly from casting aside all preoccupation with the other world. That world we may leave with perfect trust to God. We are now in *this* world — a world created by God for our sake, with God-given potentialities to develop and a God-given mission of world redemption before us.

The fundamental purpose of the Christian is to help and to serve others. To do so, men must deal realistically with the problems they actually face. The task, therefore, is to analyze the situation, to ascertain the needs to which the Christian faith is relevant, and then to bring the resources of the faith to bear upon these needs.

These ideas may not have achieved clear conscious expression in the minds of large numbers of Protestants, but they have become increasingly the presupposition of religious thinking. Most Protestants find themselves uncomfortable before the fiery insistence that all who do not meet some quite specific standards will be eternally tormented by God for their failure. Questions of the means of escaping hell-fire seem less appropriate to their minds than questions about the solution of personal and social problems here and now. The argument that nothing else matters in comparison with the one great decision that determines the soul's eternal destiny may appear objectively plausible, but it sounds hollow and artificial.

Not only has the modern milieu dethroned the values to which otherworldly religion appeals, but also many thoughtful

Protestants have become fundamentally skeptical of the reality of rewards and punishments after death. Perhaps, after all, death *is* the end, so far as individual conscious experience is concerned. If that were so, would Christianity be entirely destroyed? Would there be no meaning to the ideal of forgiving love as governing all human relations? Would there be no superiority in a life of earnest devotion to God over one of sensuous self-indulgence?

To ask such questions is to answer them. The real value of Christianity is not challenged by the doubts that arise with respect to an afterlife. For *this* life Christianity is true! But if so, the real message of Christianity must be extricated from the otherworldly teaching by which it has so often been distorted. Love of God and men must be recommended for its own sake, not as a means to saving ourselves from hell. Love must be seen as truly directed to the whole person in all his present needs and desires, not to some supposedly immortal soul that lies beyond the empirical person. Trusting belief in God must be shown to be the law of all spiritual fulfillment in time and space, not a magic key by which to procure heavenly rewards.

Although the emphasis upon the meaning of Christianity for this life may seem new or modernistic, actually it has always been present wherever Christianity has truly flourished. It is, indeed, by their spiritual attainments in their earthly lives that saints have always been recognized, and they themselves have witnessed to the truth that he who seeks merely to save his soul will lose it. Furthermore, the Bible, when approached honestly, discloses itself as an astonishingly this-worldly book.

The Old Testament knows nothing of heaven and hell. It testifies for the most part that the rewards of virtue are experienced on this side of death and that sin brings evil upon itself. But at its spiritual peak the Old Testament portrays a far nobler insight — the insight that there are higher reasons to serve God than the rewards that he offers.

In the New Testament, it is true, heaven and hell are part of the assumed background of the Jewish thought of the period. But they play no significant part in the teachings of Jesus and Paul. It is the Kingdom that is to come upon earth that grips the attention — a new world in which God's will is done, peace reigns, and love supplants force as the principle of order and government.

In the light of all this, the accusations of heresy that are so often hurled by the adherents of otherworldly points of view are seen to be arbitrary and unfair. The cultural and scientific revolutions that have done so much for us in other realms, instead of destroying religion, have freed Christianity from the shackles of medieval superstition. Only now for the first time can we see clearly the real meaning of the Scriptures, the true significance of Jesus' message for our lives.

The abandonment of emphasis upon another world is not, therefore, a retreat from Christian truth. On the contrary, it affords the finest possbility of advance. Formerly, Christians feared to develop freely the richness of their faith lest they should somehow violate the rules for gaining heaven. Now we may explore every suggestion in the teachings of our Lord, freely integrating those insights with all new knowledge of the workings of man's mind and emotions and with the functioning of the economic and political order. In this way we may find answers to man's oldest questions and the satisfaction of his greatest needs.

At one stroke, also, the terrible intolerance of Christianity, which has caused so much havoc in Western history, is wiped out. We are now free to evaluate every form of Christianity by its actual results in individual and social life. We can no longer be told that despite the horrors that a particular dogmatism inflicts upon the human race it must nevertheless be accepted because it alone provides the way to heaven. We can now frankly recognize that there is room for variety in the common quest for a new earth in which God's will is done.

With regard to other religions, too, our attitude can change. Formerly, we were compelled to believe that whatever the beauty of life and spirit manifest in non-Christian religions, whatever the similarity of their quest with ours, men who followed them were doomed by God to eternal torment simply because they did not share our creed. No wonder we Christians have shocked the religious world with our bigotry! Now we may look honestly at the achievements of all religious movements, learning from them and sharing in our turn with them. Something, we are convinced, they do lack, something that only a true knowledge of Christ can give them. And when this knowledge is provided, free from the hideous handicap of the doctrine of a vindictive deity, the hearts of sensitive men and women the world over will be glad to call Jesus " Savior and Lord."

Those who condemn the critical study of Scriptures not only are expressing a serious lack of intellectual integrity but also are seeking to discourage that development by which alone it is possible to keep the Bible a living book. As a vast collection of outdated laws, of miracle stories, and of accounts of tribal battles, the Bible cannot be taken seriously in the modern world. But when the scholar shows us the Bible as a product of increasing sensitivity to the will of God and of developing understanding of the nature of God on the part of a people gifted with extraordinary spiritual sensitivity, culminating in a vision that still dazzles our eyes by the splendid simplicity of its truth, then the Bible can live for us as it has never lived since the days in which it was written.

In the light of the new understanding of the Bible and the shift in attention to the values of this life, most of the old issues that separated Christians disappear. Many of the old denominational lines should simply be destroyed in unions of churches. When union is impossible, there must at least be active cooperation among all Christian groups. The task of world redemption is a staggering one. The Christian movement must

cease to dissipate its energies in competition among denominations and must pool its resources in the struggle against the
common enemy. That enemy, whether we personalize it as
Satan, or interpret it as materialism, immorality, inhumanity,
entrenched injustice, and spiritual insensitivity, poses a challenge of frightening proportions. Only a church united in common loyalty to the cause of Christianizing the world can be
adequate to meet the needs of the day.

Persons who adopt liberal attitudes toward the values of life
here and now, toward the world religions, toward the Bible,
and toward denominational differences, may retain a profound loyalty to many aspects of one or another of the forms
of Protestantism discussed above. They may remain deeply
permeated, for example, by the spirit of Lutheranism or Calvinism. However, the shift in focus of attention from the world
beyond the grave to the world before the grave subtly affects
the total pattern of faith and life. As the shift becomes increasingly decisive, distinctive patterns of life and thought emerge.
Although these new patterns are usually intermixed with more
traditional patterns, they may also be viewed in terms of their
own inner logic.

These patterns have much in common with each other in
their quest for the enrichment of the present life through the
use of the special resources of the Christian heritage. They
differ, however, in the conception of man's greatest needs and
in their judgment as to how these needs can be satisfied.

One view, which will be called " mystical Protestantism " is
that man's need is to live in conscious union with God, absorbed in him and plastic to his will. A second position makes
central " the quest for abundant life." It holds that man's pre-
dominant felt need is to find happiness, health, and emotional
security, and that basic principles in Jesus' teaching provide
the necessary guidance to these ends. A third orientation, " the
social gospel," sees the greatest needs in the sphere of social
relationships. Adherents of the social gospel are convinced that

only as society is re-formed in the patterns of love and justice
can individuals find true satisfaction for themselves.

The differences among these three positions need not amount
to opposition, although they are frequently presented as being
antithetical. The quest for abundant life and the social
gospel need not exclude each other, and a moderate mysticism
may be combined with either. But commitment to one goal
does imply judgments both of fact and of value that differ from
those implied by commitment to either of the other goals.
Hence, each must be presented as a distinct form of Protestant
life and thought.

No one of the three has found institutional embodiment in a
major Protestant group to the extent to which most of the patterns of Protestantism treated in previous chapters have. The
mystical tradition is strong among the Quakers and has its
followers in many denominations. Among clearly Protestant
groups, concern with abundant life has played the largest role
in Methodism, which has long emphasized the present transformation of the emotional life in religious experience. It has
played a dominant role in movements peripheral to Protestantism, such as New Thought and Christian Science, which have
been grounded as much in idealistic philosophy as in the distinctively Christian tradition. The social gospel won its most
decisive victories among the Unitarians, but Congregationalists
and liberal Baptists and Methodists were not far behind, and,
indeed, thoughtful leaders in almost all the major churches
have accepted a greater social responsibility as a result of its
testimony.

The lack of institutional embodiment of these three types of
Protestantism increases the difficulty of exemplifying each in
a single account without sheer arbitrariness. Mysticism varies
from a totally world-denying nihilism at one extreme to a
highly positive evaluation of both nature and man through the
emphasis on the immanence of God in all things. Those for
whom religion is a quest for abundant life may emphasize

social success, physical health, or emotional maturity, and may vary greatly in the techniques by which they would further the quest. The social gospel, in our day, has been sharply divided between those who insist upon the direct application of love to the solution of the world's problems and those who believe that the Christian's duty is to make his position relevant to the actual struggle for power in spite of the compromises necessitated by political involvement.

In the following chapters the effort is made to present moderate but consistent expressions of each of the three forms of liberal Protestantism. The descriptions are intentionally left indefinite in regard to many disputed questions and cannot be regarded as reflecting precisely the position of any particular leading representatives. Nevertheless, the formulations may have value in suggesting in a general way both the attractiveness and the implications of these types of Christian commitment.

MYSTICAL PROTESTANTISM

Animals are neither moral nor religious, because they live only in the world of time. Man is both moral and religious because, while he lives in time, he participates also in eternity. He stands on the boundary of two worlds and in this status inhere both his frustrations and his hope.

Man is moral because his mind grasps eternal norms by which he can judge the relative values of temporal events. He can clarify his vision and discipline his action to conform to it, or he can obscure his vision and ignore it in his conduct.

Man is religious because his deepest being belongs to the realm of the eternal and will not let him rest in time. He can obscure his awareness of this fact and live almost as if it were not so. He can even use ostensibly religious forms for merely temporal ends which ignore his real nature. But ultimately he can find no home in the merely temporal world.

True religion is the recognition of man's true being and living in terms of this recognition. It is, therefore, essentially the discovery of the spirit within us, which transcends time in its eternal unity with God, the quiet center of our existence where God always speaks his eternal Word of peace.

All religion roots in the vague consciousness of even the most ordinary man that there is within him a dimension of existence that points beyond time. It is given form by great spiritual geniuses for whom the divine eternity is vividly real and who have spoken of it with authority. Unfortunately, the purity of the message of the great leaders is often clouded by interpreters and organizers. Popular understanding and practice translate eternal into temporal truths, and men abandon all effort to achieve the heights and depths of spiritual life that are proclaimed in the original message.

Christianity has suffered as much as any religion from its misinterpretation. Jesus exemplified and offered men eternal life here and now. But many Christians rest content with the promise of a heaven beyond the grave and the hope or assurance that God will grant an eternal home there. They see in this life only suffering, and they conceive the Christian life as an endless struggle to discipline the flesh into conformity with outwardly determined principles. Even when this disciplining is acknowledged as the work of the Spirit, it is still pursued by the psychological mechanisms of repression and inhibition. The end result is often tension and anxiety expressing themselves in irritability and severity rather than flowering in true joy and love. In extreme cases the intensity of effort expended in molding conscious thought and overt actions into conformity with high ideals leads to emotional imbalance. As a result it sometimes seems that there is more of the spirit of the Nazarene among the self-indulgent children of nature than among the righteous leaders of the church.

This painful failure of Christianity really to redeem our lives results from our lack of faith. We refuse to see that the greatest gift of God, offered freely to all of us, is himself. If we are contented with the belief that he is not angry with us, or that he will give us bliss beyond the grave, we deny ourselves the attainment of heaven in the midst of life, and even our certainty of the postponed joy is likely to be dim. How many whose lives have not been irradiated with present joy have gone with real confidence to meet their death?

The history of the church likewise reflects this profound lack of awareness of the real presence of God in human life. Wars and persecutions, anger and hatred, are at least as prominent features of Christendom as are deeds of charity and expressions of brotherly concern. Nor are these evils to be blamed upon the less religious groups alone. Torture and slaughter, pillage and treachery, have all been perpetrated with deep sincerity in the name of Christ.

So long as we remain content with a part of God's gift, whatever we may believe and however rigorous our morality may be, we will remain in inmost nature unchanged. So long as we remain unchanged, we use even our service to others and our faith in God as instruments of our unregenerate passions. Worse still, we conceal from ourselves that our true motives are pride, greed, and the lust for power, for we persuade ourselves that our most vicious deeds are acts of obedience to God and his church. If, instead, we truly yield ourselves to God, not in obedience to his laws but in unity with himself, then strife and turmoil will be replaced by peace within, and peace within will be expressed in outward deeds communicating that peace to others. The only force in the world making for true peace and true righteousness is the Spirit of God, and the Spirit of God works only in the lives of those who open themselves to his working.

We can open ourselves to the transforming power of God's Spirit only when we realize in the deepest recesses of our consciousness that God is always present about us and within us. We *do* live and move and have our being in him. He is all in all, and apart from him we are nothing. He is the Alpha and Omega, the eternal ground and purpose of our existence.

We cannot achieve any vivid awareness of the presence of God in and about us by an effort of the will. Every human endeavor to feel his nearness separates us farther from him. It focuses attention upon our individual effort and feeling, and it is just this habit of self-attention which suppresses the redemptive consciousness of God. We cannot force our way into the presence of God, but in silent waiting we can become receptive to his spirit.

Since God is present everywhere, it may be possible for us to come to know him anywhere, but this does not mean that time and place are unimportant. From early childhood our minds have formed habits of thought that focus restlessly upon the changing phenomena that affect us. Memories of past occurrences and anxieties about the future mingle with present sensations to form the parade of ideas passing through our minds. To change the habits of a lifetime, to bring the parade to a halt, to cleanse the mind of memories and expectations, and to free the consciousness from the stimuli of present sensation is no simple matter. Only by constant effort and the use of every available means are we likely to gain the rich prize of eternal life.

A special time should be set aside for prayer. Whatever may be the value of prayers uttered sporadically in the midst of busy activities, they cannot accomplish the purpose of a daily period of refreshment. A special place should also be set aside, a place free from all distraction and danger of interruption, a place in which every association is with spiritual realities. When time and place become habitual, they no longer demand attention in themselves, and the mind can open itself more quickly to the Spirit of God.

Posture is important too. Bodily discomfort and muscular tension call attention to themselves, whereas a prone position on a bed is likely to induce sleep. Individual differences are to be expected, one finding in kneeling, another in sitting, the position that enables him most quickly to quit his restless thoughts and find the peace that comes from God. The sole consideration is actual effectiveness in enabling the individual to find his way into the very presence of God.

When we have formed good habits of time, place, and posture we have only prepared ourselves for the great adventure. Freedom from distraction does not in itself bring about a consciousness of God's sacred presence, though without it millions of men live in spiritual poverty. Man's mind is too habituated to activity to be changed immediately to passive openness to God's Spirit. At first it must be guided along a path that leads from symbols of God to God himself.

Perhaps a worshiper may begin by reading a passage of Scripture, dwelling with all his faculties upon the truths there presented to him or upon the picture of the Master as he once lived and moved upon the earth. Perhaps the words of some great hymn or the writings of a Christian saint may be the chosen means. Whatever the procedure, the end is the same. The mind must be filled with thoughts that lead us away from self and toward God, away from time and toward eternity.

Even when we employ all these aids to spiritual growth, we find that our minds wander repeatedly. We grow angry and impatient with ourselves for the extreme weakness of our concentration and jerk our minds back forcibly to their allotted task. But this will not do. Exasperation calls attention to our failure and stirs emotions within us that block the fulfillment of our purpose. Instead, when we note the many lapses in attention of which we are guilty we should simply acknowledge to ourselves our weakness and our inability to overcome that weakness in our own strength, thanking God for his constant help and asking him for still further outpourings of his Spirit. Thus the mind returns toward God, drawn to him by prayer rather than driven by anger.

Another pitfall of the spiritual life is that even the quest for communion with God may be more an effort to have thrilling experiences for their own sake than an attempt really to find ourselves in him. Only he who loses himself can find himself. He whose attention is constantly diverted by examination of what he feels and whether he has now achieved a new spiritual condition will not find true communion with God. He who is absorbed in the contemplation of God, forgetting his own feelings and experiences, will receive the joy and peace and new being that is the life of God within man.

Success in our effort to experience God fully comes sporadically at first and always unpredictably. It is not an achievement controllable by man, occurring whenever he meets a few precisely specifiable requirements. It comes always from God, breaking through into our consciousness and irradiating our experience. Sometimes it is only for a moment or two. Sometimes it lingers.

Even after we have been blessed with moments of vivid awareness of God's presence, there may still be long periods of spiritual drought when the same earnestness, the same technique, the same expectancy, leave us groping in darkness. The saints have told us of their dark nights of the soul. But we need not despair. In God's good time the vision vouchsafed us once will return, and he who hungers will be satisfied.

Finally the time may come, for some at least, when all shadow of darkness will be done away, the promise of the first fleeting moment of ecstasy will be fulfilled, and we will live continually in the vivid awareness of the everlasting arms that sustain us. Indeed, we will be able to say with Paul, it is not we who live, but the Christ Spirit lives in us. When this time comes all spiritual struggle will be past. We will feast continuously upon God, and wholly yield our minds and bodies to his every wish. We may scarcely know what we do ourselves. We will not feel that by an act of will we determine what we do and say. It will seem to us that we are borne effortlessly along, absorbed in God. Through us God will be speaking and acting, pouring out his love upon mankind and drawing others to himself, while we ourselves are caught up in him.

When a man has entered into the highest communion with God, spiritual powers are granted him that are undreamed of by ordinary unregenerate persons. A strange power of presence surrounds the saint. His prayers for others are answered in wonderful ways. He may have an immunity to many diseases, and may be able to mediate health to others through intercessory prayer or the laying on of hands.

Such powers are not uniformly granted to all in proportion as they achieve communion with God, for there is a variety of gifts. They astonish the unspiritual mind and draw crowds of followers. As such they may constitute a temptation even for the saint. But the saint knows that such powers are mere by-products of communion with God — to be used, of course, as he directs in the service of his children, but never for display for the satisfaction of idle curiosity.

The truly marvelous achievements of the greatest saints are inspiring demonstrations of the power of God, but the value of the disciplined spiritual quest does not lie only in the possibility of attaining the condition of total sainthood. Even when the vivid awareness of God's presence is still entirely unknown we are already becoming children of God. In the depths of our souls, beneath the level of consciousness, God is beginning his transforming work. The festering sores of repressed fear and anger are being healed. Nervous tensions are being relaxed. Spiritual energies long bottled up by inner conflicts are being constructively rechanneled. Other people become objects of love for us rather than of resentment and jealousy. We begin to endure disappointment and frustration in our daily lives without loss of emotional poise. Words like " faith " and " trust " become significant of how we actually feel toward God rather than empty sounds piously mouthed. Life is no longer an endless struggle to become righteous by controlling our appetites, for these appetites seem to wither of their own accord before the all-consuming hunger for God.

Even the hunger for God is not a painful emptiness. In all other desires, the pain of want seems to outweigh the pleasure of possession. But not so with our desire for communion with God. Even when in its full vividness communion is not granted us, the times of prayer and meditation are blessed for us. The very yearning for the greater gift is in itself cleansing and refreshing. And in those rarer moments when God does come to us, the sweetness of his coming is beyond compare.

The goal of the spiritual life is deeply personal, but it is not selfish. We should not seek eternal life for ourselves to the exclusion of the welfare of others, but we cannot benefit others by depriving ourselves of life with God. If we busy ourselves with activities designed to help our fellow men when we ourselves lack that one thing which is supremely needful, others will not be greatly benefited. As religious leaders we cannot remove the specks from our neighbors' eyes while a beam obstructs our own vision. To sacrifice our own spiritual welfare for the sake of others is to place ourselves in the position of the blind leading the blind. It is *not* selfish to ask God for his supreme gift for ourselves.

There is a still deeper reason for the falseness of the charge that the quest for our true salvation is selfish. The charge may be warranted with respect to those who seek in life after death the satisfaction of their selfish desires. But for the truly spiritual man eternal life is not self-satisfaction or the fulfillment of his natural appetites. Eternal life is neither the achievement of a wholesome and mature personality well adjusted to its temporal environment nor self-realization understood as the full development of one's manifold moral and spiritual potentialities. Eternal life is self-surrender, the negation of the selfish will, the influx of the divine Spirit, the possession of the self by its rightful Lord. To make any other end our goal, even the end of helping others, is to assert our own will. Only in the total abandonment of the self to God is self-centeredness finally and radically transcended.

Clearly, then, we can help others find eternal life only as we

ourselves learn to know the rich depths of life with God. But
it is not only in the purely spiritual sphere that the genuinely
religious man is most effective. Even with respect to social action for the improvement of man's temporal condition, he who
lives in the consciousness of the presence of God can do incomparably more than can he who regards the temporal sphere
as the whole of reality.

In the first place, only the man who knows God can show
God's tender loving concern for each of his human children.
The man of the world may busy himself with good causes from
a sense of duty or civic pride, or from a loyalty to vague ideals
or a feeling of pity for his suffering fellows. But the motives
for good deeds are in tension with his personal ambition and
often become tainted with pride. He tends to treat the objects
of his charity impersonally and thus to antagonize those whom
he seeks to aid.

On the other hand, the man who has found his true home in
eternity can pour forth his love in endless streams. To him each
individual is uniquely precious. He seeks only that God's will
be done, for his own will is wholly abandoned to God, and he
cares nothing for temporal benefit for himself.

In the second place, only the truly spiritual man possesses
the sustaining power to endure disappointment and temporary
defeat. The man of the world may have great stamina and
strength of will, but the apparent futility of his efforts and the
ingratitude of those he serves gradually embitter his spirit and
weaken his determination. His self-esteem depends upon a
success that is never assured, and anxiety creates tensions that
impede effective action.

The mystic, on the other hand, knows a security that is unaffected by the tides of fortune. He strives to help others, but
he leaves the results of his efforts in the hands of God. If those
whom he seeks to help are not appreciative, he is sorry for
them but not perturbed. Free from anxiety and inner tension,
he can deal with difficulties as they arise with objectivity and

constructive vigor. At times God uses his total dedication as a channel for the achievement of ends that transcend his own conscious aims and purposes.

Although absolute privacy with God is the major mode of mystic worship, there is much to be gained also from the companionship of other seekers. Sometimes God seems closer in the silent fellowship of meditation where two or three are gathered together. Sometimes in larger groups one person more experienced than the others can not only instruct them as to the means and goals of true prayer but can also help to direct their meditation. A " spiritual life " retreat may reveal to some the possibilities of a way of life that by themselves they would never initiate.

The services of the church need not be despised. Many services, it is true, are noisy and distracting, and we may well prefer to seek other company for our worship. But we may find that the elements of the church service, the hymns, the Scripture, and the prayers, do enable us to lose ourselves in our quest for God. Especially at the Lord's Table, as our ears, eyes, and taste are for a few moments wholly absorbed in our Lord, we may find that he draws very near indeed.

But though the service of worship may help many, and the sacraments may be a blessed occasion for true communion, nevertheless it must be candidly acknowledged that for all too many persons church and sacrament are a substitute *for* rather than an aid *to* communion with God. It is better that we separate ourselves from the church entirely than that we deceive ourselves into the belief that the outward forms of worship and communion are the reality of religion.

The church is also dangerous as a source of divisiveness and intolerance. When form or creed or even emotional experience is substituted for the ultimate reality of true communion with God, then it becomes falsely absolutized, and full fellowship is all too often denied to the fellow Christian who is in some way different. Endless theological debates and denominational jealousies replace the common quest for religious reality. Even at the Lord's Table men will refuse to kneel together because of their theories of church and sacrament!

All too often, furthermore, the approach of the churches to the other religions of the world is tainted with pride and jealousy. Instead of really striving to win others by showing them the way to find a greater spiritual reality for themselves, we seem to prefer to attack the forms and doctrines through which they have been seeking. We offer them a cold creed, or insist that only through a particular rite or institution can they find God. We bewilder them by our endless disagreements among ourselves, and finally by our folly we drive them away from the Christ Spirit that in its own power shines through the pages of the gospel writings.

Actually, God has nowhere left himself without a witness. In every land and in every age there have been those who have been touched by his Spirit and have found communion with him. To refuse to recognize this, to insist that in conformity with our rigid creeds God should have denied all spiritual light to those who do not share our beliefs, is simply to express the spirit of willful selfishness and pride. Missionaries we should indeed send to share with others what we have learned of God and of how to find him, but not proselytizers to insist that the old ways are wholly false and that only by joining a particular church can God be found.

For the Christian, Jesus always stands as the supreme embodiment of true spirituality. There have been many saints, some with wonderful powers and marvelous influence over others. All of them stand before us as a challenge to develop our own spiritual lives as they have developed theirs. But Jesus is different. He stands beyond them as they stand beyond us, not merely as the greatest among peers. Each new generation goes back to him afresh for guidance, for inspiration, and for power. Others show us what man may become. He shows us what God eternally is.

What we call him makes but little difference — Light of the World, Bread of Life, Lord, Savior, Son of God. All language breaks down here. When men insist upon defining his nature in formal creeds, they inevitably fall into absurdity. That does not matter either, unless men insist upon worshiping their creeds instead of their Lord and persecuting one another for their differences. What matters is not what we say, but that under the influence of the Christ Spirit we may enter into the abundant life of which Jesus spoke, finding through him the final avenue to God.

The Quest for Abundant Life

Many observers of the present scene agree that the greatest felt need of human beings is to find happiness. Indeed, it has been an axiom of ethical philosophy since before the time of Aristotle that this is the universal end of man. But happiness is elusive both in life and in definition, and through most of man's history it has provided but a poor guide to human endeavor.

In recent years much progress has been made in the analysis of what is involved in the satisfaction of this deepest longing of man, and although no final definition of happiness is possible, some of its ingredients may now be stated with confidence. It includes a freedom from guilt feelings, a sense of personal worth, and a feeling of adequacy to cope with life's problems. Consciously, it is likely to be identified with goals that, though somewhat removed from these ingredients in their level of generality and intrinsic value, are more readily identifiable. These include economic security, the respect of others, and success in our life's work. But these goals, important though they are, may often come as by-products of the achievement of man's real ends.

Few Christians have denied that the achievement of happiness is the universal end of man. The otherworldly emphasis on rewards and punishments has always presupposed this goal. It is true that a few extreme moralists have tried to distort their objections to selfishness into a full-fledged repudiation of personal happiness as the proper end for man to seek, but such drastic repudiation of the realities of human nature can never in practice be sustained. It can lead only to self-delusion or to guilt feelings — alike unwholesome.

In our day men have become more keenly aware of the possibility and the desirability of happiness on the one hand, and of their lack of it and their ignorance of how to secure it on the other hand. They are prodigiously hungry for guidance and help. They have looked to the church, but all too often they have found that, as an institution, it contributes more to the problem than to its solution. They have turned to psychiatrists, but psychiatry can offer only a negative treatment of cleansing from emotional illness. It can take time only to deal with the seriously ill, and even to its patients it can give little guidance in the attainment of positive happiness.

This hunger for guidance through the intricate maze of emotional development provides the opportunity for the quack to put forward many a half-baked idea and for the unscrupulous politician to play upon immature emotions for his own advantage. But it is also a God-given opportunity for the churches to recapture their traditional role of spiritual counsel, relating the profound insights of the Bible to the knowledge of modern psychology and the actual needs of men and women.

When the New Testament is read with this concern uppermost, one cannot help being amazed at the profound wisdom of Jesus and the early Christians. They perceived, for example, with an insight lost to generations of their followers, that resentment and anger, fear and anxiety, are enemies of human fulfillment even more dangerous than licentiousness and greed. Not by rigid self-discipline, but by perfect trust in God did they seek salvation. Confidence that one has been forgiven replaced for them that endless measurement of conduct by legalistic principles which inevitably leads to the guilt-ridden life.

Jesus showed that true love is redemptive both of the lover and of the one loved. To censure and scold the sinner only deepens his inner misery. To hate or despise him and to resent his injurious actions creates inner tensions that inhibit the creative forces of personality and may ultimately lead to serious mental illness. But to love the sinner even while he is a sinner, to treat him with respect and consideration, this is to give him the security that he needs if he is to grow and to find more wholesome and constructive outward expressions of his needs. At the same time, the love of others is the most powerful force in our own lives, leading to and expressing itself in self-composure and dynamic personality.

Hatred and resentment evoke hatred and resentment that lead to further injury and further hate. Each party to such feelings becomes more wretched, despises himself, and finds life increasingly empty of meaning. Only the principle of forgiving love can break through creatively into such a situation.

Love and sympathetic understanding create an atmosphere in which it is possible for the sinner to confess his faults to himself and to others without fear or self-deceit. Such confession cleanses the mind and the heart of deep-seated guilt that may for years have been hindering the flow of spiritual power and inhibiting the creative forces in the human personality. It can turn self-hatred into self-respect and thus enable the sinner to change from a spirit of bitter resentment toward others to one of affection and esteem.

Likewise, love overcomes the principle of self-centeredness that imprisons so many within the walls of their own minds. Turning in on themselves and therefore finding themselves miserable, people feel pity for themselves. Their pity for themselves causes them to blame others for fancied injury. People believe themselves victims of persecution and ultimately demand a scapegoat for their anger. But all this melts away before the first warm breeze of love. When we turn outward with real concern for the needs of others, the inner unhappiness vanishes, and the need and desire to blame others ceases.

Just as remarkably, Jesus understood the tremendous power of faith. What we *believe* will happen *will* happen. When we expect evil from others, we receive evil from them. Our expectation leads us to interpret the actions of others in a way injurious to ourselves. It creates an atmosphere that provokes others to actual injury. Still more serious, our expectation of evil damages our personalities by drying up our spiritual resources and leaving us helpless to cope with even the simplest problem.

If, instead, we expect good of others, trust them even beyond the evidence, are confident that whatever happens will work toward the benefit of all, our faith will be justified. Trust in others makes them trustworthy; generous interpretation even of their faults helps them to overcome their faults; and confidence that all will be well releases powers in ourselves that enable us to cope constructively with every exigency.

Belief in ourselves likewise tends strongly to justify itself. Doubt as to our capacities inhibits their development, whereas confidence causes them to flower even beyond expectation. Belief that we cannot change from bad habits to good ones prevents such change, whereas faith that we can reform our lives, even against the evidence of repeated failure, will bring success. Fear that others will not love us makes us unlovely, but assurance of their respect and esteem draws forth their respect and esteem.

Not only emotional and spiritual health, but bodily health as well, are affected by love and hate, trust, and fear. The marvelous healings of Jesus illustrate wonderfully the healing power of faith. Physical sicknesses are complicated and in some instances caused by emotional attitudes. Tension and nervousness produced by lovelessness and anxiety place strains upon the heart, prevent the adequate digestion and assimilation of food, cause muscular tensions that tire the whole body, and thus inhibit proper organic functioning and reduce the capacity of the body to ward off disease.

Still more startling is the fact that many illnesses are the immediate results of thwarted emotional needs. Subconscious mechanisms, which doctors are only now beginning to understand, can cause lameness, blindness, and even death. Such diseases can be truly cured only by psychological principles and especially by faith and love.

Just as in all illnesses negative emotional attitudes are likely to be contributing factors, so in all healing, confidence and concern for others are requisite for full and rapid recovery. The confident, outgoing spirit enables the inherent healing powers of the body to operate fully and effectively, often with astounding results, whereas in the absence of wholesome attitudes the best medical science may be frustrated.

That positive attitudes contribute immeasurably to health and healing is a fact now well established and generally understood. But there are other facts, still mysterious and widely doubted, that are forcing acknowledgment from reluctant minds. There seems to be a relationship between the mind of one man and the mind and body of another such that the thoughts of one when properly directed can affect the life of another. Jesus on occasion used the faith of a father to heal his distant child.

By what laws such faith operates we do not yet know. Jesus' understanding is at this point still far beyond our own. But we need not doubt that as time passes man will gain some deeper understanding of the mental and spiritual forces operative in the world and of their interrelationship with physical energy.

Though it is truly remarkable that a Jewish rabbi two thousand years ago should have grasped so profoundly the fundamental facts of human experience, it cannot be the function of the church merely to boast that this is so. Now that secular science has learned these lessons also, such knowledge cannot be the special province of the church, though it will not do wrong to continue to proclaim in modern language its ancient wisdom.

The special province of the church is the specifically re-

ligious dimension of its understanding of man's need and the
resources for meeting those needs. True happiness involves not
only trust in ourselves and in our fellow man but also trust in
God. It is not enough to love ourselves and our neighbors; we
must also love God. Without this Godward dimension, life
cannot be complete.

In spite of all our trusting, men do not prove wholly worthy
of trust. Sometimes their failure and cruelty are such that life
would indeed seem dark even to the most trusting soul if we
could not be sure that there is One who from all eternity is
wholly worthy of all trust.

Likewise, love of others and devotion to their welfare is not
a wholly adequate or satisfying end. Love must not be directed
only to a fragment here and there of our environment; it must
be directed to all of it. God himself must be the ultimate object
of love and loyalty.

Not only are love and trust toward self and neighbor inadequate apart from love and trust toward God, but they are also
often impossible. Men cannot simply will to love and trust.
These attitudes are essentially spontaneous ones which once
thwarted must be revived by new forces coming from without.
Such spiritual forces surround us always, for God is everywhere, but our exclusive reliance upon our own will and our
tense self-centeredness prevent them from giving us the new
life we need, the life we continuously seek and despair of finding. It is the special function of the church to lead men into a
new relation with these spiritual forces, that is to say, with
God. This relationship is one of humble confidence, openness,
and willingness to be helped, and when it is attained spiritual
power pours into the body, the mind, and the spirit, restoring
health and giving new strength for daily living.

The worship service of the church should be directed toward
this end. The service should radiate confidence in the truth of
the Christian message that there is a real power and willingness of God to meet every human need. It must make this truth

concrete, so that we who worship will really believe that *our* personal needs, however great or small, can be met. It must make us vividly aware that God is really there waiting to act. And finally, it must lead us through the steps of preparation and commitment by which the desired result is attained.

When this is done, the church becomes in truth our spiritual mother. We love it as the source of all that is strong and beautiful in our lives. We return eagerly week after week expecting to find still richer food for our souls. When this is not done, churchgoing becomes a perfunctory act of duty in which all too often unfortunate mental habits are strengthened, moral inhibitions are dangerously intensified, and the mind is confused by ideas incongruous with its clearer knowledge.

The church exists to fulfill a function and its success in fulfilling that function can be measured by changed lives. It should, therefore, work just as hard and intelligently to develop methods and techniques for achieving its goal as any businessman works to achieve his ends. It must develop varied forms of worship that will meet the needs of different age and social groups. It must be willing at any time to modify its techniques when new ones appear more effective. Hence, any statement of particular methods must be tentative, and their usefulness may prove transitory. Only the purpose of helpfulness is unchanging.

Despite the relativity of methods, there are certain broad principles that may be confidently affirmed. The church must recover a real certainty of the truth and immediate relevance of what it affirms, for only when it speaks with authority can it lead men to faith. The worshiper must learn to leave his anxieties and doubts outside so that he may enter into the service with a relaxed body and a receptive mind. He must be made a participant in worship, not an object of criticism or command, so that he may turn away from himself toward God. The total atmosphere of sound and sight must be such as to facilitate his realization of the immediate presence of God.

And he must be challenged, personally and insistently, to ask God's help with real confidence that this prayer is answered in those areas where his needs are greatest.

This regular ministry of the church through its service of worship should be supplemented by the provision of opportunities for personal counseling. Many persons who need help will not come to church. Some who do come are prevented by their emotional attitudes from experiencing the help they need. They require special personal attention, especially the opportunity to confess their guilt and unhappiness to an understanding and disinterested party. When they have done this, they need practical counsel geared to their individual condition. They need not only to be shown the harmfulness of their negative habits of mind and spirit; they need also to be given specific guidance as to how they can develop new and better habits. They need to be shown how they can use the resources of religion to meet their needs.

Just as in the relationship of human mind to human mind there are dimensions that are not yet understood and that transcend the expectation of contemporary science, so also in the relationship of man's spirit to God there are occurrences that are not easily explained. It seems that prayer to God, when uttered with perfect faith and commitment, can release forces not only in our own lives but in the lives of others as well. Wonderful incidents have been recorded of physical healings and spiritual conversions wrought by God at distances from the one who prays. Occasions have been witnessed in which the fury of men and even of animals seems to have been allayed by God when prayers have been directed to this end, and in many ways both the one who prays and the one for whom he prays have been marvelously preserved from danger.

Some also seem to find that through the intimacy of their relationship to God he is able to direct their action with a very special providence. They find themselves forewarned not to take a particular train headed for disaster, or they are aroused from sleep in time to escape from imminent danger. They find themselves directed to others who are in need of what they can do for them, and when they themselves are in need others are moved to help them.

These extraordinary experiences are not in themselves of supreme importance. Men can find lives of abiding happiness without such occurrences. But these happenings do testify to the fact that there are ranges of spiritual reality (governed no doubt by spiritual laws just as reliable as the natural laws that govern the physical world) that far exceed the very limited grasp of man's present knowledge and understanding. Although there may be many fakes and hoaxes, complete incredulity is a narrow and biased attitude that will hamper rather than facilitate the extension of scientific investigation into these spiritual realms.

It may be that the sacraments can be understood in part by the application of analogies from this realm of experience. Certainly most Christians have always regarded them as more than bare signs or symbols, the value of which depends entirely on the attitude of the worshiper. Many Christians have felt that these signs are really means of grace, that through them they receive spiritual power transcending that which their own attitude alone would warrant. Yet any conception of transubstantiation or consubstantiation is untenable and even meaningless. Perhaps the truth is, instead, that in the sacraments we benefit from the faith and prayers of others, of Christ himself and of all the generations of the faithful, that cluster around these hallowed rites.

In any case the real significance of the sacraments must be seen in the spiritual power that they are in fact found to communicate. The rites in themselves can have no value, and merely to conform to them because of a supposed command of Jesus is to violate utterly his own rejection of forms and ceremonies as ends in themselves. With these modes of worship as with all others the church needs to use freedom and imagination, to be ready to adapt them to changing needs, and to judge them honestly in terms of their actual results in human experience and life.

However effective the church service may be, and however wise the counsel of the minister, the individual Christian must develop resources within himself to meet the problems of daily living. For this purpose the age-old customs of prayer and Bible-reading remain the ideal instruments. To a very large extent our lives are determined by the content of our subconscious minds, which act as a storehouse of past experience. When we have for years stored this mind with bitter, angry, and fearful thoughts, we cannot find health and happiness until they are cleansed. But cleansing as a merely negative process is not enough. The storehouse must be refilled with positive thoughts or the negative will return. It cannot remain empty. Habits, therefore, of prayer and Bible-reading are of the greatest value. Prayerful thoughts and Scriptural passages, memorized and often repeated, can restore harmony and confidence to the subconscious as well as to the conscious mind. With their aid we can find the peace of heart and abundant life that are the deepest desires of our souls.

The Social Gospel

When the Christian faith is used for self-seeking ends it is perverted. This perversion is most apparent where individuals or classes cynically employ Christian doctrines for their own political or economic ends. But many who can readily recognize the evil of such practices fail to note that when they treat Christianity as a means of purely personal salvation they are in essentially the same way cheapening and perverting the true faith.

The use of Christianity as a means to a selfish end is equally corrupt whether the end is peace and fulfillment in this life or a purely otherworldly salvation. "Unselfish" acts practiced for selfish ends are not truly unselfish. Love for others that is cultivated in order that we may ourselves be more loved is not Christian love.

It is true that Christ promises rewards to those who have fed the hungry, clothed the naked, and sheltered the homeless. But he represents those in the parable who are thus rewarded as quite unaware that they have been earning a reward. It is just when they have sought only to serve their needy neighbors without thought of consequences for themselves that they have lived as Christians. Only those who have lost themselves in service to others have fulfilled the law of Christ.

The question as to rewards and punishments in a life after death is strictly irrelevant. These there may well be. But the Christian is motivated neither by fear of punishment nor by hope of reward. He is motivated by love — love of God and love of fellow man.

The question of rewards and punishments, of emotional and spiritual achievements or failures, in this life is also ultimately irrelevant. If a man is destroyed in the service of his fellow man, then he is destroyed, but this does not mean that it would have been better not to serve. As a servant of the crucified Lord he has no choice but to serve, whatever the personal cost may be.

Service to others has always been the fundamental expression of serious Christianity, but sincerity and good intentions are not enough. During many periods of Christian history, false ideas of man's nature and his needs have deflected the finest expressions of Christian love from the fulfillment of their intention of helpfulness. The modern science of man now provides us with important new tools of understanding how Christian service can be constructively channeled.

Unfortunately, much of modern Christianity has failed to make use of the new aids that are available. Many Christians still view the relationship of the individual to society in a falsely simplified way. They still assume that society is simply an aggregate of free moral agents that have reality only as in-

dividuals. Therefore, they have undertaken to present the
Christian message as a demand upon atomic wills, each of
which is supposed capable of responding or refusing to respond
quite without regard to its social environment. In so far as such
Christians have considered environment at all, they have done
so in moralistic terms, and have blamed the moral weakness
of the child upon that of the parent or guardian.

Because this evaluation is partially correct, because, that is,
men really are free moral agents, Christianity proclaimed in
these terms has been partly successful. It has succeeded in
arousing in some of the persons coming from the least promis-
ing backgrounds moral and spiritual zeal of a high order.
Sometimes it has changed individuals in sufficient number to
have a marked effect upon society as a whole. These achievements are not to be minimized.

But the results even of the successes of such Christianity
have often been paradoxical. It has saved a few individuals
from vicious habits while all the factors combining to develop
these habits in others remain to mold a whole new generation.
It has given individuals high moral ideals and deep sensitivity
to the needs of others, and left untouched an international or
political situation that has then compelled those same persons
to proceed to mutual slaughter. It has taught subject and depressed peoples to discover their dignity while allowing other
Christians to exploit and humiliate them. Even today it continues to give spiritual aid and comfort to millions, but it does
little to prevent the total destruction of human civilization.

Christianity has indeed always recognized some responsibility toward the unfortunate. It has established charitable institutions to feed and clothe the poor, cure the sick, care for
orphans and aged, and give work to the unemployed. Sometimes it has been in danger of moralization even here, helping
only those who are "worthy" by its standards, but for the
most part it has recognized all suffering as the province of its
charity.

But though Christianity has helped the sufferers, it has done little to overcome those conditions which produce suffering. It has given food to the unemployed but left unchanged the economic system that allows the means of production to stand idle while millions who need the products of the machines are eager to work. It has helped the sick, but it has not accepted any responsibility for overcoming the disease-breeding conditions of the slums or the malnutrition of the tenant farmer. It has cared for the widows and orphans of miners killed in avoidable accidents, but it has not acknowledged that it should denounce those who place higher dividends above human life and that it should demand that employers show some concern for the lives of their workers.

The failures of Christianity have arisen from the fact that, though we are free moral agents, we are also products of society. Our attitudes, our habits, our ways of thought, and even our spiritual potentialities are largely determined for us by the circumstances of our upbringing. Our freedom to choose is limited by our total personality, and this in turn is molded largely by forces not determined by our will. We are free moral agents, true. But we are German, Russian, Jew, or Arab as well. We are also members of certain economic classes and occupations, graduates of certain schools, members of certain clubs or religious groups. Each of these relationships and many more affect our personalities, our moral standards, and our strength of character.

By a heroic act of will a few men may be able to break the bonds upon thought, attitude, and action that their condition in life ordinarily produces. But the great mass of men are not heroes. If they are to be helped, the forces that mold them in patterns of vice and misery must be changed. If the few who escape are not to be replaced by many times more who cannot or will not do so, we must use our freedom to reform, not just a few individuals, but also the total social, political, and economic situation that is responsible for the evil. If Christianity cannot or will not offer the vision and motive force for such reform, realistic men of good will must look elsewhere for guidance.

But Christianity *can* offer what is needed! The church's irrelevance to man's social problems has not been due to the essential nature of Biblical religion, but rather to the church's obscuring and falsifying the full Biblical understanding of man. The church has concentrated on certain Scriptural passages taken out of context and failed to grasp the more significant truth that God dealt with a whole nation, not simply with isolated individuals within it. The church has ignored the fact that the world as a whole is to be redeemed, that the Kingdom is to be established here, encompassing all of men's activities and relationships, not just within the hearts of individuals. It has employed a dubious exegesis of Jesus' and Paul's statement about earthly authority to justify passive acquiescence to entrenched evil.

Some have supposed that although Christianity supplied the motive of love, the importance of a just order in economics and politics has been discovered for the first time by modern secular idealists. Some apparent support is lent to this view by the neglect of such questions through past generations and centuries by many of the churches. But an honest rereading of the Bible itself must forever destroy such a view.

From the very first the prophetic message coupled the demand for radical service with total social reconstruction. It was the hatred of social injustice that stirred Amos' heart to the depths and still echoes in his ringing denunciations of those in high places. Indeed, still earlier it was examples of such injustice that aroused Nathan to confront David with his sin and Elijah to risk his life before Ahab.

This does not mean that the prophets already grasped the complexity of society. We certainly cannot substitute their teachings for the modern social sciences. But this does mean that the emphasis upon the service of man through social, economic, and political action is in harmony with the whole prophetic-Biblical tradition, that this emphasis is, indeed, the form in which that tradition must express itself in the modern world.

Christianity has provided the necessary conditions for social reform. It has supplied the fundamental motivation of love; it has taught the importance of man's temporal situation and especially of his social relationships; it has afforded men the indispensable spirit of hope that better things can be. Beyond all this, Christianity has developed, confusedly but profoundly, the recognition that we share individually in a corporate guilt, that we cannot claim purity and innocence for ourselves while participating in a society that rests upon injustice and exploitation of the weak.

Yet many of the most active movements for social justice are bitterly antagonistic to the church and its teaching. They feed unconsciously upon the Biblical heritage, but they are blinded to this indebtedness by their hostility to the corrupt forms in which they find that heritage expressed in avowedly Christian churches. By returning to the full power of the prophetic message, the church can recapture its rightful role of leadership in all movements seeking to better the conditions of human life everywhere.

The return by the Christian church to its true vocation will be a costly one. Individually and collectively, we must assume responsibilities beyond our strength. We must truly bear upon our hearts the sin and suffering of all mankind. Often those for whom we labor will not understand or appreciate our sacrifices. They will add to our suffering by their ingratitude. It was thus with the Hebrew prophets and with Jesus. It will be so with us as well.

Difficulties, discouragements, loneliness, and pain must be our lot as Christians, but they are not final. Evil can never triumph in the end. God overrules all! His Kingdom will come! Love will be triumphant over hate. Peace and righteousness will reign.

Christian suffering is never hopeless or meaningless. It is a participation in the suffering of Christ, a redemptive suffering in which we can rejoice. For the gospel lived as heroically as it was lived by Jesus has world-transforming power, and he who fastens his heart upon the Kingdom of God glories in the privilege of suffering for its sake.

Emphasis upon the importance of society as a whole in no way disparages the worth of the individual. On the contrary, society is important only because it is composed of individuals and profoundly affects their well-being. Social reform is never an end in itself, but always a means to the more abundant life of men and women, boys and girls.

In the same way social concern cannot be set over against individual conversion. Without individuals converted to Christ there can be no Christian concern for overcoming the power of social evil. And, equally, without the inculcation of such a concern, we cannot speak honestly of truly Christian conversion. Those who claim to be Christian because they accept some creed or have had certain emotional experiences, but continue in their daily life impervious to the needs of their neighbors, are not truly Christian at all. Knowingly to continue to participate in a system that rests upon oppression and exploitation is incompatible with true love. To use supposedly Christian principles to suppress the cry for justice while we ourselves live in complacent comfort is the absolute antithesis of the prophetic Christian spirit. Those who claim to be converted, but who feel in their hearts and express in their lives no real concern for the needs of others are sadly, desperately mistaken.

Yet there are those who really seek to live as disciples of Christ but who have been misled as to what such discipleship involves. The sensitive Christian must therefore bring home to all who call upon the name of Jesus the gravity of their responsibility for society. Those whose hearts have *really* been converted *will* respond when the truth is made clear. The church militant will grow rapidly in strength, and when it truly fights for the cause of God no evil can long withstand its attack.

The visible church is in no sense the Kingdom of God. It is human to the core. Most of the debate as to how it should be organized, most of the endless division and dispute within it, most of its struggle for economic and political privilege, can be understood only as an expression of unconverted pride and the concern for security and power. Indeed, it must be sadly confessed that the church as an empirical institution has stood more often on the side of entrenched privilege than on the side of justice for all. It has relied for its support upon worldly instruments of force and wealth, and by them it has been corrupted. It is as often an obstacle to social progress as an instrument thereto. All too often it has encouraged hypocrisy and condoned villainy. It has made men complacently sure of their eternal well-being and callously indifferent to the suffering of their neighbors. It has initiated persecution and fought against manifest truth. All this must be acknowledged and humbly repented.

Even so, it has been the same church which has nourished the ideals and held aloft the personalities that have always had transforming power. Though the church often discouraged its people from taking seriously its own teaching, still it has not entirely concealed its light under a bushel. In every generation, in one way or another, the Christian's earnest concern to help his neighbor has been expressed.

The pulpit provides an unexcelled opportunity for the proclamation of the gospel of the Kingdom. From it the hearts of men and women can be stirred and their minds enlightened. The attitudes of the old can be changed. The young can be aroused to commit their lives to noble service. Not only can men be brought to see the vision, but they can be given the confidence that God is on their side. The God who gave his Son to die for sinners is not today unconcerned with the plight of millions of his children. He is working in the hearts of Christians to stir them into action, and when they respond to his call he will be with them in their labors.

When earnest followers of Jesus gather together for worship they do not need only to be challenged, instructed, and reassured; they need also to be refreshed. Body and mind soon grow weary of their labors, so often unrequited and unappreciated. Men need to alternate their work with worship, finding therein the renewal both of concern and of power with which they can return to their lives of service. Likewise, the fellowship with other dedicated Christians, each seeking in his own small way to serve Christ through serving man, strengthens the confidence of each in the ultimate triumph of good.

The sacraments of the church can easily become empty rites, but the Lord's Supper, especially, takes on new meaning in the context of the fellowship of suffering and sacrifice. When men of every station and walk of life, men of different races and differing creeds, kneel together to partake of the symbols of the greatest sacrifice of all, they find a sense of solidarity and strength that nothing else can give. Even when we are shut up in our class- and race-conscious churches, even when those kneeling with us around the altar do not represent the masses of mankind, still we can be conscious of the invisible fellowship of all those who through the centuries have so knelt to acknowledge their dependence upon the suffering death of a Jewish carpenter of long ago.

Private prayer can serve many of the purposes of public worship for us. When our vision grows dim, prayer brightens it. When we grow weak and discouraged, we are strengthened and assured of God's help. When we feel isolated and alone, we find again the companionship of God and the fellowship of true Christians everywhere.

The Bible is the source of knowledge and vision to be cherished and read. It does not matter whether it is perfectly accurate in every scientific and historical detail. It does not matter how we understand the miracles it records. It does not even matter that many of the writers erred in their literal expectations of the future Kingdom. What does matter is that they were inspired by God with the vision of a redeemed world that continues to have unique power to elicit our deepest devotion.

We must not use the Bible pietistically, reading only the passages that warm the heart or finding meanings relevant to merely individualistic religion where in reality they do not exist. Rather, we must honestly and accurately grasp the meaning of the whole great drama of God's dealing with mankind and of his final purpose for us in his Kingdom. In the context of this whole, personal and social religion alike find their true place.

The scholar's methods are not to be feared but to be used. He has uncovered much of the wealth of Scriptural truth hidden by dogmatic exegesis. He can set each book in its historical context and make its message come alive with meaning for its own times. And it is only as we see the meaning of each writer for his own time that we grasp his significance for our time as well.

Detailed theological commitments, on the other hand, are useless for the most part and often dangerous. Extensive debate as to the metaphysical nature of Jesus, his equality with or subordination to God, or the relation of the divine to the human nature within him, is irrelevant to the fundamental need to accept his ideals and to be stirred by his example. Such debate tends to make him unreal and to place his teaching in an unnatural light. The Biblical record speaks for itself and is enough.

Doctrinal speculations about original and actual sin, substitutionary atonement, and forensic justification are equally fruitless. They belong to the thought patterns of another generation, and in part they were unfortunate even in the past. Today they are anachronistic. Such vital significance as they have ever possessed can be stated quite simply in the language of today, and that is enough.

Since theological detail and institutional organization are unimportant in comparison with the need to transform the world according to the divine plan, denominational differences must not be allowed to hamper our service to God. The task is so vast, the resources of our separate churches so inadequate, that competition is intolerable. Friendship and co-operation alone are Christian. Exclusivism and isolation are expressions of a distortion of Christian values.

When each church recalls its members to the demand of Christ, differences will fade away, and we will move forward together as an invincible army. God's Kingdom will come and God's will be done on earth as it is in heaven.

SELECTED READINGS FOR FURTHER STUDY

MYSTICAL PROTESTANTISM

I. *Scholarly Studies in Mysticism*

Huxley, Aldous, *The Perennial Philosophy*. Harper & Brothers, 1945. A collection of sayings by mystics of all ages and religious traditions which is integrated by a running interpretation designed to show the unity of mystical thought. Written by one who found religious reality through modern Vedanta Hinduism.

Jones, Rufus, *Studies in Mystical Religion*. The Macmillan Company, 1909. One of several pertinent volumes of this great Quaker scholar. Provides sketches in the history of Christian mysticism from the first through the seventeenth centuries.

Otto, Rudolf, *Mysticism East and West: A Comparative Analysis of the Nature of Mysticism*, translated by Bertha L. Bracey and Richenda C. Payne. The Macmillan Company, 1931. Now available in a Living Age edition, Meridian Books, 1957. A major study of mystical types which focuses on the two systems of Eckhart and Sankhara.

Underhill, Evelyn, *Mysticism: A Study of the Nature and Development of Man's Spiritual Consciousness*. E. P. Dutton &

Co., Inc., 1911. Now available in a Living Age edition, Meridian Books, 1955. A pioneer work in the history and nature of mysticism which has done much to revitalize interest in this subject among Christians.

II. *Classical Exponents of Christian Mysticism*

The list of Christian mystics is very long, and to make selections among them on the basis of quality is difficult. I have selected Meister Eckhart to represent radical mysticism in the Christian tradition and for the rest have chosen representatives of moderate popular mysticism on the basis of their influence among Protestants.

Blackney, Raymond B., editor and translator, *Meister Eckhart: A Modern Translation*. Harper & Brothers, 1941. Now available in a Harper Torchbook edition, 1957. The most famous exponent of late medieval mysticism whose extreme views bring him into close relationship with non-Christian forms of mysticism.

Hodgkin, L. V., compiler, *A Day-Book of Counsel and Comfort: From the Epistles of George Fox*. Macmillan & Co., Ltd., London, 1937. A volume that serves even better than the more famous *Journal* to express and communicate the quality of spirituality that Fox impressed upon the Friends.

Thomas à Kempis, *The Imitation of Christ*. Numerous editions available. The most popular of all classics of the devotional life, reflecting the deep personal piety of fifteenth-century Brethren of the Common Life.

Brother Lawrence, *The Practice of the Presence of God*. Numerous editions available. A book that has achieved great popularity for the simplicity and purity of the life it reflects and recommends. Although written by a Roman Catholic monk, it has been at least as successful among Protestants as among Catholics.

III. *Recent Exponents of Christian Mysticism*

Fosdick, Harry Emerson, editor, *Rufus Jones Speaks to Our Time: An Anthology*. The Macmillan Company, 1951. A representative selection from the works of the best-known recent American exponent of Quaker mysticism.

Kelley, Thomas, *A Testament of Devotion*. Harper & Brothers, 1941. A beautiful and deeply moving expression of modern mystical piety which is rapidly becoming a classic.

Merton, Thomas, *Seeds of Contemplation*. New Directions, 1953. Also available in paperback edition, Dell Publishing Company, 1953. This Roman Catholic monk presents modern Catholic mysticism in its most persuasive form, exerting a wide influence upon Protestants as well.

Underhill, Evelyn, *Concerning the Inner Life, with The House of the Soul*. E. P. Dutton & Co., Inc., 1950. Representative addresses and meditations of a great authority on mystical religion. (Miss Underhill herself belonged to the Church of England and contributed greatly to the growth of mysticism within it.)

In addition to these influential statements of Quaker, Catholic, and Episcopalian mysticism there is a large literature of devotion and inspiration that combines mystical depth with the quest for abundant life and the social gospel. Typical are the works of such authors as: Georgia Harkness, E. Stanley Jones, Frank Laubach, Muriel Lester, Kirby Page, W. E. Sangster, and Leslie Weatherhead.

The Quest for Abundant Life

I. *Expression of the Movement*

Beasley, Norman, *The Cross and the Crown: The History of Christian Science*. Duell, Sloan & Pearce, Inc., 1952. An enthusiastic biography of Mrs. Mary Baker Eddy, with an appendix which includes several of her shorter writings.

Eddy, Mary Baker, *Science and Health, with Key to the Scriptures.* This and all other writings of the founder of Christian Science are available in numerous editions constantly reprinted by the Christian Science Publishing Society.

Fosdick, Harry Emerson, *On Being a Real Person.* Harper & Brothers, 1943. One of several works of this great American preacher which apply the Christian faith to the problems of living, with sensitivity, balance, and wisdom.

Johnson, Paul E., *Christian Love.* Abingdon Press, 1951. A psychological study of Christian love, informed by theological, historical, and sociological scholarship.

Peale, Norman Vincent, *A Guide to Confident Living.* Prentice-Hall, Inc., 1948. First in a series of works by this Methodist minister which have enjoyed enormous popularity and influence, giving him the foremost place in the less scholarly or less theoretically concerned branch of the general movement.

Sherrill, Lewis Joseph, *The Struggle of the Soul.* The Macmillan Company, 1951. A psychological account of Christian experience as the development of true maturity. Influenced by the insights of Paul Tillich.

Weatherhead, Leslie D., *Prescription for Anxiety.* Abingdon Press, 1956. A recent addition to the works of this English Methodist minister which brings psychology and Christian faith jointly to bear on the problems of individual living.

II. *Scholarly Discussions*
Hiltner, Seward, *Religion and Health.* The Macmillan Company, 1943. A careful investigation and evaluation of the actual practices of the churches in those areas where they effect mental and physical health, with specific suggestions for improvement.

Maves, Paul B., editor, *The Church and Mental Health.* Charles Scribner's Sons, 1953. A symposium, initially sponsored by the Department of Pastoral Service of the National Council of Churches, on historical, theoretical, and practical aspects of the church's influence on mental health by fourteen leaders in the field.

McNeill, John T., *A History of the Cure of Souls.* Harper & Brothers, 1951. A thorough study of the theory and practice of pastoral care both within and outside of Christianity. Pays special attention to the several traditions of Protestantism.

Roberts, David, *Psychotherapy and the Christian View of Man.* Charles Scribner's Sons, 1950. A theologian's investigation of the relation of Christian faith to the insights of modern psychotherapy.

Schneider, Louis, and Dornbusch, Sanford M., *Popular Religion: Inspirational Books in America.* University of Chicago Press, 1959. A sociological study of forty-six religious best sellers from 1875 to 1955, most of them of the general type suggested by the more popular titles listed in Section I above.

The Social Gospel

I. *Expressions of the Movement*

Gladden, George Washington, *Applied Christianity.* Houghton Mifflin Company, 1886. An influential work by a pioneer in the movement, discussing such problems as economics, labor relations, peace and war, and education.

Rauschenbusch, Walter, *A Theology for the Social Gospel.* The Macmillan Company, 1917. The most systematic work of the greatest exponent of the main stream of the movement. Selections from this and other books of Rauschenbusch are available in two recent anthologies of his writings.

Mays, Benjamin C., compiler, *A Gospel of the Social Awakening: Selections from the Writings of Walter Rauschenbusch.* Association Press, 1956.

Landis, Benson Y., compiler, *A Rauschenbusch Reader: The Kingdom of God and the Social Gospel.* Harper & Brothers, 1957.

Muelder, Walter G., *Foundations of the Responsible Society.* Abingdon Press, 1959. A contemporary restatement in the Rauschenbusch tradition of the responsibility of Christians in each of the areas of social life.

Niebuhr, Reinhold, *An Interpretation of Christian Ethics.* Harper & Brothers, 1935. A major early work of the central figure in the development of a more critical and less optimistic "social gospel."

Hutchison, John A., editor, *Christian Faith and Social Action.* Charles Scribner's Sons, 1953. A symposium dedicated to Reinhold Niebuhr in acknowledgment that it is expressive of the point of view of which he has been the greatest spokesman.

II. *Critical Histories of the Movement*

Carter, Paul A., *The Decline and Revival of the Social Gospel.* Cornell University Press, 1956. Traces the church's response to the attacks upon the social gospel in the twenties and its revival in relationship to the ecumenical movement and the New Deal.

Duff, Edward, *The Social Thought of the World Council of Churches.* Longmans, Green & Co., Ltd., London, 1956. A scholarly and responsible survey by a Roman Catholic of the World Council's discussions and pronouncements on social issues.

Hopkins, Charles H., *The Rise of the Social Gospel in American Protestantism, 1865–1915.* Yale University Press, 1940. An intensive treatment of the social gospel as an increasingly self-conscious movement developing to its maturity in the years just before the First World War.

Miller, Robert Moats, *American Protestantism and Social Issues, 1919–1939.* University of North Carolina Press, 1958. A thorough and scholarly study by a secular historian of the positions taken by the Protestant churches on a large number of social issues between the two world wars.

Smith, Timothy L., *Revivalism and Social Reform in Mid-Nineteenth Century America.* Abingdon Press, 1957. Maintains the thesis that the renewed social passion of the American churches which expressed itself in the social gospel was rooted in the evangelical and perfectionist revivals.

CHAPTER VI

Nontraditional Divisions

TYPES OF PROTESTANTISM have been distinguished in Chapters II through V according to concerns and perspectives internal to the religious consciousness. Each emphasis or point of view gives rise to a way of understanding the human situation that remains an enduring alternative for Protestants. These enduring alternatives, internal to the Christian faith, may be called Protestant traditions.

The nine traditions that have been presented as possible interpretations of man's existence are fundamentally independent of the changing content of empirical knowledge. However, all have been affected by the progress of historical and scientific disciplines. These effects are felt by the religious man as responses to stimuli and challenges arising outside his faith. They create divisions that cross traditional lines.

These nontraditional divisions are commonly described by terms such as " orthodox," " fundamentalist," " liberal," " modernist," " radical," " naturalist," and " humanist." Each of these terms can be given definite meaning, but for the most part they are used ambiguously and are cluttered with emotional overtones. They reflect social, economic, and cultural orientations the influence of which upon religious thought is an appropriate object of sociological investigation. However, they reflect also a deeper cleavage in spirit that results from differing responses to the greatest intellectual developments of modern times.

These responses have had revolutionary effects within each tradition in the development of man's fundamental self-understanding.

In so far as theology has been developed as a religious and intellectual undertaking in the past two centuries, it has been faced by the necessity of making, consciously or unconsciously, a basic decision. It must decide how to relate itself to the scientific enterprise which, since the sixteenth century, has increasingly dominated Western man's intellectual world.

Even when science restricted itself to the investigation of the inanimate world it created problems for the Christian who regarded the Bible as giving authoritative information about nature. Gradually, the nature that was investigated was expanded to include the organic realm and finally man himself and human society. Each step of this scientific advance created new difficulties for traditional Christian faith.

Furthermore, science as investigator of nature proved so successful that its method and results were generalized by philosophies. These philosophies posed explicitly the more profound problems implicit in the scientific development. Finally, especially in the nineteenth century, the objectivity of science and the imaginative generalizations of philosophy were applied to the reinterpretation of human history. In the process of this historical investigation the understanding of the Christian Scriptures was revolutionized.

Both modern philosophy and the modern study of history, including Biblical criticism, are in a general way products of the scientific advances. Therefore, when the theologian decides how to respond to the challenge of modern science, he is deciding also in a general way how to relate himself to modern philosophy and critical historical scholarship. In confronting this basic decision Christian leaders have divided. One group determined at all costs to come fully to grips with the problem posed by modern science. The other group has preferred to deal with the problem piecemeal, minimizing the more general implications of science and accepting its specific findings only when necessary.

The former decision, fully to confront the problem, led to the development of the whole movement of modern theology, appearing clearly first in Kant and tracing its history, or its many histories, through Schleiermacher, Hegel, Ritschl, Kierkegaard, and others of almost equal stature down through many of the theological leaders of our own day. The latter policy of dealing with science piecemeal dominated the life of the church generally, especially in America where absorption in evangelism, combined with the democratic control of the churches, insulated the rapidly growing denominations from the intellectual life of Europe. Terms like "liberal," "conservative," and "orthodox" are used to characterize differences both among those who have given serious weight in their theological development to the total implications of modern science and among those who have minimized these implications. Hence, they are not suitable for expressing this basic cleavage. The polar terms "fundamentalism" and "modernism" do suggest positions clearly defined as standing on opposite sides of the division, but the great majority of Christians even in America reject both labels, and neither term has seemed appropriate to the European scene. Hence these terms also are unsuitable. For these reasons the more neutral terms "popular" and "postscientific" will be used.

In addition to the problem now at least two centuries old as to how to deal with the implications of the natural sciences, the critical study of the Bible has produced in the twentieth century a situation that heightens an old problem of Protestantism to such an extent as to create a really new problem. This is the problem of "the scandal of eschatology."

Eschatology is the body of beliefs about man's end. In its broadest sense it may include all questions of the purpose or destiny both of men individually and of humanity corporately. In this broad sense all earnest Christians and, indeed, all serious-minded people have always recognized the importance of eschatology, and everyone will readily acknowledge that eschatology permeates the spirit of the Bible. However, eschatology also has a more restricted meaning. In its proper sense and as it will be used hereafter it refers to a temporally future event of supernatural character that will usher in a new age in which God's sovereignty will be unambiguously manifested.

The scandal of eschatology results from the theory not only that Jesus and the primitive Christian generally adhered to eschatological ideas but also that the proclamation of the imminence of the " end " was central to their message and decisive for all their thought. This appears to mean not only that the early Christians, including Jesus, were deluded in regard to their expectations but also that these false expectations determined the content of their message. What, then, is the meaning of the acceptance of the authority of the Bible or the centrality of Christ for the thought and life of the twentieth-century Christian?

The responses to the religious and theological problem posed by the scandal of eschatology are so varied and the situation is still so fluid that any attempt to categorize them is likely to be irrelevant and even erroneous. However, a serious attempt such as is made in this book to understand contemporary Protestantism cannot ignore the issues raised by eschatology. These issues have played an important role in theological discussion from the beginning of the century and a dominant role in many circles since the First World War. They have already become important in the discussions of the World Council of Churches, and are potentially of much greater importance for the life of the churches generally.

The problems posed both by the rise of the sciences and by the eschatological reinterpretation of the New Testament cut across traditional lines. Responses to the problems are determined largely by the acuteness of the awareness of their importance. They depend in the first instance on the knowledge of the content and method of science that is available, and in the second instance on the particular exegesis of certain books and passages that is accepted on relatively objective scholarly grounds. The responses are conditioned by the general socio-cultural situation and by philosophical commitments. The response to the eschatological problem is affected also by the previous response to scientific challenges.

For these reasons each problem is first presented systematically, that is, independently of the distinctions among the forms of Protestantism. The systematic presentation of the scientific problem consists in an explanation of the ways in which the rise of science has affected popular and postscientific thought and their resultant relations to each other. The systematic presentation of the eschatological problem is an outline of possible ways in which it may be treated when clearly and frankly faced, and the implications for these alternatives of the distinctions of popular and scientific thought.

However, in addition to the influences upon the responses to the scientific and eschatological problems listed above, an important and often decisive influence is exercised by the fundamental convictions that constitute the religious perspective from which the problem is viewed. Hence, in each section, in addition to the systematic presentation of the problem, the characteristic responses of each tradition are indicated.

POPULAR AND POSTSCIENTIFIC PROTESTANTISM

The greatest intellectual achievement of the modern world has been the development of natural science. It has covered roughly the same period as that of Protestantism. It has revolutionized the thought and life of all civilized men far more pervasively and far more extensively than has Protestantism or indeed any other movement.

The influence of science upon religious thought has been inescapable. This influence has taken many forms and has evoked widely different reactions. Indeed, one of the most important divisions within Protestantism today is that between those who have accepted the full implications of the sciences and have rethought the Christian faith in the light of these implications and those who have avoided so radical a theological reconstruction. For the reasons explained in the preceding section, the former response will be called "postscientific" and the latter "popular."

The term "popular Protestantism" must not be understood as referring either to an inarticulate or uneducated group or to the many who attend church occasionally but otherwise manifest general lack of interest in religious matters. The important division is that among articulate, trained leaders who are sincerely concerned with religious truth and among their more intelligent and dedicated followers.

To understand the divergence between popular and postscientific Protestantism, it is necessary first to examine the general points of view that have presented themselves as the intellectual by-products of the scientific advance. The effects of these movements on popular Protestantism can then be indicated, and the response of postscientific theology to the total implications of science can be described. Three major intellectual movements resulting from the rise of natural science may be distinguished.

The first of these is materialism, which regards itself as the world view that is the inevitable end product of the gradual extension of scientific investigation to every aspect of reality. Science portrays an orderly universe of matter in motion, each motion being traceable to preceding motions and exhaustively explicable in terms of them. To explain anything seems to mean to place it in the succession of causes and effects. These causes can ultimately be understood only in terms of the least material particles of which all things are composed. Thus the activity of mind and spirit, no less than planets and billiard balls, can be explained in terms of mechanical laws. Since the rise of the non-Newtonian physics in the twentieth century, classical materialism has been in difficulty, but the tendency remains to explain mind and spirit in terms of what is non-mental and nonspiritual.

The second major type of intellectual development given impetus by the rise of science is modern rationalism. Rationalism, like materialism, undertakes to explain all natural events in terms of intelligible laws. As a result, rationalism usually adopts the same kind of mechanistic view as materialism. Explicitly, it may not even except human reason from this reductionism.

However, rationalism gains its inspiration from science in an entirely different way, for it is impressed primarily not by the implicit world view of science but rather by the remarkable success of the human mind in probing the mysteries of the universe. Reason has won its place as final authority for all belief. The claim for belief must appeal to criteria of rationality or reasonableness. Rationalism does not simply rule out the claims of religion as does materialism, but it subjects them to its own standards of judgment. Since the viewpoint of materialism is uncompromisingly irreligious, rationalism has been the medium through which it has played its significant role in the thought of Protestantism.

The third effect of science upon general thought is in terms of its method. Science, it is thought, became successful when men limited their concepts to what they could experience through their sense organs and gave themselves over to the most careful and objective measurement of the sensory data. Thus empiricism rather than rationalism or materialism is felt by many to be the true lesson of science.

The impact of these intellectual developments stemming from the rise of science upon popular Protestantism may be summarized under three headings: first, a more or less materialistic rationalism; second, empiricism; and third, the higher criticism of the Bible.

Popular religious thought under the influence of rationalism was from the first concerned with the question of the limitation of science and of scientific reason. The limitations sought have been of two kinds. First, are there facts about the universe for which science cannot account? If so, there is room for a supernatural explanation. Or, second, does reason support belief in the suprarational status of some authority such as the Bible? If so, then independently of direct rational support, there is certain knowledge of God. If reason, which is equated with science and the scientific world view, can explain everything, and if reason does not support the idea of divine authorship of Scripture, then there is little room left for religion. However, since there are still gaps in the scientific explanation of the world, and since the Bible in one way or another can still be accepted as divinely inspired, acceptance of many of the beliefs it contains is still quite possible and very advantageous on social, moral, and psychological grounds.

In very important respects the indirect effect of rationalism upon popular religious thinking has been to push religion entirely into the realm of the supernatural. This is understood essentially as a realm of actual existence to which the findings of science can never be relevant. It manifests itself in the natural realm in breaks in the natural order of creation, in events transcendent or contradictory to that order, or in a supernatural book. The supernatural realm is primarily important in this frame of reference because upon death the immortal portion of each self enters therein, and secondarily (for some) because certain events, such as healings, may still occur by supernatural intervention in the natural order.

Intimately related to this frame of reference for many Protestants is some kind of empiricism. The final evidence of truth is experience, and from the reality of subjective experience there can be no appeal. The experience may be of God himself, of the forgiveness of sins, of peace of mind and spirit, of increased vitality, even of general personal success as a result of following a specified religious discipline. To what extent this emphasis upon the authority for belief of personal experience is to be seen as a reflection of the prestige of scientific method is certainly debatable. It arises in part out of the New Testament itself, and no period of Christian history has altogether lacked this note. Yet in more recent days, as the authority of tradition has been undermined and the supernatural evidences for supernatural truths have become less convincing, the analogy of religious experiential evidence to that employed in the sciences has been increasingly important in popular apologetics.

The application of scientific attitudes to the study of history and especially to Biblical criticism has had especially important influences on the development of popular Protestantism. Protestants were first driven by the scientific world view to a radically supernatural interpretation of Biblical authority, only to be confronted with an impressive array of facts and interpretations all tending to stress the human element in the authorship of Scripture. A minority closed their minds to this possibility, feeling that it rendered all Christian truth suspect and precarious. The majority gradually admitted the human element in the Bible, contenting themselves with the view that there is also something supernatural either in the Bible itself, or in some of the events it records, such as the resurrection, or in the personality of Jesus, or in the success of the Christian movement, or in the effects that acceptance of Biblical truth has upon the believer.

The net result of the success of science upon the popular Protestant mentality in the nonfundamentalist churches has been a gradual retreat from definiteness of conviction, an increasing distrust of logical consistency and systematic thought about ultimate reality, a growing reliance upon emotion over against reason. There has been a loss of confidence in beliefs about the supernatural sphere except in those about God and personal immortality, and an increasing identification of Christianity with bourgeois mores and with a legalistic interpretation of specific religious duties.

Postscientific Protestant theology began with the full acknowledgment of the total consequence of the scientific world view and method for religious thought in such a way as to preclude the possibility of being driven to retreat step by step before its advance. Whereas the churches were rocked to their foundations by the controversies over evolution and "higher criticism," these caused little difficulty among intellectual circles where the full effect of such developments had already been discounted. Realizing that Christianity could never rest securely upon the residue of scientific ignorance and could not remain true to its genius while engaged in mortal combat with the progress of scientific truth, many Protestant intellectuals undertook to rethink what was central to Protestant faith in the light of man's new knowledge of the world and the proved success of his method of gaining that knowledge. The concept of the supernatural as explaining those physical events which science could not explain was repudiated at the start.

Postscientific theology found open two ways of responding to the scientific challenge, and it has throughout its history tried both. Some, whom we may call naturalistic theologians, have tried to develop theology in harmony with science by portraying the activity of God in terms of the processes of nature exhibited by science. Thus, for example, the emergence of novelty in the evolutionary process is seen as God's creative work within the process, and the healing forces of nature are understood as God's gracious work of restoring us to mental and physical health.

Other thinkers have preferred to indicate the intrinsic limits of the scientific method. In this way they intend to show that there are important areas of human life and experience that can never be explored by science. It is with these areas that they concern themselves as theologians.

Both those who tried to integrate theology with natural science and those who radically distinguished them necessarily rejected the view that all parts of the Bible are inerrant. Indeed, most of them have been quite willing to abandon many of the specific teachings of the Bible not only about nature and historical events but also about moral and spiritual questions.

Postscientific theologians have been concerned to establish the truth only of that which seemed to them to be the vital heart of the Christian message whether this was understood in terms of its distinctiveness from other religions or in terms of what it shared with all religion. The vital heart of the Christian message might be seen as personal experience of God in Christ, as the Kingdom of God as the end of all endeavor, as a particular understanding of history or of the world in general, or as the full development of human personality as the real seat of the divine. Far from being disturbed by the rise of higher criticism, and of the sociology, the history, and the psychology of religion, the effort to formulate and defend what is " really important " in the Christian message has always presupposed and implied such study of the Bible, man, and history.

The difference of this point of view from that of popular Protestantism is not that one accepts and the other rejects this or that theological doctrine or scientific belief. It lies rather in the context of acceptance or rejection. Popular Protestantism when compelled to accept naturalistic interpretations of natural events and historical interpretations of historical events has done so reluctantly, even resentfully, in a spirit of defeat, feeling that each such acceptance involves the retreat of Christian faith conceived as belief in the supernatural, whereas for postscientific theology each clarification of natural and historical fact has illumined its problems and strengthened its foundations. For example, whereas the theory of evolution appeared to popular Protestantism as a momentous attack wiping out at one blow the radical discontinuities in nature on the basis of which the supernatural intervention of God had been securely affirmed, to the naturalistic theologian it made possible the concept of creative evolution through which God could be seen as even now actively at work in the universe in the interest of a greater good. Likewise, in the field of higher criticism, whereas the discovery of Egyptian, Babylonian, Canaanitish, or Greek influences in the Scripture has meant to popular Protestantism that the supernatural authority of Scripture was progressively undermined, it has meant to the post-scientific scholar the increasing possibility of determining what is distinctive about the Jewish and Christian witness.

In regard to some of their specific teachings, the edge of the antagonism between popular and postscientific Protestantism has been blunted. Despite the insistence of fundamentalists that the literal infallibility of the words of the Bible is an indispensable doctrine, the great majority of Protestants are confused in this regard and vaguely disturbed about their confusion. They demand that at least something supernatural about the Bible must be recognized, and they are quite sure that the Bible must be in some way authoritative. However, for the most part they are ignorant of its contents and frankly admit what they call their inability to understand it, by which they mean that when they read the Bible they do not find what they expect in terms of corroboration of the kinds of views that they have absorbed from their fellow churchgoers. They are receptive as never before to explanations of the Bible based upon higher criticism even though they may still abhor the term.

Meanwhile, many postscientific theologians have come to a renewed recognition of the normativeness of the Bible for Christian belief and have come to treat it with a new respect. The excitement engendered by many of the rather far-fetched theories of the past has died down. The technical, objective, critical attitude so important in the earlier phases of intellectual development has been superseded by an enthusiastic reaffirmation of basic Biblical truths.

Between the two perspectives, however, there still remains a wide gulf. The theologian for the most part "radicalizes" Biblical doctrines. That is, whatever he may regard as the probability of the literal historical or scientific reliability of a particular doctrine, he seeks instead the fundamental interpretation of life, of history, and of man's relation to God and to his fellow man that is expressed in the passage or book. It is at this level that the Scriptures have regained their real normativeness for the theological perspective. Barth, when pressed, affirms that the virgin birth " really did take place," but his interest in the virgin birth centers not in the literal accuracy of the account as miraculous evidence for suprarational beliefs, but rather in the implications of such an idea for the total conception of God's relation to man in Christ. Those adhering to the popular perspective cannot grasp this process of " radicalization." They still seek to learn what is factually true in the Biblical record and to ground their faith upon that. Because they are not accustomed to think in terms of conflicting world views but rather in terms of conflicting affirmations in regard to particular historical incidents, they are bewildered by the relative indifference of postscientific scholars to the historicity of such incidents. They may like what the theologian affirms, but they feel that there is another range of questions that must be answered first.

Another closely related aspect of the mutual misunderstanding and mistrust should be mentioned. Large numbers of contemporary American Protestants are so deeply rooted in some form of moralistic pietism that they really cannot conceive what else Christianity can be. To be more Christian is simply to be more rigorously moral and to observe more regularly the pious practices of Bible-reading, church attendance, and, above all, prayer. On the other hand, most leading theologians have either never understood Christianity in pietistic terms or have so definitely reacted against that understanding that they regard the term itself as one of opprobrium. When their views most closely approach those involved in pietism, they prefer to emphasize the remaining differences.

It is partly for this reason that matters of intense concern to the average earnest Protestant, especially in the individualistic traditions, seem naïve and peripheral to the theologian and why the matters that absorb the energies of the theologian often appear academic and peripheral to the churchman. The pietist focuses his attention inevitably on the questions: What ought I to experience? What ought I to do? How ought I to pray? How can I understand that to which I pray? How can I achieve the feelings and attitudes I believe I ought to have? The postscientific theologian, on the other hand, seeks to clarify the Christian conception of man in his relation to nature, to history, to the church, to himself, and to God. He is exercised over the interrelationships of religion with sociocultural and economic developments. He is interested in determining which of the doctrines of the church were affected by which cultural or philosophical traditions. Of late he has been deeply concerned to understand more genuinely the fundamental way of thinking of the Biblical writers. But he rarely brings all this wealth of understanding directly to bear upon the questions asked by popular piety, and when he does so he is understood with the greatest difficulty.

These general comments on the cleavage between popular Protestantism and postscientific theology can now be supplemented by consideration of how the separation has affected the nine Protestant traditions described above.

It has been within Lutheranism that scientific theology has developed most widely and most fully. This is no doubt partly coincidental, but it is also due to distinctive characteristics of the Lutheran spirit and polity. Lutheranism has always combined an intense concern for purity of doctrine with a relatively free approach to Scripture. Luther was concerned far more with the Word of God, which speaks through Scripture, than with the words of Scripture. Hence, Lutherans could tolerate those who sought new formulations of the Word even when their statements could not be harmonized literally with all of the Bible. Furthermore, the control of the church by states which at times were inclined to theological radicalism gave scholars in Germany, where Lutheranism was strongest, a measure of protection from churchmen whom they antagonized. Finally, Germany has led the world during the nineteenth and twentieth centuries in both the philosophical and the historical studies that were the indispensable tools for theological reconstruction. This leadership may have been itself partly facilitated by the special genius of Lutheranism, but whatever the cause, it provided an ideal context for the new theological developments.

Not only has Lutheranism led the Protestant world in postscientific theology, but it has also maintained a closer relationship between popular thought and theological leadership than has any other form of Protestantism. The importance attached to theology has led to the high prestige of the theologian, and the prominence of postscientific theologians has led to a much wider assimilation of their ideas than has occurred generally in other communions. This is less true of Lutheran churches in America because here popular piety has exercised greater control over theological education, but even in America the close ties to European Lutheranism have kept the channels of communication relatively open.

Nevertheless, a gulf remains between the two forms of Lutheranism. A large body has attempted to remain rather rigidly faithful to the sixteenth-century formulations, denying that changing circumstances and scientific developments have seriously affected their intelligibility or their credibility. Strict adherence to these early formulations has necessarily involved a tendency to defend even the world view of the sixteenth century, its understanding of history, and its rather naïve supernaturalism. Popular Lutheranism, therefore, though more aware of postscientific theology and more influenced by developments within it than popular Protestantism in other traditions, still remains profoundly removed from it.

At the opposite extreme from Lutheranism with respect to

the response to science stands individualistic Biblicism. Adherents of this tradition ignored or denied the implications of science for religious thought throughout the eighteenth and nineteenth centuries. This negative response was made possible by the intellectual and cultural distance that separated Biblicists from the scientific developments of the period and by the low level of the education of most of their clergy. However, when Biblicism was finally compelled to face the issues raised by science, it was divided more drastically than was any other group. It was in strongly Biblicist denominations that the fundamentalist-modernist controversy was most sharply delineated. Biblicists are least able of all groups to acknowledge the picture of the Bible as the product of the religious development of a people, which is the presupposition as well as the conclusion of modern critical scholarship. They are least able to cope with the contradiction of Biblical beliefs about nature with which the growth of scientific knowledge has confronted the modern world. Hence, they are driven, on the one hand, toward an obscurantist reassertion of Biblical inerrancy and, on the other hand, toward an explicit rejection of the old basis of authority in favor of science or reason.

The formal cleavage would have been still more serious had not the practical bent of most Biblicists, their concern to obey God and save souls, been ever greater than their theoretical reverence for Biblical authority. On strictly practical grounds the two parties may find it possible to work together, but the theoretical and religious separation remains wide.

The position of Calvinism in the face of scientific developments has been somewhere between that of Lutheranism and Biblicism. On the one hand, it has shared with Lutheranism a strong intellectual concern and high standards of theological education. On the other hand, it has shared with Biblicism a tendency toward inflexibility in its treatment of Scripture. Its polity has been more independent of secular control than Lutheranism but less democratic internally than the Biblicist churches.

As a result of factors such as these Calvinism failed to initiate postscientific movements except in connection with Lutheranism in Germany. The problems posed by science were generally minimized or ignored as long as this was possible. Only in the latter part of the nineteenth century under the influence of pervasive evolutionary thinking did Calvinist scholars in England and America begin to take seriously the theological developments of Lutheran Germany and to be profoundly influenced by them. Even then they continued to lag far behind in creative contribution to postscientific thought, serving only to mediate the more moderate results of such thought to an unprepared people.

The opposition of popular thought to the reinterpretation of the faith has been widespread and bitter, yet not so serious as in the Biblicist churches. Calvinism does not have the same necessity as Biblicism to maintain the inerrancy of Scripture in matters of detail. So long as postscientific thinkers retained basic theological affirmations about God and man, it gradually became apparent to the majority that nothing fundamental was threatened. Even in regard to these doctrines considerable freedom could be allowed so long as the basic " spirit " was retained. Thus the major Calvinist churches gradually came to tolerate in general both critical Biblical studies and reinterpretation of doctrines to fit changing scientific knowledge.

Among the reinterpretations of doctrines and the conclusions of historical research into the Biblical records, however, the Calvinists have in general exercised very conservative selectivity. A few of the more thoroughgoing postscientific thinkers have been forced out of the Calvinist churches, and minor sects have been formed to perpetuate a more rigid or fundamentalist Calvinism. But in the major Calvinist churches moderate popular thought has established a generally harmonious relationship with moderate postscientific thought.

Experientialism has been less disturbed by the natural sciences and Biblical criticism than has either Reformation or Biblicist Protestantism. However, churches that are predominantly experientialist are also in most cases greatly influenced by Biblicism, and in so far as the Biblicist influence has been strong these churches have shared in the Biblicist dilemma. Still, experientialism as such does not greatly depend upon particular doctrines about the natural world, the Bible, or Christian history.

Experientialists might acknowledge the probable accuracy of scientific and critical claims more readily than Biblicists or Calvinists, but few of their number took any constructive part in the tasks of theological reformulation. Actually, experientialism was considerably strengthened as the difficulties encountered by other groups drove them to an appeal to religious experience. Differences among experientialists certainly have existed, but for the most part experientialist groups have succeeded in maintaining working harmony on the grounds of the secondary importance of the disputed issues in comparison with the reality of Christian devotion and experience.

The most serious problem posed by science for experientialists has not yet been widely faced. This problem is posed by psychology when it undertakes to study the phenomena of religious experience. Many psychologists have purported to explain such phenomena in ways that seem to undermine their authority for religious life. This is especially true of the more emotional conversion experiences that have often been associated with experientialism, but it has seemed at times to extend more widely to religious experience generally.

The scientific study of conversion experiences has tended to strengthen the position of those who largely on other grounds preferred to emphasize developmental and educational approaches to religion. Hence, science may be partly responsible for the serious division among experientialists between those who emphasize special dramatic experiences and those who stress continual development. But experientialists have not yet been compelled to face the more drastic implications of some psychological studies of religion partly because these studies have not achieved the objectivity and definiteness of the findings of the natural sciences.

Liturgical Protestantism has been even less disturbed by scientific developments than experientialism. So long as the reality of God and his supreme worthiness for human adoration are not challenged, no serious threat is posed to a view of Christianity that makes central the act of worship. Research into the historical origins and reference of the symbols used in worship cannot undermine their symbolic or sacramental value.

At the same time there is no great incentive here for intensive work in Biblical criticism or in theological reformulation except in the study of worship itself. In this limited area scholarly work of high quality has been abundantly produced.

The position of authoritarian Protestantism is somewhat more difficult, but it has succeeded in adapting itself with remarkable facility to a changing intellectual environment. In the early days of the Oxford Movement, Newman was bitterly hostile to the critical spirit and postscientific theological reconstruction. However, within a half a century Anglo-Catholics found that the difficulties of Biblicists strengthened the hands of those who shifted the seat of authority to church and tradition. They found also that their principle of a developing tradition allowed for flexibility in the face of scientific developments. They found finally that by incorporating a strong liturgical emphasis they could employ symbolic thought and expression to escape many of the dilemmas posed by the alternatives of literal truth and error with regard to Biblical history. For these reasons, by the opening of the twentieth century authoritarian Protestantism had largely solved its problem and was participating constructively in postscientific discussion.

Mystical Protestantism has never been compelled to acknowledge that any problem existed. It gives exclusive attention to a sphere of reality that transcends the province of the scientist and historian. Hence, it develops on its own principles quite independently of external intellectual changes. Mysticism has been subjected to psychological analyses, but these are more often the poorly supported theories of those predisposed to reject mysticism than the views of genuinely objective scientific criticism. In the nature of the case, successful scientific evaluation seems extremely unlikely, for the phenomena of mysticism are not readily subject to objective study.

A more serious objection is posed to mysticism in so far as it claims to be Christian. Critical historical study has indicated the similarity of mystical patterns in different religions and has seemed to show that mysticism has received purer expression in Indian than in Hebrew religion. Indeed, many scholars have denied that the Hebrew prophets, Jesus, or Paul are mystical at all and have inferred that mysticism came into Christianity as an alien accretion. Christian mystics, therefore, face the problem of refuting these interpretations of the relationship of mysticism to world religions or qualifying their claim to being distinctively Christian.

The rise of scientific psychology which poses problems for traditional experientialism has produced what has been called above "the quest for abundant life." For the most part, this movement has been successful when older patterns have been weakened by the pervasive influence of modern scientific thought. Most of its adherents understand psychology only in a very popular way, and it is in popular terms that the position is as described above. However, many leading thinkers committed to the postscientific approach are vigorously exploring modern depth psychology and group therapy as they are relevant to the basic human problems with which Christianity is concerned. Hence, to an important degree this tradition is open to reformulation by postscientific theology.

The social gospel was directly influenced in its origin by the postscientific interpretation of the Bible and the new understanding of man and society that were produced by the social sciences in the nineteenth century. Its development has depended, therefore, in part upon the development of these disciplines. In so far, however, as it remained distinctively Christian it shared in the problems of the Reformation and Biblicist traditions. Its most acute problem has arisen only in the twentieth century as Biblical criticism has produced the scandal of eschatology.

THE SCANDAL OF ESCHATOLOGY

Eschatology as a theological topic is not new. It has long been recognized that one facet of the New Testament faith was the expectation of an end of history in which the Final Judgment would take place. Conservative Protestants have accepted this expectation as a doctrine, although their emphasis has been placed upon what Christ accomplished in his first coming rather than on what remains to be done on his return.

As the scientific world view became more widespread the expectation of a purely supernatural future event grew dim. The moral and spiritual achievements of Jesus increasingly occupied the center of consideration. Biblical scholarship devoted itself in part to minimizing the importance for Jesus of any supernatural expectations about the future. Many argued that what Jesus anticipated was the gradual victory of his Spirit over all the opposing forces of history, so that God's Kingdom would be progressively realized on earth.

However, the genuine commitment of theological scholars to honest objectivity finally asserted itself. In 1906 Schweitzer published *The Quest of the Historical Jesus* in which he demonstrated that the reconstructions of Jesus' life and teaching that had been attempted in the nineteenth century had been fundamentally false. They had portrayed Jesus after the pattern of nineteenth-century ideals rather than as he is depicted in the Gospels. Schweitzer supported the position stated fourteen years earlier by Johannes Weiss that the Jesus of the Gospels was shaped in his self-understanding and in his message by the expectation of the immediate end of the world.

The mere reaffirmation that Jesus believed in the imminent

supernatural end of history was shocking to those who wished to believe that his teaching was infallible. But in itself it posed no new problem for scholarship. Schweitzer further declared that Jesus' message as a whole centered in his eschatology in such a way that apart from this expectation none of his teaching can be understood. Jesus' ethical and spiritual ideals, then, seem to have depended for him upon beliefs that we can no longer share. This interpretation of Jesus has confronted Christian thought in the twentieth century with the scandal of eschatology.

Schweitzer's thesis has by no means received unanimous assent. Many very conservative scholars hold that Jesus predicted his return, but that his prophesies are such that they may be quite literally fulfilled even after a great interval of time. They believe, of course, that these prophecies *will* be fulfilled. Our preparation for the event in the future consists in appropriating the fruits of Christ's first coming. By this position conservatives maintain the inerrancy both of Jesus and of the Scriptural record.

Others recognize that the New Testament does teach an imminent supernatural catastrophe that in fact did not occur, but maintain that Jesus himself did not encourage this idea. Jesus' spiritual teaching, they argue, was misinterpreted during his lifetime and thereafter by his followers as well as by his enemies in terms of their false expectations. By this position Jesus' own inerrancy is safeguarded while the error of Scripture is acknowledged.

Still others have argued that Jesus accepted the prevalent expectations of his contemporaries but that his interest and that of the early Christian community lay in his present accomplishments. The work of Jesus through his life, teaching, death, and resurrection released into the world new spiritual possibilities. The exploitation of these possibilities has always been the challenge of Christianity. From this point of view both Jesus and Scripture are seen as having erred, but only with respect to an idea that was of peripheral interest.

Many scholars, however, have not been able to escape so easily the scandal of eschatology. Their reading of the New Testament indicates that the Kingdom of God is there expected in the imminent future and that the coming of the Kingdom is the heart of Jesus' message by which all else is colored.

Those who accept the view that Jesus' teaching centers in the proclamation of an imminent supernatural end face a limited number of alternatives. The most conservative may state that the apparent error of Jesus' teaching was only one of time. The end will come as he foretold, but neither Jesus nor any man, as Jesus himself said, knows when it will come. Imminence is a relative matter, and for God ten thousand years are but a day. We in our day must look for the end with the same expectancy as that inculcated in the disciples.

At the opposite extreme from these conservatives are those who regard the manifest error of Jesus' expectation as necessitating a shift away from his teaching as the locus of authority in religious faith. Since honest scholarship compels us to recognize that Jesus erred with respect to the central principle in his teaching, the norm for beliefs, even belief about Jesus, must be sought elsewhere.

One possible solution is to base religious faith upon the world views established by objective, detached reason as expressed in science and philosophy. Another alternative is to seek to find truth in the study of the history of religion generally, employing all the learning of sociology and psychology in the effort to determine the core of religious reality. However, both of these approaches lead away from distinctively Christian thinking.

Within the Christian perspective some subordinate the authority of Jesus to that of tradition or the church. For this view, too, Jesus' errors in expectation render suspect the attempt to exalt his uninterpreted teachings to supreme authority. But they do not set aside his ultimately unique significance. Truth is to be found in the developing understanding of the meaning of Jesus' teaching and work by the community that was founded by him.

Another alternative authority to Jesus' own teachings, which is acceptable to some Christians, is present Christian experience. It is in our living experience of salvation through Jesus, rather than in the teachings established by scholars as authentic, that we find safe ground for our Christian conviction.

Most contemporary thinkers who acknowledge the centrality of eschatology in the thought of Jesus seek a position between the two extremes of treating Jesus' error as merely one of date and of abandoning the authority of Jesus. On the one hand, they see that Jesus expected the end within a generation and that his authority is not protected by simply affirming that what he foretold is still to come. Most of them regard the ancient form of eschatological expectation as incompatible with our scientific understanding of the world. On the other hand, most Christian thinkers are unwilling to turn entirely from the authority of Jesus to that of reason, ecclesiastical tradition, or Christian experience. They may, therefore, either affirm the contemporary importance of the "real meaning" of Jesus' eschatology or they may hold that although Jesus' eschatological teaching was radically erroneous and this erroneous belief affected all his teaching, nevertheless, the ethical and spiritual teaching of Jesus and his actual work remain normative for Christians. That is, they may seek to employ the eschatological principle affirmatively, or they may recognize it as a stumbling block in spite of which traditional emphases on Jesus' teaching and work can be retained.

Those who regard Jesus' eschatology, despite its importance to him, as necessarily an obstacle to our appropriation of his teaching may emphasize either the residue of Jesus' teaching or the efficacy of his work.

When the teaching is emphasized, they may insist that even

though Jesus himself may have regarded his ethical and spiritual teaching as inextricably involved in his proclamation of the imminence of the end, actually his teachings can stand quite independently of such a view, as the ultimate ideal demand upon mankind. Jesus' understanding of the nature and centrality of love and of its relation to righteousness and spiritual peace and power remain permanently true and verified in the experience of every generation.

Those who emphasize Jesus' work may argue that, although Jesus expected the coming of the Son of Man on clouds from heaven to usher in the new age, in reality his own ministry, death, and resurrection performed this function. What Jesus actually accomplished, rather than what he expected, is decisive. The source and norm of Christian faith is the Christ-event — the cluster of happenings and responses reported and expressed in the Gospels.

Those who use the eschatological teaching of Jesus affirmatively necessarily state the meaning of this teaching in a way that is different from most of the Biblical formulations. This difference constitutes some form of modernization, radicalization, or demythologization. That is, the theologian restates what he believes to be central in the eschatological message of Jesus in terms that do not involve a literal future event that will bring in a new age in a strictly supernatural manner. This restatement the theologian then proclaims as the real meaning of Jesus' teaching.

Most of the discussion is beset by a serious ambiguity. What is called "the real meaning of Jesus' message" may be either that aspect of his message which is true and relevant in our day or what Jesus himself intended or regarded as supremely important in his teaching. Some hold that what was supremely important to Jesus and what is true and relevant in his message are the same. Others acknowledge that what is erroneous in Jesus' teaching may have been quite important to him and that, therefore, Jesus' intention and the modern formulation are different in important ways, although still expressive of an ultimately identical concern.

Two aspects of Jesus' eschatological teaching are often emphasized as having profound significance for our day. They are usually stressed by different theologians and often present themselves as incompatible with each other. The first of these aspects is the vivid sense of God's immediacy. Each man faces an undetermined future in which the transcendent Lord of heaven and earth is immediately related to man in grace and judgment. The significance of every decision is thereby heightened almost unbelievably. The mundane problems of daily life and social relationships tend to fade into insignificance beside the all-important encounter of man with God.

Frequently, the relation of God and man is interpreted in terms of the ancient philosophical dualism of time and eternity. The existentialism of Kierkegaard is used to throw light on the eschatology of Jesus. Eternity in these terms is not an endless extension of time but a nontemporal or changeless state of ultimate being wholly different from or other than the world of ordinary experience. Time has a secondary reality. Eternity may break into time, or, in slightly less figurative language, man may encounter the Eternal One. Such an encounter comes at a particular point in time from the point of view of temporal events, but it participates qualitatively in the Eternal. In terms of its inner nature, therefore, the encounter is a "moment" which is outside of time and utterly removed from the temporal flux. This "moment" is intensely personal, inward, and subjective. It is unrelated to the outward life in which man participates in social history. That life, therefore, and history in general are ultimately unimportant and without meaning. Eschatology proclaims the emptiness of life except as God acts, except as the solitary individual momentarily transcends the temporal flux in his encounter with the Eternal.

There is a second aspect of Jesus' eschatological teaching that is emphasized, usually by different theologians, as having profound importance for our day. This is the fact that the intensity of Jesus' perception of spiritual reality did not cause him to turn his back upon the temporal world but rather heightened the traditional Jewish expectation that the God who created the world would also redeem the world. History and individual lives alike take on meaning from the great fact that God acts in the temporal sphere to transform that sphere. God's Kingdom is not a timeless sphere of static existences of disembodied spirits. It is a new order on this earth in which righteousness, peace, and love will replace sin, war, and hatred.

It is true that the eschatological teaching of Jesus stands in radical contrast to the ideas of progress or of man's " building the Kingdom." Jesus looked for a work of God in sharp discontinuity with human history. He expected this because the qualities of life that are appropriate to the Kingdom are in sharp contrast with the highest achievements of man's moral effort. These qualities are possible only to the man whose absolute commitment places him outside all historical situations as an embodiment of that ideal which judges and at the same time gives meaning to all of history.

Although these two views tend to contradict each other with regard to the meaningfulness of history they both accentuate the responsibility of man. Each man is a self who creates himself in free decisions. In these decisions he stands directly and individually under the judgment of God. Only in his ultimate and responsible subjectivity does he find reality, and only as he renounces his past self in repentance can he find his true self in faith.

In the preceding section it has been seen that the rise of science and its impact upon Protestant thought has affected each tradition somewhat differently. For most traditions it has posed problems that have tended to divide the adherents. However, it has had a creative role in the development of some of the liberal movements, especially the social gospel.

In the same way the discussions of the importance of eschatology in primitive Christian thought have had their greatest significance in the diverse impacts that they have made in the religious traditions. However, the emphasis on eschatology seems also to be capable of producing a new Protestant movement with its own characteristic concerns and emphases. Thus far, the nearest approximation to such a development is found in Europe. There the interpretation of eschatology in terms of existentialism has not only found theological statement but has also profoundly affected large segments of the church.

It is still much too early to decide what the results of this kind of emphasis on eschatology will be. It may produce a reorientation of religious thought and life developing into a lasting tradition within Protestantism. On the other hand, it may simply lead to certain shifts of emphasis within the existing traditions. The form that a new eschatological tradition would take is still a matter for conjecture. The actual effect of the discussion of eschatology on the existing traditions is already discernible.

The response to the eschatological problem seems to be influenced by the total cultural context to an even greater degree than are religious convictions generally. The differences in this regard between America and Europe have created a marked difference in the theological climates of the two continents.

In America the problems posed by the eschatological expectations of Jesus have been largely ignored, but where they are recognized they are made acute by the popular tendency to sharp distinctions of truth and falsity. Predictions of the future are either accurate or false. Since the evaluation of Jesus' teaching according to this alternative creates painful dilemmas, it has long been customary to regard certain passages as " difficult " and to pass over them rapidly with little comment. Since historical consciousness is not highly developed, " explaining " generally *means* "rendering intelligible" in the context of contemporary experience and values, and hence always tends to modernize. For two centuries advanced Biblical scholarship and scientific theology have been disparaged and ignored; hence, it is easy to neglect their contemporary concern with eschatology.

In America, therefore, the vast majority of Christians are still little affected by the systematic problem that agitates European Protestantism and a few American scholars.

Those popular movements which do stress eschatology are developments that long antedate the scholarly absorption in the problem and are unaffected by modern critical investigation. They simply accept as literally true the prophesies of the coming end found especially in Daniel and in The Revelation. They interpret the symbolism of these prophecies so as to explain the time lapse to the present and to place the consummation in the fairly imminent future.

At least three factors have contributed to the lack of popular success of those groups which have emphasized this imminent end. The first and most important is that most Christians in America do not want to believe that the end is at hand, so that the Adventist groups have won their following chiefly among the depressed classes. The second reason is that Adventist predictions have been proved wrong in recent history sufficiently often to create a widespread skepticism even among the generally credulous. The third reason is that it is vaguely recognized that the timing suggested by the prophesies quoted is not a matter of two thousand years, and that to stress their genuineness and importance is to raise serious questions as to the wisdom of the writers. Rather than do this, it is better to ignore the whole question and to ridicule the extremists.

In European Protestantism the situation is quite different. In the first place, two world wars have weakened the love of this world and the hope of its permanence that are still strong in America. Despair of human solutions paves the way for hope of a supernatural solution. In the second place, Adventism played a less prominent role in the life of the church in the nineteenth century, and literal eschatology has been therefore less widely discredited. In the third place, the isolation of popular Protestantism from postscientific theology has been less complete. This has meant both that the simple literalism of popular American Protestantism has been partially qualified and that the ignoring of the contemporary debate is more difficult. For these reasons popular Continental Protestantism has come to terms much more explicitly with the problem of eschatology.

The difference in response to the scandal of eschatology in Europe and America is also affected by the fact that diverse forms of Protestantism predominate. In Continental Europe and in Scotland the Reformation tradition determines the context of Protestant development, whereas the American scene is dominated by individualistic and liberal traditions and in England the churchly form of Protestantism is strong. Hence, the geographical and traditional differences in response to the eschatological problem are largely parallel. Still, there are religious as well as cultural factors at work in the diversity of the responses of the Protestant groups, and these are deserving of serious consideration.

Reformation Protestantism is committed to the Word of God found in Scripture as its decisive authority. Hence, it cannot bypass the problem of eschatology by appealing to any extra-Biblical authority. At the same time, Lutheranism, at least, has avoided rigid identification of the Word of God with the words of Scripture. Hence, it has not been blinded by the dogma of Biblical inerrancy to the fact that Jesus expected an imminent end that did not occur.

Reformation Protestantism understands itself primarily as a human response to the mighty works of God. For the most part these mighty works have been seen as past, centering in the incarnation and atonement. But Calvinism, at least, has often seen the hand of the Lord of history at work in the present, as well in the cosmic and historical as in the intimately personal scene. Where these acts of God are understood in terms of a naïve supernaturalism, as is often the case in popular thought, there is little difficulty in adding to the faith in the past works of God the belief that Christ will come again to perform new and yet greater works. The individual's total response to God, therefore, is expanded to include a spirit of joyful expectancy. This expectancy is not accompanied by detailed speculation as to the time, place, and manner of the coming end, but there is real conviction that an end is to come in the temporal future. Something closely akin to the New Testament hope seems really to have been revived.

Where postscientific thought predominates, however, the problem is more difficult. On the one hand, the acknowledgment that the actual predictions of Jesus were radically mistaken in timing has accentuated the recognition of his fallibility. This has encouraged the tendency to distinguish the Christ of faith, or the risen Lord who is worshiped by the church, from Jesus, the remarkable but partly deluded son of a Galilean carpenter. The claim that events occurred which could sensuously be observed as transcending natural possibilities is widely abandoned. Hence, the events to which the Christian responds are those in which he encounters the eternal Christ of God, but are not analogous to the kind of event that would actually at some literal future time introduce a radically new order into being.

The responses to this perplexing situation have been very diverse. Indeed a large portion of the total scholarly discussion of eschatology has been carried on by leaders of the Reformation tradition. Some of them have argued that Jesus did not share the eschatological hopes of his contemporaries. Many more have acknowledged that he did share these beliefs but have insisted that he was not profoundly affected by them.

A large part of the leadership of postscientific Reformation theology has accepted the view that Jesus was seriously committed to eschatology. Major thinkers have explored all of the alternatives suggested in the systematic treatment above as available to those who take the problem with full seriousness. Schweitzer has led one group in maintaining that love, which is both the fundamental principle of Jesus' teaching and the fundamental element in his spirit, is eternally relevant despite its original association with a now untenable view. Reinhold Niebuhr has led a group of American scholars in employing the new understanding of the eschatological teaching of the Bible as a source for Christian interpretation of history.

In Europe the most vigorous thinkers have taken their clue from Barth's early attempt to state Biblical eschatology in the categories of existentialism. They have found a marked congeniality between the Reformer's sense of the awful majesty of God and the sinful corruption of responsible man on the one hand and Kierkegaard's understanding of the infinite qualitative difference between time and eternity. Furthermore, many of them have developed through the chaos and suffering of two world wars a profound contempt for all pretenses to human accomplishment and a pervasive skepticism with respect to the possibility of finding any meaning in history. Meaning is found only in the paradoxical moment in which time is negated by eternity.

Churchly Protestantism is by its very nature much less affected by the differences between the popular and the postscientific perspectives. It finds that the difficulties encountered by those who exalt the sole authority of the Bible confirm its conviction that the church as a developing community, rather than the earliest expression of the faith, is normative in doctrinal matters. The problem of eschatology was dealt with by the church long ago by being placed in proper perspective. The lessened emphasis on eschatology in Luke and John is not to be seen as a loss of true faith but rather as a developing understanding of the deeper meaning of the faith. Hence, no radical reformation of faith or practice is necessitated by the modern rediscovery of the importance of eschatology for Jesus.

When the church does undertake to clarify the enduring

meaning of eschatology, it makes use of the dualism of time and eternity in much the same way as do leaders in the Reformation tradition. A difference does exist in the usual understanding of the relation of eternity to time or of God to the temporal sphere. Whereas the Reformation tradition often stresses the separation of God from the world to such a degree that any encounter is paradoxical, the churchly tradition usually sees the world as the expression of the eternal. The eternal sustains and overrules the temporal and may be encountered sacramentally within it. The end is less paradoxically the fulfillment of time.

Individualistic Protestantism is a predominantly popular movement and is most widespread in America. Hence, in general, what has been said above about popular American Protestantism applies to it as well. For individualism inevitably the problem of personal salvation and life after death are more crucial than are questions of a new age to come. However, although the problem is still largely ignored by individualist Protestants, the positions of Biblicism and experientialism in principle vary widely with respect to it.

Biblicism has nurtured Adventism. The conviction that Christianity consists in literal acceptance of Biblical teachings has led repeatedly to the view that Jesus is to return and bring in a new age. Indeed, most Biblicists when pressed acknowledge this belief as a part of their total faith. Yet many prefer to minimize its influence upon the life of the church, stressing present obedience rather than a waiting for future events.

Some readers of the Bible have not, however, been willing to treat the Second Coming of Jesus as merely one minor and generally dispensable element in its teaching. They have stressed its importance for the Bible itself and have insisted that loyalty to the Bible involves full reinstatement of the eschatological emphasis. Thus Adventism is a natural and genuine expression of Biblicism.

The chief theoretical problem that the Biblicist faces when

he confronts seriously the Adventist's claim is found in the temporally erroneous predictions of the Biblical authors which are attributed by them also to Jesus himself. Either these must be painstakingly explained away or Biblicism must acknowledge a much larger degree of fallibility in the Bible than has been its wont. So long as all Protestantism shared with Biblicism the need to ignore some aspects of New Testament eschatology, Biblicists could obscure their problem with considerable success. Now, however, when many have insisted upon the importance of the imminent expectation of the end for the New Testament itself, Biblicists are likely to find the problem increasingly acute.

While non-Adventist Biblicism avoids the eschatological problem chiefly because of its difficulties, experientialism minimizes eschatology on principle. What is important is to experience what the early Christians experienced rather than to hold identical beliefs about the future. Such glorious spiritual achievements are possible here and now, and the hope of heaven can be so sure on the basis of what God has already done through Jesus Christ, that there seems no real need for any further divine acts instituting a radically new order. What is important is to lead men and women into the realization of present possibilities, not to urge them to wait for some future occurrences. Whatever occurs in the future, those best prepared to meet it will be those who have attained the greatest heights of Christian character and experience, not those who have given most thought to what the future will bring.

Liberalism has found itself in a peculiarly awkward position with regard to eschatology. The techniques of critical study that it had enthusiastically supported in order to uncover the eternal truth of Scripture have been used instead to show that the New Testament message is conditioned by an essentially erroneous hope. Therefore, liberalism has had to choose between continuing its earlier emphases with diminishing confidence that they are loyal to the New Testament or drastically modifying the earlier emphases in an effort to harmonize with the new understanding of Scripture. Popular liberalism has yet to face these alternatives seriously, whereas many of its erstwhile leaders have repudiated it as untenable. However, some have chosen to remain outspokenly loyal to liberalism while seeking to come to terms with the contemporary Biblical understanding.

Mystics have long recognized that the data for their doctrines have been much more extensive than the Bible and that within the Bible the materials vary widely in value. Hence, the question as to the particular beliefs of the early Christians with regard to the future are not deeply disturbing.

The widespread concern for the relevance of Christian faith to personal health has also found itself somewhat removed from the eschatological question. Regardless of the original context of New Testament teachings and early church practices, one may still derive insights and guidance for contemporary needs.

The followers of the liberal social gospel may also still urge that regardless of how Jesus expected the Kingdom to come, it was the transformation of the world into a society obedient to God and transfused with love that was his dream. This dream we must keep alive, and for its realization we must work.

Finally, liberals generally are skeptical that the new emphasis upon a supernatural eschatology is more objectively valid than was the old de-emphasis. The eschatologists are affected in their reading of the Bible by their disillusionment with historical progress just as much as the nineteenth-century liberals were affected by their optimism. Only time can bring back into focus the actual importance of eschatology for the New Testament. In the meantime the positive values of liberalism must be conserved and developed.

Thus it may be seen that although the objective problems posed by New Testament criticism are the same for all Protestants, their seriousness and the lines along which they are met are affected by the fundamental orientations of both popular and postscientific Protestantism. No basic type of Protestantism as such can be either confirmed or refuted by these conclusions of Biblical criticism, although many may be modified in important particulars.

SELECTED READINGS FOR FURTHER STUDY

POPULAR AND POSTSCIENTIFIC PROTESTANTISM

I. *Historical Studies Relevant to the Contemporary Division of Popular and Postscientific Thought*

Furniss, Norman F., *The Fundamentalist Controversy, 1918–1931*. Yale University Press, 1954. A scholarly study of Fundamentalism as a general movement and of its development in eight denominations, with a thorough discussion of bibliography.

Henry, Carl F. H., *Fifty Years of Protestant Theology*. W. A. Wilde Company, 1950. A conservative theologian's account and appraisal of the recent trends in Protestant thought.

MacKintosh, Hugh Ross, *Types of Modern Theology*. James Nisbet & Co., Ltd., London, 1937. Description of the theological positions of the major Continental thinkers in the tradition of "postscientific Protestantism."

Randall, John Herman, Jr., *The Making of the Modern Mind*, revised edition. Houghton Mifflin Company, 1940. An interpretation of the social and intellectual forces that have molded the modern understanding of man and religion, highly illuminating of the divisions discussed in this chapter.

White, Andrew Dickson, *A History of the Warfare of Science with Theology in Christendom*. George Braziller, Inc., 1955. A book that, though written in 1894, remains the most comprehensive survey of the history of the conflicts between science and Christian theology. Each theological doctrine treated separately to display how it was modified and finally displaced by scientific thought.

II. *Thoroughgoing Statements of Popular and Postscientific Views*

Henry, Carl F. H., *The Uneasy Conscience of Modern Fundamentalism*. Wm. B. Eerdmans Publishing Company, 1947. A critical but positive appraisal of fundamentalism by a leader in the Evangelical movement.

Machen, J. Gresham, *Christianity and Liberalism*. The Macmillan Company, 1923. A defense of traditional Calvinist orthodoxy and denial of the term " Christian " to those who have radically modified their views under the influence of modern thought.

Niebuhr, Reinhold, *The Self and the Dramas of History*. Charles Scribner's Sons, 1955. Accepts the full implications of the findings of all types of modern science but argues that the rational-scientific approach to man fails to do justice to the uniqueness of the individual self or to human history. The Biblical faith can contribute important insights here.

Packer, J. I., *Fundamentalism and the Word of God*. Wm. B. Eerdmans Publishing Company, 1958. A defense of fundamentalism by a leader in the Evangelical movement.

Ramm, Bernard, *The Christian View of Science and Scripture*. Wm. B. Eerdmans Publishing Company, 1954. An attempt to show that scientific findings in no way contradict the Scriptures or disprove their infallibility.

Wieman, Henry Nelson, *The Source of Human Good*. University of Chicago Press, 1946. A religious view developed through the use of scientific methods and attitudes and in harmony with the modern scientific-philosophical world view.

The Scandal of Eschatology

Barth, Karl, *Epistle to the Romans,* translated from the sixth edition by E. C. Hoskyns. Oxford University Press, London, 1933. A modern turning point of New Testament theology, which interprets the eschatology of Paul in existentialistic terms.

Bornkamm, Gunther, *Jesus of Nazareth,* translated by Irene and Fraser McLuskey and James M. Robinson. Harper & Brothers, 1959. Interprets Jesus' eschatological message and the kerygma of the church as essentially continuous.

Bultmann, Rudolph, *The Theology of the New Testament,* translated by Kendrick Grobel, 2 vols. Charles Scribner's Sons, 1951–1955. The New Testament eschatological faith here demythologized and presented in the categories of modern existentialism.

Cullmann, Oscar, *Christ and Time,* translated by Floyd V. Filson. The Westminster Press, 1950. Emphasizes the linear conception of time in the Bible and the importance of the chronological end.

Dodd, C. H., *The Parables of the Kingdom,* third edition. James Nisbet & Co., Ltd., London, 1952. Argues that Jesus viewed the consummation as already present in himself. Dodd has modified this position somewhat, but "realized eschatology" continues a living point of view.

Kummel, W. G., *Promise and Fulfilment: The Eschatological Message of Jesus,* translated by Dorothea M. Barton. Studies in Biblical Theology, No. 23. Student Christian Movement Press, Ltd., London, 1957. Emphasizes that the eschatological promise of a future Kingdom is understood only in terms of the fulfillment already realized in Jesus.

Minear, Paul S., *Christian Hope and the Second Coming.* The Westminster Press, 1954. A careful study of the hope and expectations expressed in the New Testament. Designed to help American Protestants understand the theme of the Second World Council Assembly.

Niebuhr, Reinhold, *The Nature and Destiny of Man.* Charles Scribner's Sons, 1947. An interpretation of man and his situation from the point of view of a Christian faith influenced both by the recovery of Reformation insights and by the eschatological interpretation of Jesus and the New Testament.

Robinson, James M., *A New Quest of the Historical Jesus.* Studies in Biblical Theology, No. 25. Student Christian Movement Press, Ltd., London, 1959. A reappraisal of the abandonment of the quest for the historical Jesus based on full acceptance of the eschatological character of Jesus' message.

Schweitzer, Albert, *The Quest of the Historical Jesus: A Critical Study of Its Progress from Reimarus to Wrede,* translated by W. Montgomery, third edition. A. & C. Black, Ltd., London, 1954. The great classic study that brought the eschatological interpretation of Jesus to the forefront of modern discussion.

Wilder, Amos N., *Eschatology and Ethics in the Teaching of Jesus,* revised edition. Harper & Brothers, 1950. The imminent expectation of the end is seen as decisive for Jesus' ethics, although the doctrine of interim ethics is rejected.

CHAPTER VII

The Unity Beyond

THE FOREGOING CHAPTERS have suggested something of the complexity and variety of Protestantism. The actual variety is far greater than has been indicated, for individual Protestants combine elements of a number of traditions with greater or lesser consistency in their total view and are influenced by postscientific modes of thought and the implications of New Testament eschatology to varying degrees with respect to each part of their faith. Furthermore, most Protestants are equally subject to classification in other categories: businessmen or farmers, Americans or Germans, socialists or capitalists, introverts or extroverts; and their Protestant attitudes and convictions are intertwined with attitudes and convictions deriving from all these other factors. There are virtually as many forms of Protestantism as there are individual Protestants.

Confronted by this bewildering diversity, many thoughtful Protestants have been deeply troubled. How can there be an effective witness to Christ on the part of those who cannot agree as to the gospel message? Can any one of us really believe that his own understanding is correct when the great majority of other sincere Christians disagree? Should we simply close our minds to all positions different from our own, assuming them to be in error? Or should we say that all are good and no one truer than the other? But the former way leads to fanaticism and dogmatism, and the latter leads to loss of all commitment. Surely there must be some better way!

Protestantism generally has become remarkably awake to the twin dangers of dogmatism and the uncommitted life. One hundred and seventy different institutions have agreed to recognize one another as in some sense genuine parts of the church through joint membership in the World Council. This act of mutual recognition, hedged about though it is with qualifications, still seems to conflict with some of the doctrines otherwise maintained by member churches. The desire of these churches to avoid dogmatic exclusivism has overcome the concern for rigid consistency in following all the implications of some of their doctrines. The willingness to recognize one another seems to imply the acknowledgment of the possibility of error or incompleteness in each view, even at very fundamental points, and the hope that through mutual interchange the truth may be clarified.

This openness to the ideas of others has not resulted in a loss of commitment by each group to its own distinctive principles. On the contrary, the sense of the richness of each tradition has been enhanced on the part of its more thoughtful leaders. The paradox of the movement toward unity has been its production of a greater consciousness of diversity and a revival of interest in the distinctive heritage of each group. This phenomenon needs to be explained.

The initial approach to co-operation, harmony, and mutual acceptance typically takes the form of seeking a common platform. It is remarkable how much can be said to which all will agree. The more aggressive leaders of a generation ago often felt that these common beliefs were quite sufficient and that the divisive beliefs should be ignored or minimized.

Christians found, however, that verbal agreements were deceptive. Many had supposed that the differences in verbal formulations of faith among the Protestant groups concealed a unity of conviction that needed only to be uncovered. When they found that verbal agreement on most important points could be secured, they were convinced that union would be readily attainable. They discovered, however, that in fact verbal disagreements had expressed profound spiritual divergences that were concealed but not altered by agreement on propositional statements of belief. The apparent unity of the conference room fell apart most painfully at the Lord's Table. There the fundamental spiritual diversity has prevented delegates to ecumenical meetings from kneeling together.

The inability to share together in the most sacred act of Christian worship has revealed both the emptiness of verbal agreements and the error of the opinion that points of difference are peripheral. Liberals who had supposed that doctrine could be wholly subordinated to spirit have rediscovered deep-seated beliefs supporting their particular attitudes. Traditionalists have been strengthened in their convictions of the unique preciousness of their own heritage.

Nevertheless, the hunger for unity and the faith that in Christ unity already must exist have continued to grow. The reinvigoration of the separate traditions has not encouraged complacency with sectarian divisions, for the founders of these traditions consistently appealed for unity. Indeed, the longing for unity is commonly transferred by the renewal of traditional thinking from the level of practical considerations and brotherly sentiment to that of profound theological concern for the expression in the visible church of the unity of the invisible church.

Heightened emphasis upon our separate traditions temporarily separates us from one another, but it may eventually bring us together. The road to mutual understanding may be through more sensitive self-understanding. Genuine mutual understanding may lead to that deep spiritual unity which is genuinely important.

Self-understanding enables us to distinguish three levels in our religious faith. We find first a great cluster of attitudes, habits, and opinions that seem to constitute our religious lives.

We have difficulty in explaining or justifying many of these, but we cling to them tenaciously, feeling that to abandon or modify any of them is dangerously disloyal.

Nevertheless, we do perceive a difference of importance and centrality among them. As life places us in contact with different points of view and practices, we find that we can modify our religion here and there without damaging what is really important to us. We recognize the genuineness of other Christians who are in many ways quite different. Gradually, therefore, we begin to distinguish between what is really essential to us and what is derivative or peripheral. We may be able to state quite clearly what to us seems the irreducible kernel of Christian faith.

The more highly trained can carry the analysis another step, and most of us can recognize the validity of the further distinction. The smaller cluster of beliefs and attitudes that seem essential have this appearance because they are rooted in and expressive of our deepest self-understanding and experience. Often we have never tried directly to express this perspective which we have upon life, for we have never questioned it sufficiently to make it the object of our thought, but it remains all the more decisive for our religious life.

These three levels of our religious existence we may call in reverse order from their treatment above, our " perspective," its " expression," and its " elaboration." From the point of view of this distinction we may hope to understand one another more clearly and to throw light upon the path to unity.

Since our perspective as such is rarely an object of conscious consideration, its expression is not critically controlled. Hence, patterns of thought more or less accidentally absorbed may become identified by us with our deepest understanding of reality. Because of their close association with our largely unconscious perspective, the importance that inevitably attaches to the perspective attaches quite naturally to the particular expression as well.

Our perspective is the point of view from which all of life is seen and given unity. To the extent that we identify a verbal expression with the perspective, the particular form of that expression colors the way in which unity is achieved. There develops a large cluster of beliefs and customs that elaborate the implications of our expression of religious faith for wide areas of life and thought. In this way the whole of our experience achieves integration and meaning. The satisfaction that is derived from the achievement of this meaningful synthesis further enhances the sense of certainty and absoluteness that attaches to the whole.

It is clear that the systematic elaborations of Protestant faith are often painfully contradictory to one another. However, it is also clear that they are not in detail the necessary expressions of the perspectives of those who hold them. Hence, we may hope that many of our differences can be overcome by the slow and painful process of distinguishing the fundamental from the secondary, the essential from the accidental. If we can discover a unity of perspective, we can seek a unity of its expression and tolerate painlessly some diversity of elaboration.

But this goal is an elusive one. Self-consciousness about our deepest self-understanding and experience does not lead immediately to unity. It uncovers for us instead the deeper rootage of our diversity. This diversity is most marked between Christian and Hindu, Mohammedan and Buddhist, mystic and secularist. But it is found also within Christianity and within Protestantism, between European and American, German and English, socialist and capitalist. What, then, of the hope for unity?

If we take each man's perspective as simply and ultimately given, there is little that can be said except that they differ. But perspectives can be changed, indeed are constantly being changed; and one of the factors in such change is understanding of the causes or sources of the perspective. When the man who wills to be molded in his inmost being by devotion to God discovers that in fact the point of view from which he interprets life is largely determined by his economic situation, he wills to overcome what he regards as a distortion of his perspective. In some measure, if never completely, he will succeed. Thus there are secular sources of our perspective that are from the religious point of view accidental. In so far as our diversity of perspective arises from these secular sources, it can in principle be overcome.

Intellectual differences pose a somewhat different problem. When the earnestly religious man finds that his perspective is conditioned by beliefs about the empirical world, he will recognize the need of testing these beliefs against the evidence. Since some beliefs about the empirical world are ingredient in every perspective, he cannot will to rule them out entirely, however earnest may be his desire to let God be all in all. However, he must desire that his beliefs be in harmony with the evidence, and he must will to cleanse his perspective of all elements that have been shown to be false by objective investigation. Furthermore, when beliefs of a factual character are neither required nor disproved by empirical evidence, the religious man will not wish his perspective to be affected by them unless he feels that they are demanded by his religious convictions. Thus, the intellectual sources of our perspectives need pose no insuperable barrier to unity. On the contrary, natural science and historical research by correcting our opinions about our environment and our past, should help us overcome many of those differences of opinion which still divide us.

Victory over the diversity of perspective that arises from secular and intellectual sources is far from simple, and it will never be complete. Its approximation will require great patience, rare spiritual discernment, and profound humility, but in principle such victory is possible. The question remains whether even this great accomplishment would reveal a true unity, or will we find that we differ also in the purely religious aspects of our perspective?

Chapters II through V of this book are written in part to show that our Protestant perspectives do differ for religious as well as for secular and intellectual reasons. Nine types of Protestantism are displayed as elaborations of the expression of nine different ways of understanding the human situation in its relationship to God revealed in Jesus Christ. Each of them rings with sincerity and each can show us martyrs to its cause.

The Lutheran sees himself as one alienated from God, needing above all else the assurance of God's gracious forgiveness. The Calvinist sees himself as a creature worthless in comparison to the majesty of the sovereign God, but finding meaning in devotion to God's glory.

Some churchly Protestants find that their souls turn properly to the adoration of God and that only as they share with others in worship that is enriched by the whole Christian tradition can they adequately develop and express those attitudes which are appropriate to the creature's relation to the Creator. Other churchly Protestants find that their deepest spiritual problem is the chaos and the emptiness of all ideas for the direction of life which can be found apart from revelation, and that revelation can give them the direction which they require only as mediated through the church.

Biblicists are so awed by their vision of an everlasting life beyond the grave that their greatest felt need is to learn and to meet the conditions for gaining beatitude rather than suffering in that life. The experientialist is impressed by the experienced possibilities of entering into a state of righteous blessedness in this life and experiencing here and now the conscious assurance that this new life will be consummated beyond the grave.

Mystics see the problem of human life primarily in terms of the meaninglessness and unreality of the merely ephemeral phenomena of the sensuous world and have experienced the possibility of transcending that world to find union with the reality which is God. Other liberals find the needs of this life so insistent that their problems center in achieving human success and personal health of mind and body here and now both for themselves and for others. They find in the Christian heritage resources that, when properly utilized, are adequate to their needs. Still others see themselves in a relation of solidarity with their fellows and feel that only as men can rise together in their total social relationship can they truly rise individually.

It is the discovery of this deeply spiritual diversity among us which is most baffling. We cannot ask that by seeking further understanding the religious man undertake to erase from his perspective this religious element as well. It is precisely by virtue of his hold upon this fundamental religious self-understanding that he is a religious man. If he is persuaded that this understanding is either an illusion or the result of purely accidental factors, he may indeed change or lose his faith. But in so far as he continues to experience his own existence before God in a given way, this will properly constitute for him the determining principle of all elaboration of his faith.

We seem here again, at the end of a long analysis, to be confronted by the same impossible alternatives we faced at the outset. We may either insist upon the final truth of our own perspective or simply abandon all claim to truth in favor of a pure relativism. But Protestants rebel at both alternatives, and in this rebellion lies our hope.

Though each of us cherishes his own perspective deeply, as Protestants we recognize its incompleteness and ultimate inadequacy. When we are surrounded by others who share our perspective, we may almost forget the finiteness of our faith, but when circumstance drives diverse groups of us together, as in the modern world, we are compelled to recall what we should never have forgotten.

Many of us, when we are confronted by a sympathetic expression of a perspective other than our own, feel threatened.

When we thoroughly understand a point of view we almost inevitably accept it as true. Therefore, we dare not allow ourselves to listen openly lest we be unsettled in our own faith.
We prefer to locate the "error" in the alien position, which
gives us moral justification for its rejection.

But if we understand ourselves and our Protestant situation
more fully, we *will* dare to listen. We will recognize an authentic Christian note often where we least expected to find it.
When we recognize a view as authentically Christian we will
accept it also as somehow akin to our own perspective, however
different it may initially appear.

We may be inclined at first to seek a simple conjunction, to
say "both . . . and," and to suppose we have thus done justice
to all. But we soon find that this is not enough. There must be
some principle of unity that is deeper than both, some synthesis that still eludes our intellectual and spiritual powers.

Since the simple conjunction of several perspectives is not
enough, and each synthesis that is proposed appears upon inspection as the imperialism of one perspective, it is better for
us to acknowledge our bondage to our perspective while keep-
ing alive the consciousness of its incompleteness. We can believe that the conflict we feel between our habitual perspectives and what we have recognized as authentic in others is
apparent only, that if we will probe far enough into our own
understanding, we will find a place there also for what we
have found elsewhere. Indeed, what seems novel would not
have sounded true had it not been somehow already present
within us.

Our open interchange with one another will not lead to easy
agreement, but it will have two effects that may pave the road
toward unity. Each will gain a deepened appreciation of the
other, and through enrichment by varied emphases each will
grow more genuinely catholic.

As each tradition grows through its appreciation of others,
it may be compelled to modify some of the aspects of its posi-

tion that are accidental, but it will not feel itself to be disloyal to its heritage. On the contrary, the enrichment of a heritage through the broadening of its sensitivity to spiritual reality must always be the highest expression of loyalty to that heritage.

The process of mutual enrichment among the Protestant traditions is already far advanced, but it has progressed thus far on a largely unintentional and accidental basis. Generally the results have been wholesome, but at times there has been loss of spiritual distinctiveness through increasing superficiality rather than genuine enrichment. The time now seems ripe for a more thoughtful effort to learn from one another and to profit from the lessons of history.

The course of development that will occur in any tradition as it seeks to incorporate into itself what is authentically Christian in other traditions cannot be predicted. For a long time it is not likely to lead to conspicuous reduction of diversity of spirit and practice. Yet, from the first it must reinforce the faith that beyond and above all diversity lies an ultimate oneness. Eventually, one may believe, as each modifies his own tradition by incorporation of what he sees to be valid in the others, all will grow into a clearer manifestation of their real unity.

The long process of growing together should be further aided by the external problems that Protestants face in common. The rise of the natural and social sciences has already compelled Christians to acknowledge that many of their long-cherished beliefs are accidental rather than essential to their faith. The findings of Biblical scholarship, though still chaotic in many respects, gradually leave a precipitate of reliable conclusions with which all the traditions must come to terms. The histories of the continents have been merged into a history of the planet, and the common history will continue to confront Protestants with unforeseen problems with which all must deal.

In this process some of the forms of Protestantism now current may give way to others as their distinctive focuses appear inadequate to serve as centers around which a deeper and more catholic faith can develop. However, we cannot safely prejudge in this matter. Each perspective has an inner vitality that enables it to adapt its expression and elaboration to widely changing circumstances.

We realize that the unity toward which we grow is rooted in the unity from which we come, and out of this awareness there emerges in outline an enriched understanding of the church. The church is that fellowship called into being by the acts of God in history, supremely by God's giving of himself in Jesus Christ. Whenever men respond affirmatively to this event by acknowledging the Lordship of Jesus for their lives, the Spirit of God is present leading men into the fullness of Christian faith. Where the Spirit of God is at work, there is the church.

The total meaning of God's acts and the ideal personal response to them can never be known by any one man. On the other hand, none who acknowledge the Lordship of Jesus, none in whom the Spirit of God is at work, can be wholly wrong. Among Christians there can be only degrees of breadth and clarity of understanding, not absolute knowledge and absolute error.

For this reason, doctrine, however elementary, can never be the criterion of Christianity. No human formulation of Christian belief can be finally binding. Agreement cannot be demanded even with regard to " the existence of God " or " the deity of Christ." Both are subjects of legitimate debate among Christians. Thus Paul Tillich protests that the affirmation of the existence of God places God as an object alongside of other objects and obscures God's utter uniqueness. Many sensitive thinkers are convinced that the attribution of deity to Christ either separates the eternal Christ too far from the temporal Jesus or obscures the distinction between the man Jesus and the God who manifests himself through Jesus.

These are subtle and difficult issues, and our present need is not to settle them but simply to note that they exist *within* the church rather than separate the church from the world beyond it. Furthermore, even if agreement could be achieved, it would be superficial. Men would agree because they were already Christians and would not be Christians by virtue of their agreement. In addition, their agreement would be a verbal one, concealing differences in meaning rather than leading to genuine mutual understanding.

Although there can be no doctrinal statement of the unity of all Christians, there must be some principle of delimitation, for not every religious man is a Christian. This principle must have reference to Jesus, but it must not be a statement of belief about him. It must therefore be a relationship to him.

Any perspective is Christian when it includes the serious acknowledgment of Jesus as Lord. This acknowledgment is not the statement of a belief about Jesus' nature but the submission of ourselves to him. Even if we dislike the term "Lord" and prefer to describe our relationship to him in some other way, we may still be Christian. The acknowledgment of Jesus as Lord means that our lives and thoughts are opened to his positive influence as supremely worthy and important. Understanding Jesus' Lordship in this way, we may assert that its acknowledgment constitutes the invisible church.

Wherever the attitude of receptive openness to Jesus is adopted, the faith that results is authentically Christian, however much it may be conditioned by secular and intellectual factors. But not every authentic expression of Christianity is equally true, profound, or adequate. Some of the criteria for evaluating the varied expressions have been suggested above.

That expression of Christian faith which is truest to the purest Christian perspective is better. Among those which are equal by this standard, that is better which can more freely acknowledge and more adequately encompass what it finds authentic in other perspectives. To these criteria we may add the requirement that every expression of Christian faith should remain conscious of its incompleteness and open to the discovery of new significance in Jesus' Lordship.

These norms arise out of the very nature of Christian faith as response to God's acts. Relative failure as measured by them means that though the faith is in part authentic, nevertheless the irrelevant circumstances by which it has been affected have corrupted it and made it partly destructive of the response in which it arose. Such relative failure is the rule rather than the exception, and this failure is the reason for the need of the prophetic voice in every generation.

Not all that the prophet attacks is really un-Christian, and not all that results from his own work is truly Christian. Wherever there are major divisions within the church from the Reformation to the present day we may expect to find authentic Christian reasons for loyalty to the parent body as well as for revolt in the name of truth and purity. Likewise, we may be sure that among both groups the purity of Christian response is partly corrupted by elements of class and individual interest.

This understanding of the church is truly inclusive or catholic. It prejudges no group or point of view that acknowledges seriously the Lordship of Jesus, however diversely the Lordship is expressed in life and thought.

The church is holy in principle but never in fact. It is holy, that is, in that the response to God's act in Christ in which Jesus is acknowledged as Lord is the expression of the Holy Spirit. That response is holy and that response constitutes the church. But the church as the fellowship of those human beings who have experienced this holy response expresses not only this unity in discipleship to Jesus but also the individual and corporate interests of its members. The church expresses its faith, therefore, above all, in repentance for its continuing sinfulness.

The church does not possess the truth, yet it is the bearer of the truth. The truth is that into which man is led by the

Spirit as he seeks to make the Lordship of Jesus the sole rule of his life. He who is led into this truth is already in the church. The fullness of the truth is never attained by one man since the particularities of his condition and the limitations of his experience are never overcome. But in the total community through time these particularities and limitations can be transcended, and collectively the inclusive and purer truth can be manifested. Although every effort to give the Christian message final expression must ultimately fail, the need to state and re-state it is enduring. While no statement is final, some may be far more sensitive to wider ranges of the Christian response to God than are others and, as such, must approximate more closely the truth.

The unity that we seek is first the unity of response to God's calling and only secondly the unity of expression of the meaning of God's acts and our response. The greatest enemy to the attainment of this unity is the enemy of all deepening of the Christian life — complacency. So long as we are content with what we have and are, so long as we accept our present response to God as adequate, so long as we seek only to maintain those views with which we can remain comfortable, we will be divided one from another.

Our need is for honesty. We need to be honest about our moral condition, about our efforts to serve both God and Mammon, about the spiritual pride with which we corrupt the promptings of the Holy Spirit. We need to be honest also intellectually, to face squarely the baffling problems that are posed by the widening horizons of scientific and historical knowledge, and to abandon the pretense to believe what is no longer credible. Out of moral and intellectual honesty may come an inner unity or integrity of the Christian spirit that will heal the divisions alike within the individual Christian and among the Protestant traditions.

A church that finds unity in honesty and spiritual depth can command the attention of the world for the Word of God.

SELECTED READINGS FOR FURTHER STUDY

I. *Historical and Apologetic Works*

Garrison, Winfred E., *The Quest and Character of a United Church*. Abingdon Press, 1951. An interpretive survey of Christian history in terms of the methods employed to seek unity.

Horton, Walter Marshall, *Christian Theology: An Ecumenical Approach*. Harper & Brothers, 1955. A formulation of Christian theology indicating both the consensus that has developed in ecumenical discussions and the points where debate continues.

Macfarland, Charles S., *Christian Unity in the Making*. The Federal Council of Churches of Christ in America, Inc., 1948. A history of the first twenty-five years of the Federal Council, 1905–1930, by its General Secretary Emeritus.

Minear, Paul S., *The Nature of the Unity We Seek*. The Bethany Press, 1958. The official report of the North American Conference on Faith and Order, Oberlin, Ohio, September, 1957.

Morrison, Charles C., *The Unfinished Reformation*. Harper & Brothers, 1953. A vigorous attack upon denominationalism and an appeal for moving rapidly forward toward the achievement of a united church.

Nichols, James H., *Evanston: An Interpretation*. Harper & Brothers, 1954. A sensitive appraisal of the state of the ecumenical movement as of its last great assembly.

Rouse, Ruth, and Neill, Stephen C., editors, *A History of the Ecumenical Movement, 1517–1948*. The Westminster Press, 1954. A thorough survey of the historical expressions of the desire for Christian unity. Prepared by a group of highly competent historians and published on behalf of the Ecumenical Institute.

Visser 't Hooft, W. A., editor, *The Evanston Report.* Harper & Brothers, 1955. The official report of the Second Assembly of the World Council of Churches.

II. *Evaluations and Interpretations of Ecumenicity*

Bradshaw, Marion J., *Free Churches and Christian Unity.* The Beacon Press, Inc., 1954. A liberal's expression of serious concern at the danger to theological freedom inherent in the quest for unity.

Bromiley, G. W., *The Unity and Disunity of the Church.* Wm. B. Eerdmans Publishing Company, 1958. A conservative Calvinist's view of the problem and the reality of Christian unity.

Nicholls, William, *Ecumenism and Catholicity.* Student Christian Movement Press, Ltd., London, 1952. Written by a scholar of Anglo-Catholic background who explains his conception of the church as it has developed out of contact with and study of the ecumenical movement.

Outler, Albert C., *The Christian Tradition and the Unity We Seek.* Oxford University Press, 1957. A book by an American Methodist who treats the meaning and importance of Christian unity from the perspective to which he has been brought by participation in the ecumenical movement.

Tavard, George H., *The Catholic Approach to Protestantism,* translated by the author from the French. Harper & Brothers, 1955. Written by a sympathetic Roman Catholic observer who explains the Protestant situation and the ecumenical movement to his fellow Catholics.

Zander, L. A., *Vision and Action,* translated by Natalie Duddington. Victor Gollancz, Ltd., London, 1952. A book by an Eastern Orthodox leader in the ecumenical movement who inquires sympathetically into its problems.

Appendix and Index

Guide to Topical Comparison in Chapters II to V

This guide is provided to facilitate comparison of the several Protestant traditions on specific aspects of their teaching. However, the reader must be cautious in its use. In the chapters, no effort was made to give comprehensive coverage of a list of topics. The effort was, rather, to explain the fundamental understanding of what it means to be a Christian and to illustrate with respect to a few doctrines for which this understanding has special relevance. The omission or very limited treatment of a topic in any section does not mean that adherents lack interest in that topic. It may suggest that what they have to say on that subject is not especially *distinctive* of their tradition.

PERSONAL SALVATION
The situation in which we find ourselves:
    26–27, 31–33, 48–49, 60–63, 71–72, 75–76, 89–90, 109–110, 117–118, 132–133, 158–159, 169–170, 177–182
God's act in revelation and redemption:
  in nature and general religious experience:
    50–51, 60–61, 155–168
  in Scripture:
    41–42, 50, 51–53, 77–78, 113, 118, 129, 139–140, 170–173, 182–183
  in Jesus Christ:
    27–28, 33–34, 39, 41, 42, 50, 78–79, 90, 95–96, 99, 102, 107, 118, 122, 132, 135, 143, 159, 168–169, 170–173, 184, 185, 187

General Bibliography on Protestantism

HISTORIES OF PROTESTANTISM

I. *General*

All histories of Christianity, as a whole, include the history of Protestantism more or less adequately. However, only two are listed here, because of their special usefulness.

Dillenberger, John, and Welch, Claude, *Protestant Christianity Interpreted Through Its Development*. Charles Scribner's Sons, 1954. An excellent one-volume history of Protestantism, giving attention to both institutional and theological developments.

Ferm, Vergilius, *Pictorial History of Protestantism*. Philosophical Library, Inc., 1957. An extensive collection of pictures with a running commentary on Protestant history.

Latourette, Kenneth Scott, *A History of the Expansion of Christianity*, Vols. III–VII. Harper & Brothers, 1939–1945. Five volumes of a seven-volume work which provides extensive information on Protestant history, focusing on the faith's missionary expansion.

Nichols, James H., *History of Christianity 1650–1950: Secularization of the West*. The Ronald Press Company, 1956. A penetrating analysis of the major trends of development within Christendom in the three centuries indicated by the title, chronologically developed with rich detail. Serious attention paid to Eastern Orthodoxy and Roman Catholicism as well as to Protestantism.

Norwood, Frederick, *The Development of Modern Christianity Since 1500.* Abingdon Press, 1956. A highly readable survey of the history of the Christian church, with special emphasis on the division of Protestantism into denominations and the recent expression through the ecumenical movement of the latent desire for unity.

Troeltsch, Ernst, *The Social Teachings of the Christian Churches,* translated by Olive Wyon, Vol. II. The Free Press, 1931. A classic analysis of extraordinary scholarship with insights into the deepest spiritual principles of the Protestant groups as well as their more specifically social teachings.

Whale, J. S., *The Protestant Tradition.* Cambridge University Press, Cambridge, 1955. A study of the origins of the major Protestant denominations and the problems they now confront.

II. *American*

Bates, Ernest, *American Faith.* W. W. Norton & Company, Inc., 1940. A history of the American churches up to the Civil War, in terms of their European backgrounds.

Brauer, Jerald C., *Protestantism in America: A Narrative History.* The Westminster Press, 1953. A readable but scholarly account of Protestantism in America from the colonization to the present.

Curran, Francis X., S.J., *Major Trends in American Church History.* The American Press, 1946. A perceptive interpretation of American church history written by a Roman Catholic but focusing primarily on Protestantism.

Drummond, Andrew L., *Story of American Protestantism.* Oliver & Boyd, Ltd., Edinburgh, 1949. A Scotch historian's sympathetic account of the history of Protestantism in America from its founding to recent times.

Garrison, Winfred E., *The March of Faith*. Harper & Brothers, 1933. A highly readable account of Christianity in America from 1865 on. Set against the general cultural background.

Hudson, Winthrop S., *The Great Tradition of the American Churches*. Harper & Brothers, 1953. Focuses on the Christian responsibility for society and appeals for a revitalization of the church and its outreach.

Niebuhr, H. Richard, *The Kingdom of God in America*. Willett, Clark & Company, 1937. Now available in a Harper Torchbook edition. A selective history of American Protestantism in terms of its inner spiritual dynamic.

Stephenson, George M., *The Puritan Heritage*. The Macmillan Company, 1952. Interprets American church history to the middle of the nineteenth century in terms of the Puritan tradition from which its vitality has stemmed.

Sweet, William Warren, *The Story of Religion in America*, revised edition. Harper & Brothers, 1939. The standard work by the dean of American church historians.

DISCUSSIONS OF PROTESTANTISM AS A WHOLE

I. *General Expositions*

Anderson, William K., editor, *Protestantism: A Symposium*. Commission on Ministerial Training, The Methodist Church, 1944. A collection of essays on the history, interpretation, and present prospects of Protestantism by a large group of contemporary leaders.

Bouyer, Louis, *The Spirit and Forms of Protestantism*, translated by A. V. Littledale. The Newman Press, 1950. A brilliant statement of the strengths and weaknesses of Protestantism as seen by a French Catholic priest converted from Calvinism.

A truly remarkable sensitivity to the deepest spiritual values of Lutheranism and Calvinism.

Cannon, William R., *Our Protestant Faith*. Tidings, 1949. A brief statement of normative Protestant teaching, guided chiefly by Reformation thought.

Clyde, Walter R., *Interpreting Protestantism to Catholics*. The Westminster Press, 1959. A treatment of both the agreements and divergences of Protestantism and Catholicism. Designed to help Protestants present their case to Catholics.

Davies, Rupert E., *Why I Am a Protestant*. The Epworth Press, London, 1957. A statement by an English Methodist of his Protestant convictions and his attitude toward the Roman Catholic Church.

Easton, W. Burnet, Jr., *The Faith of a Protestant*. The Macmillan Company, 1946. A simply written statement of Christian beliefs designed to clarify for laymen the content of the Protestant faith.

Ferm, Vergilius, editor, *The Protestant Credo*. Philosophical Library, Inc., 1953. A collection of ten essays by leading liberal Protestant scholars. Intended to communicate to laymen the heart of the Protestant message.

Flew, R. Newton, and Davies, Rupert E., editors, *The Catholicity of Protestantism*. Muhlenberg Press, 1954. A report presented to the Archbishop of Canterbury by a leading group of English Free Churchmen which defends Protestantism as being genuinely catholic in its faith and practice.

Garrison, Winfred Ernest, *A Protestant Manifesto*. Abingdon Press, 1952. A vigorous statement of the common elements in the faith of all churches rooted in the Reformation tradition, both those elements which are shared with other Christians and religions generally and those which are distinctive of Protestantism.

Hamilton, Kenneth G., *The Protestant Way*. Essential Books, Inc., 1956. A thoughtful and scholarly effort to formulate a normative statement of the distinctive affirmation of Protestantism understood as the tradition of the Reformation and the Free Churches.

Jenney, Ray Freeman, *I Am a Protestant*. The Bobbs-Merrill Company, Inc., 1951. A plea to Protestants to reaffirm the liberal and unifying principles in their heritage.

Kerr, Hugh T., Jr., *Positive Protestantism*. The Westminster Press, 1950. An appeal to Protestantism to recapture its Reformation heritage in order to regain its affirmative message.

McElroy, Paul Simpson, *Protestant Beliefs*. Abingdon Press, 1940. A popular statement of what the author says is "what many Protestants believe in certain of the great questions of the Christian faith."

Munro, Harry C., *Be Glad You're a Protestant!* The Bethany Press, 1948. A brief statement of Protestant doctrine prepared for use as a text in lay study groups.

Nichols, James H., *Primer for Protestants*. Association Press, 1947. An excellent introduction to Protestantism which provides both historical understanding of its sources and a persuasive statement of its principles. A shortened version now available in a Reflection Book edition (Association Press).

Pauck, Wilhelm, *The Heritage of the Reformation*. The Beacon Press, Inc., 1950. A scholarly study of the origins of Protestantism, its relation to other movements, and its present position and prospects.

Protestantism. Tidings, 1947–1949. A group of pamphlets including *What Is Distinctive About Protestantism*, by Albea

Godbold; *A Protestant Platform of Our Goodwill*, by R. W. Sockman; and *Why I Am a Protestant*, by Roy L. Smith.

Seidenspinner, Clarence A., *A Protestant Primer*. Tidings, 1947. A popular presentation of the source and character of Protestantism. Written especially for Methodist students.

Union Theological Seminary (Richmond) faculty, *Our Protestant Heritage*. John Knox Press, 1948. Essays interpreting the Christian heritage from the Protestant, and especially Calvinist, point of view.

Wilburn, Ralph G., *The Prophetic Voice in Protestant Christianity*. The Bethany Press, 1956. An appeal to Protestants to find their unity of spirit in the dynamics of their prophetic heritage.

II. *Evaluation of American Protestantism*

Bach, Marcus, *Report to Protestants*. The Bobbs-Merrill Company, Inc., 1948. An evaluation of the current strengths and weaknesses of the standard American denominations in relation to the sects and Roman Catholicism. Interestingly written in the form of autobiography.

Eckardt, A. Roy, *The Surge of Piety in America*. Association Press, 1958. A description, analysis, and appraisal of the revival of folk religion in contemporary American Protestantism.

Morrison, Charles Clayton, *Can Protestantism Win America?* Harper & Brothers, 1948. Evaluation of the strengths and weaknesses of American Protestantism in terms of its relations to secularism and especially Catholicism.

Osborn, Ronald E., *The Spirit of American Christianity*. Harper & Brothers, 1958. An interpretation of popular Protestantism in America in terms of its history. Designed especially for Europeans.

Parker, T. Valentine, *American Protestantism: An Appraisal.* Philosophical Library, Inc., 1956. An impressionistic but interesting and sometimes perceptive survey of the strengths and weaknesses of American Protestantism today.

Pfeffer, Leo, *Creeds in Competition.* Harper & Brothers, 1958. Shows how the religious diversity of America has affected its institutions for good.

Schneider, Herbert W., *Religion in Twentieth Century America.* Harvard University Press, 1952. A perceptive discussion of the changes in the American religious scene in the first half of the twentieth century.

Sperry, Willard L., *Religion in America.* The Macmillan Company, 1946. A description of American Christianity, its history, diversity, and thrust toward unity; with appendices giving factual and statistical information.

III. *Comparisons of Protestantism with Other American Traditions*

Abrams, Ray H., editor, *Organized Religion in the United States.* The Annals of the American Academy of Political and Social Science, Vol. 256, 1948. Accounts of the contemporary situation, problems, activities, and future prospects of Protestant, Catholic, and Jewish Churches by authorities in each field.

Finkelstein, Louis, and others, *The Religions of Democracy: Judaism, Catholicism, Protestantism.* The Devin-Adair Co., 1941. Essays by Louis Finkelstein, J. Elliot Ross, and William Adams Brown on Judaism, Roman Catholicism, and Protestantism respectively.

Herberg, Will, *Protestant-Catholic-Jew.* Doubleday & Co., Inc., 1955. Subtitled "An Essay in American Religious Sociology." Has been widely acclaimed as illuminating the present religious situation in America, especially the similiarities and differences of its three major faiths.

264   APPENDIX AND INDEX

Johnson, F. Ernest, editor, *Patterns of Faith in America To-day*. The Institute for Religious and Social Studies, 1957. Distributed by Harper & Brothers. Essays on: Classical Protestantism, by Robert McAfee Brown; Liberal Protestantism, by Edwin E. Aubrey; Roman Catholicism, by Charles Donahue; Judaism, by Simon Greenberg; and Naturalistic Humanism, by John Herman Randall, Jr.

Sperry, Willard L., editor, *Religion and Our Divided Denominations*. Harvard University Press, 1945. Chapters on Roman Catholicism, Protestantism, Judaism, and Humanism by exponents of each, preceded by an introduction by the editor.

THE DIVERSITY OF PROTESTANTISM

I. *Inclusive Surveys and Interpretations*

Hardon, John A., *The Protestant Churches of America*. The Newman Press, 1956. A carefully documented description for Roman Catholic readers of the history, organization, teachings, and doctrine of fourteen major denominational groups and a large number of minor ones. Based chiefly on the official documents of each denomination discussed.

Kerr, Hugh T., Jr., *What Divides Protestants Today*. A Reflection Book (Association Press), 1958. A popular but responsible discussion of the theological and social sources of Protestant disunity and the prospects of unity.

Landis, Benson, editor, *Yearbook of the American Churches for 1959*. National Council of the Churches of Christ in the U.S.A., 1958. Among other valuable data are included lists of all religious bodies in the United States and Canada, with names and addresses of officers.

Mayer, F. C., *The Religious Bodies of America*, second edition. Concordia Publishing House, 1956. The most thorough and comprehensive treatment of American religious groups available. Discusses their history, organization, and teaching.

Mead, Frank S., *Handbook of Denominations in the United States,* revised and enlarged edition. Abingdon Press, 1956. Brief studies of all religious bodies in America. Arranged alphabetically.

Neve, J. L., *Churches and Sects of Christendom.* Lutheran Literary Board, Inc., 1940. The only available comprehensive survey of the organization, history, and official teaching of the Christian bodies of the world. Although somewhat outdated, remains indispensable.

Niebuhr, H. Richard, *The Social Sources of Denominationalism.* Henry Holt & Co., Inc., 1929. Now available in the Living Age Books series (Meridian Books), 1957. The classic study of Protestant divisions in America as affected by such nonreligious factors as race and economic class.

Whalen, William J., *Separated Brethren.* Bruce Publishing Co., 1958. A Roman Catholic survey of the denominations and sects of Protestantism and discussion of the possibility of reunion.

II. *Comparative Studies of Major Denominations*

Bilheimer, Robert S., *The Quest for Christian Unity.* Association Press, 1952. A brief characterization of each of nine major Christian bodies in the United States by a spokesman for each follows a survey of American Protestantism in the last fifty years with special focus on the ecumenical hope and achievement.

Church, Brooke Peters, *A Faith for You.* Rinehart & Company, Inc., 1948. Brief descriptions of the doctrine and practice of thirty-two religious bodies in the United States preceded by a discussion of their historical background and common origins.

Ferm, Vergilius, editor, *The American Church of the Protestant Heritage.* Philosophical Library, Inc., 1953. Twenty-two essays, each contributed by a scholar, which discuss the history and practice of various American Protestant denominations.

Hedley, George, *The Christian Heritage in America*. The Macmillan Company, 1946. Appreciative statements of the history and genius of ten American Protestant traditions in addition to Roman Catholicism, Greek Orthodoxy, and Judaism.

Herklots, H. G. G., *These Denominations*. Student Christian Movement Press, Ltd., London, 1946. A description of the religious bodies of England in terms of their historic origins.

Maxwell, Reginald D., and Foles, Sophia Lyon, *The Church Across the Street*. The Beacon Press, Inc., 1946. A treatment of fourteen religious groups in America which stresses the lives of those regarded as founders or dominant figures in each.

Potter, Charles Francis, *The Faiths Men Live By*. Prentice-Hall, Inc., 1954. A humanist's interpretation, containing chapters both on the world religions and on the main branches of Christianity. Includes nine chapters on Protestant denominations.

Rosten, Leo, *A Guide to the Religions of America*. Simon and Schuster, Inc., 1955. Statements by nineteen religious leaders of different churches explaining their respective positions. With an extended appendix of factual and statistical information.

Stuber, Stanley I., *How We Got Our Denomination: A Primer on Church History*. Association Press, 1948. A sketch of Christian history prefaces brief characterizations of the major Protestant denominations. A shortened revision entitled *Denominations — How We Got Them* now available in a Reflection Book edition (Association Press).

Williams, J. Paul, *What Americans Believe and How They Worship*. Harper & Brothers, 1952. A thoughtful presentation of nine major patterns of American religion. With additional brief statements on a number of lesser movements.

In addition to the above, reference should be made to two series of books: one published by Thomas Nelson & Sons, entitled *Why I Am a Methodist, Why I Am an Episcopalian,* etc., and the other published by Prentice-Hall, Inc., entitled *The Methodist Way of Life, The Episcopalian Way of Life,* etc. In both series each volume is written by a spokesman for the denomination and presents its faith and activity in attractive, popular form.

III. *Studies of Minor Groups and Movements*

Bach, Marcus, *They Have Found a Faith.* The Bobbs-Merrill Company, Inc., 1946. A sympathetic treatment of eight minority movements on the fringes of Protestantism. Based on firsthand study of their living practices.

Braden, Charles S., *These Also Believe: A Study of Modern American Cults and Minority Religious Movements.* The Macmillan Company, 1949. An original study of thirteen religious movements rooted in American Protestantism but standing somewhat apart from the main stream of Christianity.

Clark, Elmer T., *Small Sects of America,* revised edition. Abingdon Press, 1949. Also available in an Apex edition (Abingdon Press). Treats smaller churches both within and outside of the main stream of American Protestantism.

Davies, Horton, *Christian Deviations.* Philosophical Library, Inc., 1954. Expounds the tenets of Theosophy, Christian Science, Spiritism, Seventh-Day Adventism, Jehovah's Witnesses, Mormonism, British-Israel, Moral Rearmament, Astrology, and " open-air religion " to distinguish them all from genuine Christianity.

Ferguson, Charles W., *The Confusion of Tongues: A Review of Modern Isms.* Zondervan Publishing House, 1940. Nineteen movements, mostly on the fringes of Protestantism, are described.

Ferm, Vergilius, *Religion in the Twentieth Century*. Philosophical Library, Inc., 1948. Emphasizes American Protestant groups of relatively recent origin as well as characterizing currents of thought in the major denominations. Twenty-seven scholars, each state the case for one of twenty-seven forms of religious life in America, not all institutionally distinguished, and many not Christian. Also available in the New Students Outline series (Littlefield, Adams & Co., 1956), under the title *Living Schools of Religion*.

Martin, Walter R., *The Rise of the Cults*. Zondervan Publishing House, 1955. Brief histories, analyses, and criticisms of Jehovah's Witnesses, Theosophy, Mormonism, Christian Science, Unity, Father Divine, Spiritualism, and Bahaism.

Rhodes, Arnold B., editor, *The Church Faces the Isms*. Abingdon Press, 1958. A discussion of recent movements, including Protestant sectarianism, by members of the faculty of Louisville Presbyterian Theological Seminary.

Van Baalem, John Karen, *The Chaos of Cults: A Study of Present Day Isms*, second revised and enlarged edition. Wm. B. Eerdmans Publishing Company, 1956. A conservative Protestant critique of fourteen movements, most of them on the fringes of American Protestantism.

————, *The Gist of the Cults*. Wm. B. Eerdmans Publishing Company, 1957. A shorter paperback work otherwise similar to *The Chaos of Cults*.

Index of Persons and Subjects